KANPAI

KANPAI

THE HISTORY OF SAKE

ERIC C. RATH

REAKTION BOOKS

To my wife, Kiyomi, for her support, assistance and wisdom,
which made this and all my work possible.

Published by
REAKTION BOOKS LTD
2–4 Sebastian Street
London EC1V 0HE, UK
www.reaktionbooks.co.uk

First published 2025
Copyright © Eric C. Rath 2025

EU GPSR Authorised Representative
Logos Europe, 9 rue Nicolas Poussin, 17000, La Rochelle, France
email: contact@logoseurope.eu

Printed and bound in India by Replika Press Pvt. Ltd

A catalogue record for this book is available from the
British Library

ISBN 978 1 83639 115 9

CONTENTS

NOTE TO READERS

Throughout the book, Japanese names appear Japanese style, family name first, except for authors writing in English or for Japanese brewers living outside of Japan. For most of the book, I use the word 'sake' following the rules for Japanese language, meaning sake, like sushi, can be singular or plural. The last chapter makes an exception because North American brewers often say 'sakes', indicating how that Japanese word and others have become American English. While writing this book I frequently referred to Timothy Sullivan's essential 'sake glossary', maintained online by Urban Sake (www.urbansake.com).

One of the aspects of sake history that struck me early as a historian of Japan was that brewers still measured production in terms of capacity with the traditional unit called a *koku* (180 litres/47½ U.S. gallons). Students in my Japanese history classes learn that to be called a 'warlord' (*daimyō*) in early modern Japan required holding land with an income of 10,000 koku. Samurai were said to have lived on 1 koku of rice a year, although they actually needed twice as much grain and other foods to survive. I have retained koku as a unit of measurement, but I have translated other traditional Japanese measurements into modern equivalents. Unless otherwise noted, the translations from Japanese texts are my own.

INTRODUCTION

In Japanese the word 'sake' can refer to any alcoholic beverage, but this book focuses on the most famous of these sake, the fermented drink called sake and known technically as *Nihonshu* or *seishu*, which in its purest form consists of rice, a mould called kōji and water. To call sake a 'rice wine' highlights one of its main ingredients, but sake is brewed like a beer rather than fermented like a fruit wine. Wine relies on the sugars already available in the grapes or other fruit, but both beer and sake need something else to unlock the sugars in grain. Beer accomplishes this through malting. Sake uses the mould kōji.

Sake is made by mixing rice, kōji and water to make a starter called a *moto* or *shubo*. Yeast might be added unless the brewer is relying on ambient yeasts, wild yeasts existing in the natural environment, as sake was made for most of its history in Japan, from at least the eighth to the early twentieth century. In an innovation discovered in the late sixteenth century, more rice, kōji and water can be added in increasingly larger amounts over time, in three stages that in Japanese are called *sandan jikomi* or *sandan*

Glass of sake filled to the brim and overflowing into the *masu* cup below. *Masu* were traditional measuring cups, but the one used here catches the overflow, indicating that the restaurant is giving a full pour.

shikomi – a solution to the desire to produce a larger amount of sake without overwhelming the yeast. Pressing separates the liquid from the lees (*kasu*), and beginning in the fifteenth or sixteenth century sake was usually pasteurized to end the fermentation process and stabilize it. Methods used to clarify the sake to remove any remaining rice lees and produce a clear beverage came into wider use in the seventeenth century. Other innovations in the twentieth century made sake brewing faster and the recipes more foolproof.

Seishu, to use sake's legal name and definition in Japan, is an alcoholic beverage made from rice and the kōji mould *Aspergillus oryzae*, but other moulds and grains were used historically in Japan.[1] Some might not consider these beverages as 'sake' today, but that would ignore the diversity of sake's past that this book means to uncover. Chapter One, for instance, introduces sake in the tenth century made with malted wheat and possibly other varieties of kōji besides *Aspergillus oryzae*. Up to the twentieth century a sake from Takarajima, an island 370 kilometres (230 mi.) south of Kagoshima, used a version of the kōji mould usually used to make miso and soy sauce to brew a 'wheat sake' called 'women's sake' locally because it had lower alcohol content than the sake made with rice that men drank.[2] When rice was in short supply during the Second World War some parts of Japan made sake from other grains like barnyard millet (hie); foxtail millet

'Sweet sake' (*amazake*).

(*awa*) and barnyard millet sake were typical ingredients for sake in places that could not grow much if any rice. The Ainu people also used barnyard millet and foxtail millet in their brewing.[3] Finger millet (*shikokubie*) was the main ingredient for a version of sake from Gifu prefecture where barnyard millet was also used for brewing.[4] But there are many advantages to using rice due to its higher starch content, ease of milling compared to wheat and millets, and taste. Still, non-rice sake have their place in the history of sake in Japan and they will be introduced in this book. This book does not include beverages sometimes described as 'rice wines' from outside of Japan. Chinese Shaoxing wine and Korean Makgeolli have similarities to sake in that they are usually, but not exclusively, rice-based, but Shaoxing wine uses glutinous rice and also incorporates wheat while Makgeolli is often flavoured with other ingredients. That both of these beverages might be distant cousins of Japan's sake is probable, but Japanese sake evolved separately from them. Chinese primary sources, which provide resources on the origins of many aspects of Japanese foodstuffs, unfortunately do not shed light on the history of sake in Japan.[5] Sake is no longer made exclusively in Japan, but its roots and long history in that country are the focus of this book, except for the last chapter on sake in North America.

Besides the legal seishu, two other members of the sake family deserve introduction: 'sweet sake' (*amazake*) and *doburoku*. Amazake is a sake in the sense that it can be made by warming rice, water and kōji, and it derives its sweetness from kōji mould transforming the starches in rice into glucose as in sake. In sake making the glucose feeds yeast essential to alcoholic fermentation. Amazake is not fermented. There is an alcoholic version of amazake, developed in the twentieth century, made from the leftover lees from sake making. However, the chefs who are experimenting today with amazake as a sweet substitute for cane sugar prefer the non-alcoholic version.⁶ Amazake is a sweet drink that the whole family can enjoy, not an adult beverage like sake.

Doburoku refers to a sake with a cloudy appearance thanks to the presence of lees in the liquid. In other words, doburoku is an unfiltered sake. Since doburoku was historically made at home instead of in a modern brewery, it usually has a lower alcohol content of 10–12 per cent ABV (Alcohol by Volume) compared to sake (seishu) at 13–17 per cent ABV. Higher alcohol content and the techniques of professional brewers like pasteurization give sake a longer shelf life than doburoku, which was meant to be consumed immediately after it was made.⁷ References to doburoku, also called *dakushu*, date from the ninth century, but before the seventeenth century most sake was cloudy, so the distinction between sake and doburoku is often hard to draw historically.⁸ Some experts dismiss all ancient and medieval sake as doburoku, but that ignores the variety of brewing styles in those periods, as Chapter Two reveals.⁹ Brewers of the early modern period (1600–1868) used the same recipe to make a version of doburoku as they did a style of sake; the only difference is the former was not pressed to remove the lees.

The distinction between sake and doburoku became clearer in 1899 when the Japanese government banned both home brewing and cloudy sake. Once an inexpensive beverage that was part of daily life in cities and the countryside, the law made doburoku an illicit drink, one that the government later warned might cause birth defects. Doburoku, however, never disappeared. In 1964, around the time that one newspaper described illegal home brewing as a 'national pastime', sake brewers invented *nigorizake*, a style of sake that even used the same Japanese characters for doburoku but pronounced them differently.

A variety of doburoku served at Konohano brewery, Tokyo.

Nigorizake was legal because it was filtered. It simply used a coarser filter than for typical sake, which allowed nigorizake to retain some lees. Despite the debut of a legal version of doburoku, sake professionals, writers, advocates of rural culture, and voices on the political left began a campaign from the late 1960s to recover doburoku and legalize home brewing. Yet home brewing remains illegal even though sake was a home-made beverage centuries before it was a commercial one. Compare the wholesomeness of home-made doburoku, made with just rice, kōji, water and yeast, to much of the commercial sake sold in Japan from 1943 to 1992 (as Chapters Six and Seven detail): a 'sake' (technically called sanzōshu or sanbaijōshu) made with two-thirds brewers' alcohol, sweeteners, artificial flavourings including monosodium glutamate (MSG) and salicylic acid, a preservative banned in foods in Japan because it was known to cause headaches, seizures and heart attacks but allowed in sake making until 1969. Doburoku serves as an example not only of how the official definitions of sake change, but that if we limit the history of sake to the legal or commercial variety of today, we will miss the stories of other important types of sake that challenge these norms.

At the same time that this book takes an inclusive approach to styles of sake, it also considers the wide variety of sake makers. Much attention today is rightly given to the few female master brewers (tōji) working in the male-dominated sake industry, such as the brewer Imada Miho (b. 1961), who is president and tōji of Imada Shuzō in Hiroshima prefecture.[10] Women brewed sake for centuries in Japan, but they are usually omitted from the history of sake apart from the false tales told of 'virginal' shrine maidens who supposedly long ago made a beverage with their spit, a story that fascinates some male sake experts. The contributions of women brewers in premodern Japan are hard to document due to a lack of sources, but so too are the historical claims on many breweries' websites.[11] Nonetheless, women were synonymous with sake brewers in ancient and medieval times, and to be clear, there were no laws or rules or taboos that prevented women from brewing or entering breweries in the early modern period. However, when brewing increased in scale in the early modern period, its labour force also shifted from a family operation that women sometimes managed to a seasonal male workforce dominated by men, as Chapter Four explains.

Tales of shrine maidens brewing with their spit remain prevalent in writings about sake because there is a lot of imaginative speculation about the origins of the drink in Japan but little hard evidence. Chapter One explores the 'cloudy' beginnings of sake, while Chapter Two examines the rise of commercial brewers in Kyoto and in temples in the Nara region in the fifteenth and sixteenth centuries. Sake can be called an industry in the early modern period, not in the sense of using modern technology, but in terms of the production scale of breweries, some of which produced 180,000 litres (47,600 gall.) annually with a highly skilled seasonal labour force, sending their sake across country in specialized transport ships. The Meiji government (1868–1912) relied on taxes on sake brewers to fuel modernization and to build its armed forces, and the government also invested in sake brewing, creating in 1904 the National Research Institute of Brewing (NRIB). The NRIB made new strains of yeast commercially available and suggested improvements to traditional brewing methods. Chapter Five contends that the word 'Japanese sake' (Nihonshu) is the appropriate term for sake in this era, reflecting the ways in which the national government shaped sake in the modern period. Sake's value as a tax resource was expressed in a ranking system introduced in 1943 and lasting until 1989 that rated sake higher simply if the brewers paid higher taxes. This ranking system had nothing to do with quality, as sake writers observed beginning in the late 1960s, and advocates of home-made doburoku and the local sake (jizake) movement of the 1980s sought 'real sake' apart from the higher ranked commercial brands, as Chapter Seven describes.

The final chapter traces sake's journey to North America via Hawaii in the early twentieth century, leading to the California sake boom of the 1980s when major Japanese brewers built plants in the United States, and the craft sake movement that has emerged in the last two decades, especially in the last five years. One of the questions that all brewers in North America grapple

Selection of sake bottles in a Japanese supermarket.

with is the extent to which sake remains a Japanese beverage or is evolving into something new in the United States, where brewers are adapting and experimenting with recipes and innovating ways to connect with customers – such as in brewpubs. Chapter Eight developed from my conversations with sake makers whose words capture the dynamism of North American craft sake at an exciting moment. Craft sake will likely evolve further in coming decades in the United States and spread widely elsewhere; the lessons learned in the United States now will prove influential to the spread of sake globally.

Sake's history is not just the story of its production but also of its consumption. Chapter Three spotlights drinking in the ancient and medieval periods (700–1600) in elite culture, by virtue of the extant sources. Primary texts expand exponentially in the early modern period, and a comprehensive discussion of drinking in early modern and modern Japan would take more than just a chapter or two to do it justice. So, Chapter Six narrows the lens of drinking culture in these periods to focus on *izakaya*, commercial establishments for drinking and eating, tracing their development from food stands in the 1600s to chain restaurants in the twentieth century.

Sake is becoming increasingly familiar outside of Japan, and this book will help readers understand not only sake's long history within Japan, but how the story of the production and consumption of sake provides a lens through which to view Japanese history. Despite often being described as a 'traditional beverage made with a few ingredients', which in its purest form it is, sake has changed through the centuries. For instance, although it has been essential to any banquet and integral to dining out for centuries in Japan, the notion of pairing sake with food, as with wine, is very recent in sake's long history.[12] I worked in an upscale traditional Japanese restaurant in Kyoto in the 1990s, where meals cost the equivalent of hundreds of dollars at the time, but we sold only two brands of sake, and most customers chose beer.

This book is not meant to endorse different brands of sake or to tell readers how to drink it. There are enough magazines, books and blogs that advise which sake to purchase, and sake can be consumed at almost any temperature. Indeed, one of the advantages sake has over other alcoholic beverages like wine or beer is the way that temperature affects sake's flavour profile in wonderful ways. So, drink sake warm. Drink it cold. Taste the difference and decide for yourself which brands and temperatures you like best.

There has been a campaign in Japan since 2004, spurred by the national organization of sake brewers, the Japan Sake and Shōchū Makers Association, to encourage people to say 'cheers' (*kanpai*) and toast each other with sake once again instead of with beer or any other beverage.[13] 'Kanpai', which I took for the name of this book, is a modern term, likely an effort to indigenize the Western word 'cheers', or specifically the toast that British naval officers made to their sovereign and country at the start of their formal meals.[14] Today, raising a glass and saying 'kanpai' can mark the start of many different meals and occasions within and outside of Japan. Recalling that 'kanpai' in Japanese was initially synonymous with drinking sake and that sake was once a central part of special occasions is a good idea considering sake's long history and its influence on Japanese culture, notwithstanding the distressing fact that sake amounts to only about 5.3 per cent of the alcoholic beverages' sold in Japan today.

Varieties of sake rice growing as a display in Kamotsuru Brewery, Saijō, Hiroshima.

ONE
CLOUDY BEGINNINGS, 1000 BCE TO 1000 CE

The first alcoholic beverages in Japan, the earliest sake and the first use of kōji, are all cloudy subjects, matters more of speculation than of clear facts, but this chapter will endeavour to shed some light on these topics. Unfortunately, primary sources are few and far between, and the earliest Chinese records reveal little about the history of brewing in Japan.[1] But that has not prevented – or perhaps it has even facilitated – some scholars from conjecturing about the history of alcohol and the origins of sake in Japan. Despite the prevalence of some of these theories, the sources are more suggestive than definitive. The assumption is that since most people enjoy alcohol today, the prehistoric ancestors of the Japanese must have as well. It seems it is hard for some to imagine a past without alcohol, given its long importance to Japanese culture and prevalence today. However, it is impossible to develop a clear picture of sake or alcohol in Japan before the eighth century.

ALCOHOL IN JAPANESE HISTORY

Sake is a beverage made from grain, chiefly rice. Scholars date the arrival of rice in Japan from the continent to the beginning of the Yayoi period, a date that was once accepted as 300 BCE but has been pushed back further with new archaeological discoveries to the second or first millennium BCE. Beyond the arrival of rice and the technology to grow it in paddies, the Yayoi period ushered in many changes, arriving with settlers from the continent, including the introduction of bronze and iron tools and weapons and fortified settlements. Farming takes time to reap its rewards, and the Yayoi people built moats, pits, stockades and towers to defend themselves against neighbours who might have been out to steal their crops.

The Yayoi people enjoyed alcohol, at least according to one Chinese record, *The Chronicle of Wei* (*Wei zhi*), which describes how between 238 and 265 CE the Chinese court tried to establish diplomatic ties with the people living in Japan, whom the Chinese called the 'dwarf people' (*Wa*). Chinese envoys visited the Japanese islands, describing how the land was divided into small kingdoms controlled by chiefs. One of the largest kingdoms was Yamatai, ruled by a woman named Himiko. The directions that the Chinese envoys gave to Yamatai remain confusing, so there has been a long scholarly debate about Yamatai's location, and archaeologists have yet to find the tomb of Himiko described in the Chinese records that would pinpoint it. The Chinese chronicles describe Yamatai as a land devoid of cattle, horses and sheep, where rice and vegetables were staples and the people 'made no distinction between father and son or between men and women'. But for scholars of sake, the most important note from these records about the people of Wa is that 'it is in their nature to have quite a taste for alcohol.'[2] The question is: what was this alcoholic beverage?

Some scholars assert that alcohol existed in Japan before the Yayoi period, dating it to the Jōmon era that began around 10,000 BCE. Besides being hunter-gatherers, Jōmon were a pot-making culture, perhaps the earliest in the world, firing their unglazed ceramics in pits in the earth. The holes around the rim of some Jōmon pots have suggested to some scholars that they may have been used in fermentation, allowing carbon dioxide to escape.[3] However, Jōmon vessels were neither airtight nor could they retain liquid well, since they were not fired at high enough temperatures. The particular pots with holes around the rim, which date from the mid- to late Jōmon period, do not have pouring spouts, which has given rise to the supposition that cups were used to scoop out the fermented drink inside them. However, such drinking cups have not been found either, which leads defenders of the vessels to claim the lost cups were made of wood and have not survived.[4]

Turning from the evidence of pots to native fruit has given rise to theories that the Jōmon made alcohol from red elder (Japanese *niwatoko*, *Sambucus sieboldiana*), crimson glory vine (Japanese *yamabudō*, *Vitis coignetiae*) or raspberries.[5] Fruit will naturally ferment, even on the vine. It is easy to imagine a Jōmon hunter-gatherer putting aside some berries and discovering later that they had fermented, tasting them, liking the euphoric results, and then deciding to reproduce the concoction. However, the fruits native to Japan will not yield much alcohol. Native grapes (*yamabudō*), for instance, are small, the largest measuring no more than 8 millimetres (⅓ in.) in diameter, and too low in sugar to produce wine by themselves thanks to Japan's heavy rains and high temperatures. Japan's famous *Kōshū* grapes, grown in

Yamanashi prefecture, arrived in the Kamakura period (1192–1333), and those grapes were not used in alcoholic beverages in Japan until the early modern era (1600–1868), when they were added to some drink recipes for flavouring. Kōshū grapes were grown for the table.[6]

Sake historian Yoshida Hajime has reviewed the possible ways in which people in prehistoric Japan could have made alcohol and has found them all wanting except for rice. Japan's other indigenous wild grape, *ebizuru* (Vitis flexuosa), is likewise low in sugar. Nuts, especially chestnuts and horse chestnuts, were key staple foodstuffs for both the Jōmon and Yayoi and for later periods in Japanese history, but they will not naturally ferment like fruit. After removing the tannins, the nuts need to be further processed to break down their starch into sugar, a task too cumbersome for primitive technology, according to Yoshida. Japan's

Model of a kamado created as a funerary offering, Kofun period (300–538). Fire placed within the kamado (right) heats water in a cauldron (*kama*) on top. The steamer (*koshiki*; left) is placed on top of the cauldron to steam rice.

native tubers, taro (*satoimo*) and yam (*yamanoimo*), were not well suited for alcohol either. White and sweet potatoes, which arrived in the seventeenth century, were the ones historically used for making the distilled beverage *shōchū*, but only after the know-how to distill was introduced in Japan in the late 1500s. Wheat and barley both arrived with rice in the Yayoi period, but Yoshida concludes that they were much more difficult to process compared to rice either for fermentation or the table, so those grains were usually grown as animal fodder in the ancient period. The popularization of wheat and buckwheat had to wait until the arrival of stone mortars in the Kamakura period to transform the grains into flours. Stone mortars were not common appliances in Japanese farm homes until the late seventeenth century. Yoshida acknowledges continental and domestic examples of alcoholic beverages made from foxtail millet (*awa*) and barnyard millet (*hie*), but he explains that these grains were used for brewing in Japan only when rice was unavailable.[7]

By a process of elimination, Yoshida Hajime posits rice as the best ingredient for brewing in prehistoric Japan. Sake brewing begins with soaking and steaming rice. The people living near the end of the Yayoi period had the technology to steam rice using an earthenware stove (*kamado*) that could support a wood or ceramic steamer (*koshiki*).[8]

Rice can also be steamed by putting it in a wet bag, placing it in a hole, and putting hot rocks on top.[9] Glutinous steamed rice can be pounded into a rice cake. Non-glutinous rice, the kind used for sake, is best boiled then steamed if it is being prepared for eating, but just steaming the rice is optimal for sake brewing. However, simply steaming the rice will not produce alcohol because the sugar needed for fermentation somehow needs to be extracted from the starch.

THE QUESTION OF CHEWING BREWING

Modern sake brewers use the mould kōji to break down the starches in the steamed rice, but it has been posited that the Japanese once used chewing to accomplish this task, relying on the amylase in saliva instead of kōji. The evidence lies in a single textual source and in ethnographic comparisons. The textual reference is the eighth-century *Gazetteer of Ōsumi* (*Ōsumi no kuni fudoki*), which provides information about the eastern part of modern Kagoshima prefecture.

Gazetteers were regional reports responding to an order from the central government in 713 to list local stories, resources and other lore. Only a few of these gazetteers survive and only one is complete. *The Gazetteer of Ōsumi* exists only in a few lines of text. Like other official texts of the eighth century, such as *The Records of Ancient Matters* (*Kojiki*), compiled in 712, and *The Chronicles of Japan* (*Nihon shoki*), completed in 720, the gazetteers value myth and legend as much as factual information such as lists of local products. Both the *Kojiki* and the *Nihon shoki* mention sake but not how it is made. The *Kojiki*, for instance, includes a story of the Korean immigrant named Susukori who made sake for Emperor Ōjin. However, it is uncertain the degree to which sake-making technology came from Korea.[10] Although the stories within all of these eighth-century texts cannot be taken at face value, that has not always been the case for sake history and the *Gazetteer of Ōsumi* in particular. The passage about sake making in the *Gazetteer of Ōsumi* survives because it was quoted in a thirteenth-century text called *The Rubbish Bag* (*Chiribukuro*), where it is used to define the word *kamu* in a question-and-answer format typical of that text:

Kamu refers to brewing sake. What is the meaning of that?

 In the province of Ōsumi, a household prepared rice and water and called together the people of the village. When the men and women had gathered, they chewed rice and spat into a larger container for sake making, going home their separate ways. When it began to smell fermented, they came together again to drink what they had chewed and spat. The name they gave this was 'chewed sake' (kuchikami), according to what the gazetteer states.[11]

The point the author of *The Rubbish Bag* was trying to make – that the word for 'brewing' (*kamu*) derived from the word for 'chewed sake' (*kuchikami*) – is inaccurate. The words for brewing and chewing might seem similar but they are different verb forms that were not historically linked.[12]

 Despite appearing in a thirteenth-century text, the quote from the *Gazetteer of Ōsumi* is accepted as authentic for the eighth century. However, without the remainder of that document, it is hard to place the story in context. Perhaps Ōsumi was considered a land of many fantastic practices not found elsewhere? Gazetteers included information about local myths and legends as well as explanations for place names, so it is possible that the chewed sake story appeared in that context as local lore and hearsay, not actual fact.

 Yet some scholars attribute considerable significance to the story of chewed sake, viewing it as the origin of sake in Japan.[13] Their faith is notwithstanding the fact that there are no other references in the main Japanese islands to *kuchikami* sake in the premodern period, and there is no way to determine with archaeological evidence if chewed grains were used for fermentation.[14] Despite the absence of any evidence, a few scholars go as far as to project the practice of chewed sake back to the Jōmon period, before rice even arrived in Japan.[15] The assumption is that the Japanese, like everyone else, drink alcohol today, so they must have imbibed in prehistoric times, some way, somehow.

Examples of using chewing in fermentation can be found throughout the world, especially in South America, reaching a peak of productivity under the Inca empire (1438–1533), as historian Jeffrey Pilcher explains.[16] Sake scholars in particular point to the practice among the Ainu people of Hokkaido of using rice and corn for brewing and to the Ryukyu Islanders, who made a chewed sake up to the Meiji period (1868–1912).[17] According to a description of the practice on Ishigaki Island in southeastern Okinawa prefecture in the Meiji period, locals made a beverage called *mishi* for festival occasions, both as an offering to the divinities and as part of banquet celebrations for rice planting and the harvest. Residents prepared raw, non-glutinous rice and a flour made from it, chewing both and spitting the results into a cistern holding water. They then scooped up any rice solids from the bottom of the container and rechewed them. The ingredients were then ground in a stone mortar, strained with a coarse sieve and placed in a vessel to be allowed to ferment. The concoction was mixed three times a day and consumed after three to four days. The time and hard labour needed to process a lot of rice made the women's teeth tired, their mouths rough and their jaws ache, according to ethnographic accounts.[18] The use of a stone mortar makes it unlikely that a similar process was employed in the eighth century, when such technology was not widespread.[19]

A further twist of the chewed sake story is that it was made by virgins. Ishige Naomichi, one of Japan's foremost food scholars, expressed this view in *The Cambridge World History of Food*, writing, 'This primitive technique survived until the beginning of the twentieth century in Okinawa. By tradition, virgins prepared this type of liquor for special religious ceremonies.'[20] By 'surviving', Ishige implies that chewed sake was once more widespread in Japan and that it endured in Okinawa thanks to the area's remoteness. A long-held view among some scholars of Japanese folklore and anthropology, including Ishige, is that regions far from the political centre are 'primitive', holding on to customs that have disappeared in the mainstream.[21] In other words, the same folklorists believe that travelling away from the city into mountains or distant coastal villages was the same as travelling back in time, and no areas were more peripheral and therefore more 'ancient' than Hokkaido and the Ryukyu Islands because they were furthest away from the 'civilized' centre of Japan.[22] Ishige has used the same line of reasoning to argue that sushi originated in Southeast Asia due to ethnographic accounts of similar dishes in remote areas of Thailand and Laos today. Yet there is no written evidence that speaks to the age of these Southeast Asian culinary traditions or of their connection to Japanese sushi.[23] In short, the customs of the Ainu or Ryukyu Islanders may have nothing to do with past practices in mainland Japan. Indeed, most experts in the history of Japanese food culture view the foodways of the Ainu and of the Ryukyu Islands as distinct from that of the main islands of Japan.[24]

   That kuchikami sake was not only ancient but prevalent seems to have swayed sake expert Gautier Roussille, who writes about the supposed connection of the brew to virginal women:

> In Japan, *kuchi-kami-sake* ('chewed sake') was produced during
> Shinto ceremonies and consumed quickly. Depending on
> the period, the place and the specific ceremony, the work
> of mastication was carried out either by young virgins, by

the *miko* ([female] diviners and guardians of the sanctuary), or by the whole village.[25]

Such statements make kuchikami sake sound much more important historically than it was, but even more problematic is the way the beverage is gendered and sexualized. Modern sake brand names that include terms like 'beautiful woman', 'maiden', 'daughter', 'bride' and 'beauty' could be seen to evoke a similar gendering and sexualization of sake, a fantasy of young women of yore chewing rice and spitting into containers in what could be mistaken for a sex act. Such impressions contribute to sake's reputation in Japan today as an 'old man's drink', despite efforts to market to other consumers. Japanese people in the eighth century may not have viewed virginity as a specific life stage for women or men, or even thought about virginity at all, and the process of chewing grain to make sake as described in *The Gazetteer of Ōsumi* indicates that both men and women – neither of whom were called virgins – participated. In creating a false history of chewed sake, one scholar went as far as saying that the fourth-century Chinese record cited earlier for the people of Wa's love of alcohol also described how young girls, 'especially virgins', made chewed sake.[26] However, that Chinese record says nothing of the kind.

Thinking more of the mechanics behind chewed sake, scholar Yamashita Masaru endeavoured to reproduce it, but rather than chew the rice himself, he enlisted his students, which was a wise choice. Chewing raw rice, after all, is hard work. Yamashita hypothesized that with ten minutes of chewing, his students could produce a beverage with 2 per cent alcohol by volume (ABV), but the students reported the difficulty of the task and the rice they chewed failed to produce alcohol. To resolve the question of whether young women might have higher amounts of amylase or yeast in their saliva efficacious for brewing, Yamashita surveyed his students and concluded that there were no differences in the amount of these compounds among men and women of different ages, although there were variations among individuals and depending on whether or not they had brushed their teeth in the morning.[27] Other scholars have tried and failed to reproduce chewed sake, and I certainly would not recommend someone to try to make it at home.[28] Save your teeth!

That some communities in ancient Japan may have chewed grains and drunk the results is plausible given the *Gazetteer of Ōsumi* reference, but sake made that way would be difficult to produce in large amounts. The idea that chewing sake was a woman's task or that it was a practice dating to the Jōmon period even before the arrival of rice into Japan is as hard to swallow as a beverage made from someone else's spit. Thus to uphold chewed sake as the 'origin' of sake in Japan is a risky bet. Kuchikami sake seems instead a convenient way to imagine how there could have been sake in Japan before the advent of kōji. And the image of drinking virginal women's spit makes it too exciting a topic for many male sake historians to fail to mention.

DEFINING KŌJI

Instead of saliva, kōji is the essential ingredient for sake, but before delving into the history of kōji, it is important to know what it is and how it functions in making sake. Kōji is a filamentous fungi (mould) of the genus *Aspergillus*, so named because its asexual spores looked like an aspergillum, an instrument used for spreading holy water, according to the eighteenth-century botanist and priest who identified them. Some modern experts compare the appearance of the spores to toilet brushes.[29] Of the more than 250 species of *Aspergillus*, A. *oryzae*, aka kōji, has become well known beyond the world of sake. Chefs, and makers of charcuterie, are experimenting with the mould to facilitate fermentation and impart sweetness and umami notes to foods, aspects celebrated in the Japanese children's 'Song of Kōji' (*Kōji moco moco*) by the self-styled fermentation designer Ogura Hiraku, who promotes and markets the mould.[30] Kōji is a key ingredient in creating traditional Japanese flavourings like soy sauce and miso. More recently it is finding use in tenderizing and curing meat and fish, washing detergents and even pet foods. Approximately two-thirds of the bread produced commercially in the United States uses *Aspergillus oryzae* to facilitate yeast growth.[31] Kōji has been consumed as a stomach medicine in Japan for over a century and it might be employed in the future to biodegrade plastics.[32] Fans of the fungus gather for the annual Kojicon convention

Homemade *Aspergillus oryzae* kōji on rice.

online. Given kōji's importance to Japanese culture, many within Japan claim it as a 'national mould'. Kōji has been called Japan's 'national enzyme' from as early as 1957, and in December 2024 the Japanese government successfully lobbied the United Nations Educational, Scientific and Cultural Organization (UNESCO) to add Japanese sake brewed with kōji to its list of 'intangible cultural heritage'.[33]

As in the 1950s and earlier, the word kōji is most often used in Japan and elsewhere to refer to *Aspergillus oryzae*. However, in 2013, the Brewing Society of Japan, founded in 1987 to promote the scientific study of fermentation, argued that kōji as a national mould should be considered in the plural. Besides *Aspergillus oryzae*, the Brewing Society laid claim to three other types of kōji as 'national fungi': black kōji (*Aspergillus awamori*), necessary to make the distilled beverage Awamori, famous in Okinawa; a white variation of that kōji called *Aspergillus luchuensis mut. Kawachii*; and *Aspergillus sojae*, sometimes used in place of *Aspergillus oryzae* in making the distilled beverage known as shōchū.[34] For clarity, unless otherwise noted, use of the term kōji in the discussion that follows refers to *Aspergillus oryzae*.

THE FUZZINESS IN KŌJI'S PAST

There are a lot of mysteries in the history of kōji. In *The Arts of the Microbial World: Fermentation Science in Twentieth-Century Japan*, scholar Victoria Lee describes *Aspergillus oryzae*'s modern history, specifically how kōji makers developed pure cultures of their mould.[35] However, there are no equivalent monographs that cover kōji's premodern history in Japan. Scientist Ichishima Eiji, one of the main advocates for calling *Aspergillus oryzae* Japan's 'national fungus', devoted a 2007 book to kōji, but that work offers very little information about the mould's history, focusing instead on the origin of the Japanese race, the arrival of rice to Japan and sake brewing, before discussing kōji from a scientific perspective. Ichishima's study attests to the impact of the mould on Japanese civilization, but it also demonstrates the difficulty of writing the history of kōji beyond the various products it is used to create.[36]

Despite the close association between kōji and *Aspergillus oryzae*, the word kōji has other meanings, which complicate writing about the history of the mould. In sake making, kōji can designate the 'mould spores' (*tane kōji*) of *Aspergillus oryzae* sprinkled on steamed rice, which itself will be called kōji once the mould grows. The scientific name *Aspergillus oryzae* designates a mould found growing on rice (Latin *oryza*), but as described in more detail below, in Japanese the word kōji can also encompass other moulds with different scientific names that grow on a variety of media. The Japanese use the character 麹 to refer to kōji, which combines graphic elements signifying barley, rice and wrapping. That character was invented in China to refer to moulds there called *qu*. In the Meiji period, Japan modernized, and the Japanese sought to distinguish their culture from China and the West linguistically; this included popularizing a different character for kōji (糀), invented in the eighteenth century, to disentangle 'native kōji' from continental versions.[37] This Japanese character for kōji, comprised of elements meaning rice and flower, was comparable to the neologisms 'Japanese cuisine' (*washoku, Nihon ryōri*) and 'Japanese sweets' (*wagashi*), coined in the same period to nationalize food culture. Japan's kōji, in other words, 'flowered on rice', in contrast to the continental moulds grown on other media. The late nineteenth century thus marked the starting point of the effort to nationalize kōji in Japan, although that new character is still not as widely used as its predecessor.

Chemically, *Aspergillus oryzae* is a mould that produces more than fifty enzymes, of which amylase and protease are the most important for their culinary applications including sake. Amylase breaks down starches into sugars very effectively. Amazake, a non-alcoholic beverage made from kōji and now used in some recipes as a replacement for refined sugar, contains five to eight times more glucose than 100 per cent fruit juice.[38] Protease degrades proteins, releasing savoury amino acids. Though kōji also contributes sweetness and rich umami notes to sake, without that mould there would be no way to transform the starches in rice into sugars needed for alcoholic fermentation.

WHERE DID KŌJI COME FROM?

References to kōji in Japan can be traced back at least 1,200 years, and some claim that moulds now called kōji were first domesticated 9,000 years ago in China.[39] Since kōji can be found in soil and on plants there remains some debate about whether or not it emerged through domestication. If it did, then domesticated kōji later escaped into the wild.[40] The domestication of animals and plants is well studied and can be defined

> as a sustained, multigenerational, mutualistic relationship in which humans assume some significant level of control over the reproduction and care of a plant/animal order to secure a more predictable supply of a resource of interest and by which the plant/animal is able to increase its reproductive success over individuals not participating in this relationship, thereby enhancing the fitness of both humans and target domesticates.[41]

However, 'the evolutionary paths traversed by domesticated microbes [like kōji] remain poorly understood.'[42]

The argument that kōji emerged as a domesticated fungus traces kōji's origins to the wild mould *Aspergillus flavus* that grows on grains, nuts and dead plant and animal tissue.[43] The genomes of *A. flavus* and *A. oryzae* share a 99.5 per cent identity.[44] It is estimated that speciation of *Aspergillus* occurred 20 million years ago, and *A. flavus* emerged 5–8 million years ago.[45] *A. flavus* is not only older than kōji, it is far less benign, because it produces the carcinogenic compound aflatoxin, which is a 'nemesis to worldwide agriculture' as it can grow on any food or crop.[46]

In premodern Japan, sake brewers, producers of soy sauce and miso makers, as well as home chefs making sushi and pickles, certainly knew how to cultivate and use kōji, but they lacked the understanding that they were using a domesticated microorganism. The author of a late seventeenth-century guide to sake brewing compared kōji to a yōkai, a 'ghost' or 'an uncanny presence'. There is a wide variety of Japanese ghosts, but yōkai are phantoms that appear at a certain time and place for reasons not readily understood. Kōji qualified as a yōkai for that sake maker because, although its manifestation might be predicted, the mould sometimes behaved beyond human control or complete comprehension – to the point that kōji might delay its arrival, fail to appear or even grow malevolent. The brewer, for example, described how healthy yellow kōji might turn black, becoming detrimental to sake making. Such transformations could be so dire that the sake maker must temporarily stop using the room for making kōji in order to clean and fumigate it.[47] Kōji, in other words, was a mould that sometimes proved difficult to tame.

The Japanese word kōji has become synonymous with the mould that has the scientific name *Aspergillus oryzae*, but kōji in a wider sense encompasses other moulds and fermentation media besides rice. Japanese scholars differentiate *Aspergillus oryzae* from the kōji in the rest of Asia, which they divide into two other types depending on how they are made. What the Japanese call 'dumpling (*mochi*) kōji', used in brewing in China, is made from wheat dough that is shaped into bricks and allowed to grow mouldy. 'Grass (*kusa*) kōji' mixes grain flour with powdered vegetable material and this is also formed into shapes and allowed to get mouldy, a technique used in the Himalayas, northeast Asia and China.[48] Each of these approaches produces different moulds from *Aspergillus*, respectively *Rhizopus*, the same mould used for tempeh, and *Mucor*, also found in some cheeses from the French Alps. Kōji nationalists argue that Japanese kōji is distinct from the other moulds used in Asia not only in fermentation, but in the supposedly indigenous Japanese 'loose (*bara*) kōji' method of propagating *Aspergillus oryzae* by sprinkling it on steamed rice without forming it into bricks. However, there are examples of similar 'loose kōji' methods in Taiwan, Korea, Indonesia and Nepal.[49] All this begs the question of whether Japan's national mould is native to Japan or if it was imported, and if so, when and from where?

There is archaeological evidence of kōji fermentation to make alcohol in Early Neolithic (*c.* 9000–7000 cal. BP) China using grains such as broomcorn millet, Job's tears and rice around the time that rice and millet were domesticated. People of the Yellow River and Yangtze River valleys also innovated new types of ceramic vessels that presumably would have supported their passion for brewing, and evidence of fermented beverages made from rice, honey and fruits have been discovered in Henan. The people of the Early Neolithic period experimented with a wide variety of types of alcoholic fermentation in China long before the first possible literary mention of kōji (Chinese, *qu*) in the *Book of Documents* circa 500 BCE.[50]

There are several theories about when kōji first appeared in Japan. One is that it arrived along with rice paddy agriculture around the second or first millennium BCE, which would make sense given that *Aspergillus oryzae* is grown on rice in Japan.[51] However, there is no evidence to verify this claim, so the main purpose of this theory seems to be to link kōji to a historical moment many perceive to be foundational to Japanese civilization – helpful to claims that kōji is Japan's 'national mould'. A second hypothesis is that Japanese kōji, whenever it arrived, was a reinvention of imported continental fermentation techniques.[52] It is conceivable that the Japanese experimented first with methods of brick and grass kōji as used in other parts of Asia. But, when they replaced wheat with steamed rice as a medium, they discovered that the moulds *Rhizopus* and *Mucor* did not grow well, but that *Aspergillus oryzae* thrived.[53] As noted earlier, wheat would have been difficult to process for brewing in ancient Japan due to the rarity of stone mills. Rice, in contrast, can be polished using a wooden mortar and pestle.

Notwithstanding modern attempts in Japan to nationalize fungi and questions about kōji's origins as a domesticated version of *Aspergillus flavus*, kōji is found in soil and on plants. So, a third possibility for kōji's origins in Japan is that while the fungi are universal, the 'loose' method used to cultivate the mould on rice developed in Japan either independently or with influence from abroad.[54]

The discovery of kōji in Japan might have been a happy accident. Even without being inoculated by spores, *Aspergillus oryzae* will grow on steamed rice.[55] The earliest reference to kōji in Japan, a passage from the eighth-century *Gazetteer of Harima* (*Harima* fudoki), describes how someone used mouldy rice to brew sake. The reference is meant to explain the name of a village called Niwato in Harima (modern Hyōgo prefecture):

> Niwato Village was once called 'Sake for the Deities' (Niwaki). Food offerings for the deities had grown mouldy and sake was brewed from them. The 'Sake for the Deities' was offered to them and used at banquets. So the village was called Niwaki, although people currently call the place Niwato.[56]

A similar method of using mouldy rice can be found in Taiwan where leftover cooked millet or rice is spread in the bottom of a basket, covered with another basket, and hung on a stand and kept warm. After three to four days, mould appears. This black, yellow or red fungus is mixed with steamed rice or millet to create an alcoholic beverage.[57]

The ancient Japanese name for kōji is kabitachi, meaning 'mould appearing', and besides cooked rice, kōji can be found elsewhere in the environment and cultivated for use. Sake expert, scientist and author Suminoe Kinshi (1889–1972) describes how every autumn the elderly master brewer (tōji) at his family's sake business would gather twigs from deciduous trees, which he burned to make ash. Then he would steam brown rice, cover the rice with this ash and place the mix in a tray used for cultivating kōji (kōji buta). The tōji put leaves on top of the mix and placed it in the brewery's kōji making room. Kōji grew on the ferment, which the tōji gathered and dried to be used for brewing the following year.[58]

Kōji can also be harvested from mouldy rice plants growing in a paddy, which the Japanese called 'kōji flowers', 'rice kōji' or 'rice flowers'. This kōji, found on rice ears, has a deep green colour.[59] Kōji specialist Koizumi Takeo described the example of a kōji maker from Yamagata prefecture who, before the Second World War, gathered kōji from rice fields, mixed it with wood ash, waited half a year, and used that as the basis for kōji making. Koizumi documented similar examples of people gathering kōji to make miso, especially in the Kyoto–Osaka region.[60] Even after the advent of commercial kōji sellers in the medieval period, people in rural areas of Japan likely used similar techniques to gather and cultivate kōji for use in making miso and sushi and in home brewing. From these examples, we can further hypothesize that the Japanese experimented with moulds found naturally on rice plants and steamed rice and then gradually domesticated *Aspergillus oryzae* from them. When or how this may have occurred, and whether it was influenced by continental know-how or was an independent discovery, remains a mystery.

In summary, existing evidence does not allow us to know when or how kōji first appeared in Japan, but by the eighth century we can conclude that kōji had become an ingredient used in alcoholic fermentation. How to cultivate and brew with kōji would have been important skills, which is why they became closely guarded guild secrets later in the medieval period – as described in the next chapter.

SAKE BREWING IN THE ENGI SHIKI

Although kōji is a main ingredient in sake, any history of brewing, or of kōji, needs to recognize that when it came to making alcohol, the ancient Japanese were as experimentally minded as the people of Early Neolithic China, as shown in the tenth-century

Procedures of the Engi Era (Engi shiki), one of the most important historical sources for the early history of brewing in Japan.[61] The *Engi shiki* is not a brewers' manual but rather a collection of laws, Shinto regulations and descriptions of government offices, including those charged with brewing sake for the court and festivals. The *Engi shiki* lists types of sake and the resources used to make them, including brewing equipment, but it does not include recipes that allow us to reproduce these varieties of sake. It is possible that these recipes used different types of kōji besides *Aspergillus oryzae*.[62]

Most remarkable for the history of both kōji and sake in Japan is that some of the descriptions of beverages in the *Engi shiki* make use of both kōji and sprouted wheat or barley, ingredients typical for beer brewing.[63] Using kōji in conjunction with sprouted grains may have been the original meaning of the word kōji (Chinese, *qu*) in China.[64] In fact, some scholars are quick to call the use of sprouted grain a 'Chinese' method.[65] However, the sake descriptions found in the *Engi shiki* are different from the methods used in China in the same period.[66] So rather than identifying these methods as foreign, they instead speak to the variety and experimental nature of brewing in ancient Japan. There might have been even more diverse types of brewing in ancient Japan that were never described in writing.

Besides sake making, the ancient Japanese were familiar with using sprouted grain in confectionery. The sweet called *ame*, mentioned in eighth- and tenth-century sources including the *Engi shiki*, was made from sprouted rice or barley.[67] However, it is uncertain if those Japanese following the directions in the *Engi shiki* also malted the germinated grains, heating them to stop the germination process and so make the grains last longer – a technique used in beer brewing.

The *Engi shiki* lists the following sake and the ingredients used to make them, with blank spaces indicating that some information was not included:

SAKE NAME	INGREDIENTS				
	Steamed Rice	Kōji	Water	Sake	Sake Produced
Goshu 御酒	1,000	400	900		800
Goishu 御井酒	1,000	400	600		400
Reishu 醴酒	40	20		30	90
Sanshusō 三種糟					
Version 1	500	100 + 100 sprouted wheat or barley		500	500
Version 2	500 glutinous rice	100 + 100 sprouted wheat or barley		500	500
Version 3	500 non-glutinous rice or foxtail millet	100 + 100 sprouted wheat or barley		500	500
Kachisō 擣糟	1,000	700	1,700		1,000
Tonshu 頓酒	1,000	400	900		800
Jukushu 熟酒	1,000	400	1,170		1,400
Reishi 醴斎	180 white rice flour	90		50	200
Ōshi 盎斎	130 brown rice flour	60		50	200
White and Black Sake 白酒、黒酒	714	286	500		178.5 each

Sake in the *Engi shiki*

The unit of measurement used in this table is the gō (0.18 litres/ just over ⅓ U.S. pint). There are 1,000 gō (180 litres/47¾ gall.) in a modern koku, but in the tenth century, 1 koku measured just 83 litres (22 gall.). Hence the above measurements are best understood to reflect proportions.[68]

Several of the sake, including the style goshu, used a method – called shiori – for building up the alcohol content in which some sake was produced, then more ingredients were added to the brewed sake, typically up to four more times. The eighth-century *Records of Ancient Matters* (Kojiki) includes the story of the storm god Susano'o defeating a giant snake by causing it to drink a sake made with eight more additions of ingredients.[69] The shiori method was eventually discontinued because it took time to produce sake that way and the sake could easily spoil.[70] Instead, breweries added more ingredients in stages as the sake was fermenting, a process first documented in the Muromachi period (1336–1573), as described in the next chapter.[71]

Goshu was the top-grade sake used by the imperial court and for rituals.[72] It was produced beginning in the tenth lunar month, which roughly corresponds to November today. Making goshu used a high ratio of kōji to rice, so it would be called a sweet sake by modern standards. The name goshu signified high-quality sake through the medieval period, and a recipe for it is found in the earliest brewers' manual, *Sake Journal* (Goshu no nikki), as described in the next chapter, although the directions differed from the *Engi shiki* version here.

Goishu was a late summer sake made in the last ten days of the seventh lunar month (late August). Like goshu, this sake had a high kōji ratio, but it would have been even thicker since less water was used. This sweet summer sake may have been cooled in a well if goishu is translated literally as 'well sake'.

Reishu was a sweet sake made quickly from the beginning of July to August. This was another shiori sake created by adding kōji and rice to existing sake. With a high kōji ratio, this sake would have also been sweet, and probably consumed cooled. Reishu might be similar to mirin, a sake-like beverage made with glutinous rice and distilled alcohol used as a sweetener in cooking today.[73]

Sanshusō, literally the 'three varieties of sake', were made for the New Year with the shiori method using equal parts kōji and sprouted wheat or barley. What differentiated them was the type of rice or non-glutinous millet (awa, Setaria italica) used.

Kachisō was another sweet sake that, according to the name, featured a mash pounded in a wooden mortar. It was produced from July to September.

Tonshu and Jukushu – what differentiates these two seems to be the period of time they were brewed. Judging from the names, Tonshu was produced quickly and Jukushu more slowly.

Reishi and Ōshi were two sake produced four days in advance for a ceremony honouring Confucius in March and September. Reishi used white rice flour, which facilitates the growth of kōji and alcohol production, and Ōshi used brown rice flour. Both were sweet sake.[74]

The sake makers for the imperial court, introduced below, also brewed a white and a black sake for the imperial enthronement rites and the annual harvest festival. The latter was darkened with ash from the Clerodendrum plant (kusagi, Clerodendrum trichotomum), used also for dyes in the ancient period.

Based on the list of tools in the Engi shiki, a wooden mortar and pestle was used for dehulling and polishing the rice. Unglazed jars were used for brewing and storage, and these would have had a maximum capacity of 540 litres (143 gall.). Most were probably one-third that size. The list of tools in the Engi shiki includes bags and a press (*fune*), so some of the sake at least would have been added to the bags and pressed to separate the liquid from the dregs. Still, most of the sake would retain some sediment, contributing to the sweet flavour profile that aristocrats of the tenth century favoured.[75]

THE IMPERIAL SAKE BREWERS

Sake described in the *Engi shiki* were the product of the Imperial Household Agency's Sake Bureau (Miki no tsukasa, Sake no tsukasa). *Ryō no shūge*, a collection – dating from the ninth century – of commentaries on administrative codes, sheds further light on the Sake Bureau, as do archaeological excavations that have yielded wooden slips (*mokkan*) and the site of the bureau at the imperial palace in Nara.

The imperial court employed artisanal groups called *be*, which provided goods or services in lieu of paying taxes in goods. Among these be were performing artists, specialized craftspeople such as lacquerware makers, and brewers known as the Sake-be (*Sakabe*). Members of the Sakabe consisted of 160 households from Yamato, Kawachi and Settsu provinces (modern Nara and Osaka prefectures including a portion of Hyōgo prefecture). The Sakabe produced sake for the imperial court two to three times a year, and they also supplied vinegar.[76] In a given year, sixty members of the Sakabe came to court to perform their duties, which also included serving sake at some court parties. Excavations of the Sake Bureau near the remains of the imperial Heijō Palace in Nara in 1993 revealed a building with a pounded earth floor, a tile roof and a well 1.4 metres (4½ ft) in diameter lined with wood. Fragments of stoneware and wooden slips about sake making were also discovered, which confirmed the purpose of the site. The

Sake Bureau well, Heijō Palace.

brewing jars were partially buried in the ground for stability, a practice that continued through the medieval period.[77]

JAPAN'S FIRST HOME BREWER, PRINCE NAGAYA

There is also evidence of sake making at the residence of Prince Nagaya (684–729) in Nara, where some 50,000 wooden slips with writing dated to the early eighth century were discovered in 1988 during construction of a department store.[78] The wooden slips indicate that Prince Nagaya had five ceramic vessels of various sizes for sake making. Unfortunately, we only know the dimensions of two of these containers: a middle-sized vessel of 406–31 litres (107–14 gall.) capacity and a small vessel with a 206-litre (54 gall.) capacity. The prince had his servants make sake for his own use, but he also sold some of his home brew commercially in Nara.[79] Thus, besides his important role in eighth-century politics, which ended poorly with his death at the hands of political rivals, Prince Nagaya may have been Japan's first documented home brewer and sake seller.

WHEN ALL TŌJI WERE WOMEN

Prince Nagaya was hardly the only person to brew sake for home use or commercially in the eighth century, a period when the word tōji was synonymous with women. Today, tōji refers to the 'master brewer' in charge of all aspects of production at a brewery, but when the term first appeared in the eighth century it referred to a female chief of a provincial social and economic unit called a clan (*gōzoku*). Only women were tōji. The male chief was called an *obito*. More than simply the spouse of the clan head, the tōji held authority over her clan. Use of the word tōji to signify a married woman continued in parts of Japan into the twentieth century.[80]

By the ninth century, the usage of tōji expanded and the meaning changed to refer to the female head of a wealthy household. As the term became more widespread, the authority of the tōji diminished, since the title now became synonymous with wife. However, the tōji continued to have important duties in managing the household that included brewing sake. One story in the early ninth-century collection of Buddhist tales *Record of Miraculous Events in Japan* (Nihon ryōiki) describes an impoverished woman who prays to the bodhisattva Kannon for help in finding a wealthy husband. Through the divinity's intervention, she is wed, and her spouse provides her with gifts befitting her new status as tōji. She receives cloth to make clothes and rice to brew sake.[81] A similar story is in a twelfth-century collection of Buddhist stories, *Tales of Times Now Past* (Konjaku monogatari), in which a woman devoted to Kannon miraculously receives rice to brew sake and silk so that she can impress a suitor.[82] Sake brewing, it seems, was a sought-after skill that distinguished a good female partner.

Women not only brewed at home, but sometimes sold their sake. The *Record of Miraculous Events in Japan* includes a cautionary tale of a woman brewer who went to hell for selling watered-down sake.[83] Not to dilute the sake too much was probably good advice for any brewer (from the perspective of the sake drinker), but the fact that the sake maker in the story was female provides further evidence of women's prominence in the trade. By the 1400s, some women managed their own brewing operations, as outlined in the next chapter, which also charts the rise of brewing at Buddhist temples and cities in the medieval period.

Two centuries after its first appearance in Japanese records the island's brewers were making a variety of sake, most with rice and large amounts of kōji, giving the final beverage a sweetness only enhanced by the minimal pressing. Sake in the ancient period was in a process of becoming in the sense of the development of the processes to make it, and experimentation continued in the medieval period, as the next chapter describes. Although the recipe was evolving, sake was already central to Japanese culture – an aspect covered in Chapter Three.

TWO
ENLIGHTENED BREWS: MEDIEVAL TOWN AND TEMPLE SAKE BREWERIES, 1400-1600

After the era of the tenth-century *Engi shiki*, mentioned in the previous chapter, there are few sources for tracing the history of sake until the fourteenth century, due to the famines, epidemics and social problems that plagued Japan from the eleventh to the thirteenth century.[1] A chronicle of the Kamakura shogunate (1192–1333), *Mirror to the East* (*Azuma kagami*), records in the ninth month of 1252 how officials found 37,274 jars for sake brewing in Kamakura residences, and subsequently limited each household to just one brewing jar. Clearly there was both considerable home brewing and commercial sake sales in medieval Kamakura because the shogunate simultaneously prohibited the sale of sake. The Kamakura shogunate sought to limit brewing so that resources like rice would be used for food and not alcohol.[2]

That the Kamakura shogunate's prohibition of sake was an attempt to direct grain towards food and not alcohol is evident in its subsequent prohibitions against selling sake in 1264, 1284 and 1290, which came in the wake of famines. There were 21 famines from 1150 until 1280, of which the Kangi famine (1229–32) and

Storage jar (*tsubo*), Muromachi period, 1400s, stoneware with natural ash glaze (Shigaraki ware).

Shōga crises (1257–60) were particularly devastating. After the Kangi famine, the shogunate went so far as to allow families to sell their children into slavery. Lawlessness was so endemic that the jails filled up, but the warrior government had to release the prisoners because it could not afford to feed them.[3] In this context of limited resources, 'the prohibition of sake making became a fundamental policy of the Kamakura shogunate', explains the pre-eminent sake historian Yoshida Hajime.[4]

Japan's social and economic outlook was much better by the late fourteenth century, leading to a decline in the number of famines thanks to better climatic conditions and improvements in agriculture such as new rice varieties and double cropping, which provided resources to boost the population. Culturally too the late fourteenth century was a renaissance, with the new Muromachi warrior government, now headquartered in Kyoto, spurring trends in architecture, patronizing Zen Buddhism and Noh theatre, and enjoying new pastimes such as tea tasting (which developed into the tea ceremony) and new types of dining that stimulated the creation of a cuisine suitable for banquets. The Muromachi shogunate (1336–1573) also understood that sake could be an important revenue source for the government rather than being a drain on the economy. Thus the Muromachi shoguns began a long relationship of government facilitating sake production to reap tax benefits. That sake was an important source of revenue was a lesson the shogunate learned from religious institutions and wealthy urban entrepreneurs.

MONASTIC BREWERIES

Although the Kamakura shogunate viewed brewing negatively, the other two powerholders in medieval Japan, the imperial court and religious institutions, recognized its revenue potential. The aristocracy and religious institutions (temples and shrines) derived income from landed estates and received payments in kind for rents. Rice was one of the most important products that any estate could produce because the grain functioned as a currency that could be exchanged for other goods. Rice could also be transformed into a higher value finished good, namely sake.

Brewing required space, expertise and manpower, which religious institutions had in abundance. Although Buddhist monks took vows to eschew alcohol – a point that the shogunates and ecclesiastical authorities sometimes felt they needed to be reminded of – in Japan, Buddhism was inseparable from Shinto, meaning that temples also supplicated Shinto deities that required sake as part of their daily offerings. Shinto divinities, like their Greco-Roman counterparts, enjoyed alcohol. As early as the eighth century, Japanese temples began making their own brews, and sake production became more widespread in the major temples of Nara in the tenth and eleventh centuries.[5] Buddhism's tacit approval of sake brewing is seen in the *Essentials of Salvation* (Ōjōyōshū), completed in 985 by the Tendai monk Genshin (942–1017), a work in which the author offered a guide to escaping the world of suffering by being born into the Pure Land of Amida Buddha after death. Instead of condemning sake brewing in this highly influential text, Genshin instead warned brewers not to dilute their sake with water, threatening that those who did would be punished in the afterlife in the Hell of Fire and Worms, where besides suffering from four hundred diseases, worms would emerge from their bodies to consume them, a fate also destined to befall anyone who killed an animal. To hammer the point home further, Genshin warned that anyone who adulterated sake would suffer endless thirst in their next life, taking the form of a hungry ghost with an enormous belly but a needle-thin neck.[6] Genshin brought the full force of Buddhist damnation to bear, not to stop brewing or drinking, but to try to scare brewers and sake sellers into maintaining the purity of their products.

Besides serving the temple's own internal religious needs in Shinto worship – and the occasional tipple for the monks as well – sake was an important way for religious institutions, which were vast landowners, to transform rice paid in rents and tribute into a finished good that could be sold at a profit. From the late fourteenth to the end of the sixteenth century, several religious institutions became noted for their sake, chiefly the wealthy Nara temples of Kōfukuji and Shōryakuji; Amanosan Kongōji and Kanshinji in modern Osaka prefecture; Hyakusaiji in modern Shiga prefecture; and Toyoharaji in Fukui prefecture.[7] The brewers of Shōryakuji, introduced in more detail below, became particularly famous in the 1440s, but were later surpassed by Kōfukuji in the sixteenth century.[8]

THE GROWTH OF URBAN BREW SHOPS (SAKAYA)

While many religious institutions were brewing their own sake, aristocrats in Kyoto derived income from granting rights to secular brew shops (*sakaya*), which made and sold sake. Kyoto was known for the number and prominence of its sake brewers, according to passing references in texts from the tenth and thirteenth centuries. Besides being the capital, Kyoto was well situated to become a centre for brewing because of the city's two rice markets, where rice received as rent, taxes or payments from around Japan was exchanged for other goods or coins.⁹ Many of Kyoto's brewers made payments to the area's most powerful temple, Enryakuji, located on Mount Hiei northeast of the capital, for the right to operate. The prominence of clerical and religious-sounding names among these brewers in historical documents evidences the close ties between urban brewers and the monastic establishment. Other Kyoto brewers developed similar relationships with powerful aristocrats, who often granted rights of production and/or monopoly to groups in and near Kyoto in return for payments in cash, kind and service. Such links explain why, in the first decades of the fourteenth century, the capital's aristocrats tapped brewers to pay for the restoration of a shrine and its festival floats.¹⁰

By the end of the fourteenth century, the shogunate, which was always eager to limit both the revenue and the authority of the imperial court, took away the payments from sake brewers from the aristocrats. In 1372, on the pretext of paying for the enthronement of Emperor Goen'yū, the shogunate demanded that sake makers pay a yearly operating fee as well as a separate 'pot tax' on the number of vessels they used for sake making. In 1393, the shogunate affirmed its right to tax all brewers, even those under the operation of temples. Beginning in that year, Kyoto's brewers collectively made a yearly payment of 6,000 coins to the shogunate, which was an enormous sum.¹¹

In the early fifteenth century, Kyoto's brewers came from the ranks of wealthy merchants, a fact confirmed by a list of 342 brewers compiled in the years 1425–6. The wealthy merchants who had the financial resources to engage in brewing were called *dosō*, which referred to the storehouses that held their wealth, consisting of products paid to them in kind, rents, and to secure loans. Like the brewers of Kamakura, Kyoto's brewers created their beverages in pots called *kame*, which had a capacity of 2–3 koku (360–540 litres/95–142½ gall.) and were partially buried in the earth for stability. A typical brewing operation consisted of 120 pots, but larger businesses had upwards of 200 pots.[12] An archaeological survey by the Kyoto City Archaeological Research Institute in 2005 uncovered a brewery from the Muromachi period consisting of two hundred holes for sake pots, each 0.6 metres in diameter and 0.4 metres deep (2 ft × 1 ft 4 in.). The same brewery had nineteen wells, four of which were lined with stone.[13] In the fifteenth century, most of Kyoto's breweries were located so that they were able to draw water not only from wells but from the Horikawa River. Another cluster of brewers lay east of the Kamo River in the areas near Yasaka Shrine, Kiyomizu Temple and Kenninji Temple. Seventeen more brewers found a home in the Saga area in the west of the city, close to the Katsura River, an important water route to Osaka and the coast.[14] Ceramic containers, such as the one behind the woman sake seller depicted overleaf, were also used to age sake, as the preference in the fifteenth and sixteenth centuries was for sake aged up to a decade.[15]

Kyoto's first famous brand of sake was called Willow (*yanagi*), a favourite beverage of the capital's aristocrats and clerical elite, who mentioned it in their diaries.[16] Willow's producers stamped their barrels with six stars as a way to distinguish their product, and later called their brew Great Willow (*dai yanagi*) to differentiate it further from imitators.[17] The Willow Brewery paid the warrior government taxes that amounted to one-tenth of the shogunate's annual revenue – testimony to the wealth of the brewery and the dependence of the shogunate on the sake trade.[18]

WOMEN BREWERS

Much is made today, and rightly so, of women brewing masters (tōji) in a trade which has, since the early modern period (1600–1868), been male-dominated, but women had a prominent place in medieval brewing. The aforementioned list of brewers from 1425/6 includes three breweries owned by women, two of which were operated by nuns and one by a lay person. Likely all of these women were widows, which was why their names were listed. Women likely assisted or jointly managed other breweries in this period even if the ownership appeared under their husband's name.[19]

Sake-maker next to a pot seller, detail from *Poetry Competition of Seventy-One Artisans*, copy dated 1847.

The prominence of women brewers is evidenced further in a picture scroll dated to 1500, *Poetry Competition of Seventy-One Artisans* (*Shichijū ichiban shokunin uta'awase*). The painting depicts 142 tradespeople with accompanying poems, and the sake maker is a woman. Pictured next to a pot seller, the caption above the sake maker reads: 'Try my sake, and I have the popular *usunigori* too.' One of the sake maker's containers is open, allowing customers to see the *usunigori*, a sake clarified when the lees (*kasu*) have naturally settled to the bottom. *Usunigori* (also called *nakagumi*) would have fetched a higher price than cloudy sake since it was more refined. However, the sake maker's real prize is in the decorated containers behind her, which likely hold a higher grade of sake, perhaps *koshu*: sake aged for upwards of ten years that wealthy customers preferred in that period.

THE KŌJI WARS

Although the Muromachi shogunate asserted its right to tax the capital's brewers, it also recognized the authority of religious institutions, specifically Enryakuji and its affiliate Kitano Tenmangu Shrine, to continue to derive income from sake through the kōji trade in return for helping the shogunate collect taxes from sake makers. In the fourteenth century, the city's kōji makers paid the imperial court fees for the rights to operate in the city, but in 1387 the warrior government directed kōji producers to pay Kitano Shrine instead. The same edict declared that all of the city's sake producers had to buy their kōji from makers affiliated with Kitano Shrine and that they could not produce kōji themselves.[20] Kitano's kōji makers were shrine functionaries (*jinin*), a group of people who assisted in religious ceremonies, management and tasks like collecting rents for the shrine. Kitano Shrine's functionaries enjoyed the sole right to produce and sell kōji, and in return they collected the taxes from sake brewers, which they remitted to the warrior government.[21] Sometimes Kyoto's brewers needed a reminder that they had to purchase all of their kōji from the Kitano Shrine guild. In 1419, the shogunate reiterated that law and emphasized the point two days later by destroying the kōji rooms of 52 brewers and kōji producers, including 25 members of Kitano's own guild guilty of violating guild rules.

Facing further resistance from brewers in 1443, the Kitano kōji guild called again for the shogunate to affirm their monopoly

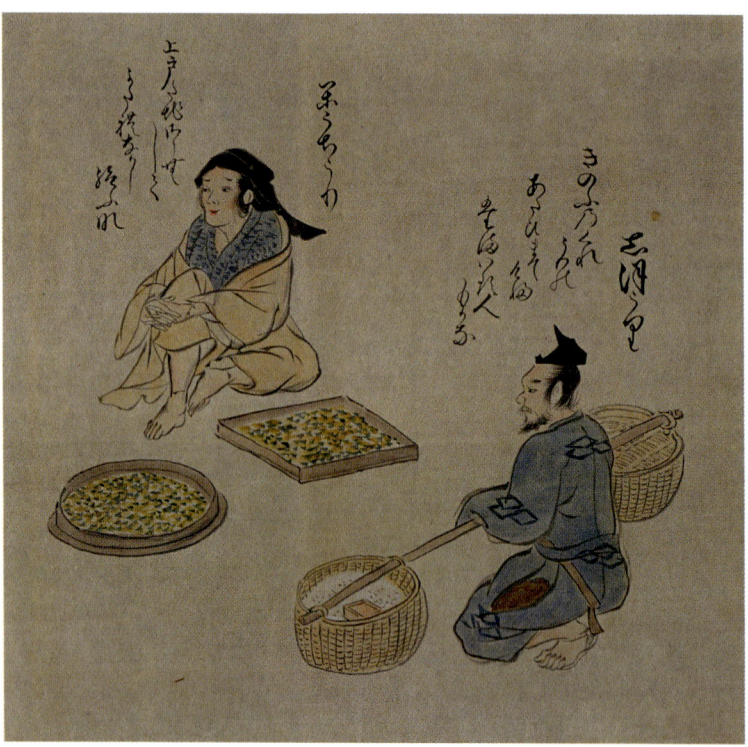

Kōji seller, detail from *Poetry Competition of Seventy-One Artisans*, copy dated 1847.

rights. Guild members then locked themselves in a hall in their shrine and threatened to kill themselves unless their monopoly rights over the kōji trade were upheld. Hearing rumours that they had lost the support of both the warrior government and their religious patron Enryakuji Temple, the kōji makers took over the shrine again in 1444. When the shogunate intervened to force the guild from the shrine, fighting ensued, leading to the deaths of forty people and the burning of Kitano Shrine. Ultimately, the guild preserved their monopoly rights to kōji making. A century later the shogunate reaffirmed the guild's sole right to produce and sell kōji in and around the capital.[22]

The picture scroll *Poetry Competition of Seventy-One Artisans* reveals that women were involved in the kōji trade. The caption above the kōji seller reads: 'Sake drinkers look, but please don't drool.' Though kōji is a key ingredient for making soy sauce, miso and versions of sushi, the kōji seller calls out directly to sake brewers, suggesting that they are her main customers. Judging by the image, her kōji is not in powdered form (*tane kōji*) but rather as rice that has already been 'inoculated' with kōji, allowing buyers to use it immediately for sake making.

ASH IN SAKE BREWING

Medieval kōji guilds discovered the importance of ash in kōji production and preservation. The ash was mixed with steamed rice to cultivate kōji, contributing phosphorus and potassium to help the kōji grow. Ash also improved aeration and helped to maintain the alkalinity of the kōji-inoculated rice, thereby preventing contamination from other microorganisms since kōji is more tolerant of alkaline conditions than other moulds. In addition, ash neutralizes acidic organisms that could inhibit kōji's growth. Kōji makers sought out ash from centuries-old Japanese oak, camellia and chestnut trees to which they added ash from leaves and branches they had harvested and dried for years. The ash was usually burned twice to make it very fine.[23]

In premodern Japan, besides the ancient 'black sake' (kuroki) mentioned in the previous chapter, ash was also sometimes added to sake to make it less acidic. Medieval sake makers kept their fermentation pots busy all year round, but sake produced in the summer ferments quickly and takes on a bitter taste. So, brewers often added ash to the sake before diluting it, a method surviving in the traditional sakes of Izumo (Shimane prefecture) and sake made in Higo (Kumamoto) and Satsuma (Kagoshima). Brewers preferred the ash from camellia and evergreen trees, and speciality ash dealers who sold to brewers were active through the early modern period.[24] Adding ash improves the shelf life of the sake but can negatively affect the taste. Warlord Toyotomi Hideyoshi (1537–1598), who unified Japan in 1590, ordered the temple Amanosan Kongōji to stop adding ash to its famous sake, which was one of his favourites.[25]

YEAST

Since medieval brewers did not have a modern understanding of science, they knew that kōji was essential for brewing, but they did not know that the mould was a microorganism, and they did not know about yeast. Before Yabe Kikuji discovered sake yeast in 1897, most brewers and brewery scientists believed that kōji alone was responsible for fermentation.[26] Yabe's discovery came more than a decade after Emil Christian Hansen's isolation of pure yeast at the Carlsberg Brewery in Copenhagen in 1883.[27] But, even without a scientific understanding of brewing, good brewers are like good chefs who tinker with recipes. Given that medieval brewers made sake in small batches, when one pot failed spectacularly but another flourished they took notice. Observing the connections between foam and fermentation, they may have discovered how to encourage fermentation in a new vessel by transferring foam from another. They might even have thought to soak the foam with a cloth and dry the cloth so that they could use it another time. Both techniques for transferring yeast were described in a twelfth-century Chinese text, although there was no evidence that Japanese brewers had access to that work.[28] For their part, Chinese brewers did not understand the scientific role of yeast in brewing until the modern period.[29]

THE MEDIEVAL SAKE OF THE GOSHU NO NIKKI

A more in-depth view of medieval brewing can be gained from the text *Sake Journal* (*Goshu no nikki*), which presents six recipes for making sake, directions for pasteurizing it and other notes. Notwithstanding the information about brewing found in the tenth-century *Procedures of the Engi Era* (*Engi shiki*), which do not provide enough detail to reproduce ancient recipes, the *Sake Journal* is the earliest guide to brewing in Japan that allows us to take the measure of the brewers' art in the medieval period.[30] The oldest extant version of the *Sake Journal* is a copy in the collection of the University of Tokyo's Historiographical Institute that dates to 1566, but the text may have been composed as early as 1355 or 1489, depending on how one interprets the calligraphy for the date on the manuscript. Before reading the translated text provided below, a few background observations about the *Sake Journal's* history and contents are needed to explain its significance and contents.

The anonymous author of the *Sake Journal* presents the text as 'an oral secret that must be kept completely private'. Before the chemistry of sake making was understood, brewing methods would have been discovered from a trial-and-error approach, making technical knowledge of how to brew sake precious. The *Sake Journal* reaffirms the importance not just of oral instructions but of physical – such as sensory – learning for sake brewing. As the directions translated below reveal, successful brewers had to be able to use their senses to judge the taste and appearance of sake, from the clarity of the water used to wash the rice to the progress of the ferment to the correct temperature for pasteurization. For example, the directions for the sake called goshu remind the reader to add more ingredients 'when the brew becomes sharp tasting', which would signal to the brewer that the sugars had been transformed into alcohol. The *Sake Journal* also provided guidance for gauging temperatures by touch alone. A brewer also had to keep seasonality and weather in mind, since environmental factors could affect the outcome of the product.[31]

TRANSLATED EXTRACTS OF
SAKE JOURNAL (*GOSHU NO NIKKI*)

Sake Journal is an oral secret that
must be kept completely private.

• [Goshu]
Allow 18 litres [1 to; 4¾ gall.] of white rice to soak overnight in water; then steam it thoroughly. Add 10.8 litres [6 shō; 2¾ gall.] of kōji at body temperature. Add the water used for soaking the

rice the previous evening to the ferment (tsukuri). That water should be at body temperature, and 18 litres of it should cover [the ferment]. Cover the bucket with a mat for a lid and allow it to rest for about six days. Once the fermentation is activating in the bucket, mix and stir it. Make sure to mix carefully, including the ferment on the edges of the bucket. Stir it twice at midday. When the brew becomes sharp-tasting, add kōji mixed with water (mizu kōji).[32] Then steam 18 litres of rice thoroughly as before and cool it completely. Add the rice into the centre of the fermenting sake. After that, stir it twice daily. If it settles, churn it with the stirrer. Cover with a lid you have made. There are [additional] oral secrets.

• Amano Sake

Allow 18 litres of brown rice to soak overnight.[33] Steam it thoroughly the next day. Since this is a sake brewed in winter, allow the rice to cool to body temperature and combine it with 10.8 litres of kōji, placing it in the ferment. Measure and add 18 litres of water, cover with a mat for a lid and allow to rest. Within about four or five days, when the grains of the rice begin to dissolve and the fermentation occurs, stir it gently. When it starts to taste fermented, take 18 litres of rice, soak it overnight, and steam it well on the following day; then cool it thoroughly on a straw mat. Combine this with 10.8 litres of kōji and add it to the sake made earlier. Add 18 litres of water and stir. When the fermentation progresses and it starts to bubble, divide it into two vessels (kame). Then add 5.6 litres [3 shō; 1½ gall.] of steamed rice to each vessel. The kōji [added] is 10.8 litres, as before. Because this is a transcript of an oral instruction, it must remain secret.

• Font of Enlightenment (*Bodaisen*)

Wash 18 litres of polished rice until the water is clear. Remove 1.8 litres [½ gall.] of rice from that and cook it.[34] In the summertime, be sure to allow the rice to cool completely. Put that cooked rice in a bamboo basket and soak it in water, positioning it in the middle of the [remaining] uncooked rice. Seal the container for a day and allow to stand overnight.[35] On the third day, place a bucket (*oke*) off to the side and remove any clear water at the top of the vessel. Then remove the cooked rice from the centre and place it in the bucket off to the side. Next, remove the uncooked rice and thoroughly steam it. In the summer, be sure to allow that rice to cool completely. [From that rice prepare] 9 litres [5 shō; 2½ gall.] of kōji and set aside 1.8 litres [1 shō] of it. Combine that 1.8 litres of kōji with the 1.8 litres of cooked rice [that had been soaking in the basket in the water] and place half of it flat on the bottom of a bucket. Combine the remaining [4 shō] of kōji with the rice, mixing these together and placing them in the ferment (*tsukuri*). Measure off 1.8 litres of the [clear] water removed earlier and add that on top. Then spread the [other half of the] cooked rice [and kōji] from earlier on top of that. Cover the opening with a straw mat; let it rest for seven days. The sake is usually done in seven days, but if you do not need it yet, wait up to ten days.

• Kikaki

Soak 18 litres of brown rice overnight. While the rice is still hot, place it into a vessel [either a large bucket (*koga*) or a ceramic vessel (*koka*)]. Measure out 1.8 litres of hot water and pour that on top. Stir it using a mixing stick. Remove the rice and allow to cool overnight. Prepare the usual 10.8 litres of kōji. Combine that with the rice and place it in a container. Stir it twice a day. If the ferment quietens, mix it with the stirrer. Cover the container. The sake is ready in twenty days.

• Glossy Silk (*Nerinuki*)

Do not produce this sake in the eleventh lunar month [December]; instead, make it after the New Year. Measure out 18 litres of polished rice and wash it until the water is clear. Set aside 1.8 litres of rice from that and cook it, allowing it to cool completely. Put the cooked rice in a bamboo basket and soak it in water, placing it in the middle of the uncooked rice. Seal the container and let it stand for seven days. On the seventh day, remove all the mould (*kabi*) from the top of the water, then scoop out the water and fill up a rice cauldron (*kama*) with it, boiling it until it is reduced in volume to 80 per cent.

Take the remaining 16.2 litres/4¼ gall. of rice, steam it, and while it is still hot place it in a separate large vessel [*koka* or *koga*]. Measure out 1.8 litres of the hot water and pour it on top. Let it stand for an hour, and then agitate it with the stirrer. Mix with the stirrer and allow it to cool overnight.

Combine 10.8 litres [more] rice with the same amount of *kōji* and place them in the ferment. Stir this twice a day. Stir when it stops bubbling. Cover with a mat and allow it to rest for seven days.

Combine the 1.8 litres of rice prepared the first day with *kōji* and add them to the existing ferment. [Wait] twenty days.

• Pasteurizing 'Glossy Silk' (*Nerinuki*) and Kikaki[36]

On the 25th day of the fourth lunar month [May], heat the sake to the temperature warmed for drinking (*nomikan*); on the 25th day of the fifth lunar month [June], the sake should be hot to the touch (*tehikikan*); carefully remove all the foam at the top.

Likewise, on the 25th of the sixth lunar month [July], the sake should be warmed until drinking temperature, then covered so it is airtight for approximately seven days.

A second method of pasteurizing for these two types of sake is to heat the sake so that it is hot to the touch regardless of the time of year, and carefully remove any foam that rises to the top when it is being heated. This will enable the sake to last up to a year. This is a transcription of an oral secret, and it should be kept secret.

ANALYSIS OF THE RECIPES

While translated here as *Sake Journal*, the title of the manuscript comes from the name of the first recipe for a sake called goshu (御酒), which could also be read as miki in other contexts – as when a sake is used in offerings to the deities. Goshu was a thick, sweet sake made with a relatively large initial ratio of kōji to rice, approximately 60 per cent according to the directions, as compared to the 20–25 per cent used today. The 'Go' in the title is an honorific – one usually not translated. Goshu was brewed for the emperor's use for seasonal celebrations in the ancient period, as described in the previous chapter. However, the version in the *Sake Journal* is different from the recipe in the tenth-century *Procedures of the Engi Era*. The ancient version used a method called shiori in which rice, kōji and water were added several times to previously made and pressed sake as a way of raising the alcohol content. The *Sake Journal*, by contrast, adds ingredients to the sake in stages, while it is still brewing.[37] By the early modern period, brewers included two more stages of adding ingredients to the starter so that there were three stages in total (*sandan jikomi*), and that is the way sake is generally made today, with a possible fourth stage to produce a sweeter sake. Modern brewers usually produce sake at 20 per cent alcohol by volume (ABV), which they water down to about 15 per cent; however, we can only guess at the strength of goshu and other medieval sake.

The other two recipes for sake, Amanosake and Bodaisen, purport to be in styles produced at temples. Japanese temples were brewing sake as early as the eighth century and were at the fore-front of sake brewing by the sixteenth century. Amano-style sake refers to the brand made at Amanosan Kongōji, a temple in Kawa-chi province (modern Osaka prefecture). Amano sake was the fam-ous brand for which the warlord Toyotomi Hideyoshi ordered that ash should no longer be used as a preservative.[38] The origins of Amano sake are uncertain, with the earliest references to brew-ing at the temple dating from the year 1234. The name 'Amano sake' first appears in an aristocrat's diary in 1432. Amano sake, like Willow sake, often appears in diary references mentioning it was given as a gift. The Hatakeyama warrior house presented the sho-gun with Amano sake three times a year in the Muromachi period.[39]

The other temple sake in the *Sake Journal*, Bodaisen, can be translated as 'Font of Enlightenment' (菩提泉). The name refers to the Bodaisen River near Shōryakuji Temple. Shōryakuji, founded in 992 and located 5 kilometres (3 mi.) south of Nara City, was a branch of Nara's Kōfukuji Temple. Like Willow and Amano, Bodaisen was often gifted in the medieval period, as when the sake was first mentioned in 1444. Apparently, the temple subcontracted merchants to distribute the sake in Kyoto.[40]

Amano sake was a winter brew using brown rice, but Boda-isen could be brewed in the warmer months and made with pol-ished rice using a method called 'enlightened starter' (*bodaimoto*), in which steamed rice is placed in a cloth bag or a wicker basket and then submerged in raw rice and water for several days. The so-called bodaimoto method produces lactic acid, which helps to eliminate bacteria that are harmful to sake brewing. Brewers continued using variations on the bodaimoto method until the 1920s.[41] Today, only a few sake makers take this step, preferring instead to add lactic acid directly, an innovation discovered in 1910 – as described in Chapter Five.

Due to changing economic conditions in the late sixteenth century, such as the loss of income from agricultural landholdings and the transition to a new political order that authorized only artisans and merchants to engage in manufacturing and trade, temples ceased brewing sake in the early modern period; but Shōryakuji has revived its tradition of bodaimoto brewing. In 1998, the temple received a licence from the Nara prefectural government to produce sake.[42] Instead of opening its own brewery, the temple partners with local sake makers, who create a small batch of bodaimoto starter each January on the temple grounds. The brewers then take this starter to their own breweries to finish making the sake, and the temple sells these brands on site. One other element distinguishes the Bodaisen recipe from the previous ones in the *Sake Journal*: Bodaisen uses a lower ratio of kōji to rice, which would have produced a bolder tasting, more acidic sake.[43]

The fourth sake, Glossy Silk (nerinuki), also makes use of the bodaimoto method but directs that the cooked rice be soaked for seven days instead of three. Nerinuki was a type of 'white sake' (*shirozake*) similar to the modern nigorizake that retains some of the lees. The cloudy appearance of Glossy Silk must have set it apart from the other sake in the *Sake Journal*, although the text does not provide any indication about how all the sake were pressed and finished, which would have played a key role in their appearance. Finishing involves separating the liquid from the solids, a task that begins with pressing the sake by placing the liquid and lees in a cloth bag and either hanging the bag to allow the liquid to drip out or applying force with a press to expel the liquid from the bag. The tenth-century *Engi shiki* includes sake presses (fune) in its list of equipment for sake making, so we can assume these were in general use in medieval times.[44] After pressing, medieval brewers probably understood that they could add a little ash to their pressed sake to separate the liquid from the solids further, a clarification technique that may appear in written records from the fourteenth century but came into more widespread use in the sixteenth century.[45] Unfortunately, the *Sake Journal* sheds no light on pressing and fining the sake, the process used for clarifying the liquid by adding compounds like ash to bind to leftover solids so that they can both be removed.

Nerinuki was one of several different types of white sake in premodern Japan, such as the sake called *shiroki* used for imperial enthronement ceremonies (daijōsai), where it was served in conjunction with black sake (kuroki) darkened with ash. A different white sake written with the same characters as shiroki but pronounced shirozake, not to be confused with the shirozake mentioned earlier, was made from a blend of glutinous and non-glutinous rice. Hakata (in modern Fukuoka prefecture) and Bungō (modern Ōita prefecture) were famous for it in the early modern period.[46]

Perhaps because of the many varieties of white sake in premodern times, the one described in the *Sake Journal* has a prestigious name to distinguish it. Nerinuki was the term for a silk fabric made crisp, light and glossy by removing the protein sericin in the silk by submerging it in an alkaline solution, usually ash, which also brightened any dye colours used on the fabric. Nerinuki silks were much in vogue in the era when the *Sake Journal* was created. They were used for short-sleeved kimono (*kosode*) and the elaborately dyed garments worn by powerful warlords such as Toyotomi Hideyoshi.

Nerinuki sake is mentioned in several fifteenth-century diaries.[47] It seems the glossy white appearance of the sake gave rise to the name, at least according to the theory of the noted philosopher and botanist Kaibara Ekiken (1630–1714) centuries later. Writing about *nerizake*, which was another name for neri-nuki, in the *Latter Gazetteer of Chikuzen* (*Chikuzen zokufudoki*), Kaibara observed: 'We do not know when this sake originated, but the sake's appearance like glossed silk gave rise to the name.' Kaibara elaborated that there were two versions of this sake. The first was called nerizake because of the way the liquid was separated from the solid dregs when the sake was pressed. Presumably, some of the solids remained floating in the sake to give the sake a whitish, glossy look comparable to a modern nigorizake. The second type of nerizake he identifies, which he calls the 'authentic' version, combined glutinous and non-glutinous rice, similar to the afore-mentioned shirozake. In fact, Kaibara seems to be equating nerizake with shirozake because he identified the beverage as a speciality of a city in his home territory, Hakata, where shirozake was produced. Kaibara boasted that brewers from neighbouring lands came to Hakata to learn how to make it. Nerizake was the variety that the warlord controlling Hakata gifted to the shogun annually in the early modern period – another sign of the sake's fame and quality.[48] Today, Wakatakeya Brewery in Kurume City, Fukuoka, produces a nerizake that it advertises as a revival of the medieval sake. Packaged in a 50-centimetre (1½ ft) container that looks similar to a milk bottle, the beverage has the appear-ance and consistency of a yoghurt drink, making it much thicker than a typical nigorizake, and with a much lower alcohol content (3–4 per cent ABV).

To Kaibara's list we can add a third type of nerizake from a recipe in *Tales of Cookery* (*Ryōri monogatari*, 1643), the first Japanese printed cookbook for a general readership. The directions read: 'Add white sugar to an egg and mix it well with cold sake. Serve hot.' The egg was likely raw when added to the sake but cooked when the beverage was warmed. This recipe was one of nine suggestions in the cookbook for serving sake with different flavourings that sound today like remedies for hangovers.[49]

Another element that made Glossy Silk a prestigious sake was that it used polished rice where the recipe for Amano sake in the *Sake Journal* called for brown rice, which had to be 'thoroughly steamed'. Brown rice is generally not used for commercial sake today. In fact, the extent to which the white rice is milled is mainly what legally defines various grades of sake, with the most refined versions (*daiginjō*) featuring rice in which at least 50 per cent of the kernel has been polished away. The use of brown rice and wild yeasts would have given medieval sake a much rougher and tangier flavour profile than commercial sake today. Of course, the 'white' rice mentioned in the *Sake Journal* recipes, as for goshu, would have also been less polished than modern table rice.

While we do not know the exact polishing rates to be used for the recipes in the *Sake Journal* or in the medieval period, in the early modern period the scholarly consensus is that people living in cities ate rice that was 70 per cent milled, meaning it retained 30 per cent of the bran, compared to modern table rice in which the bran is completely polished off. City dwellers in early modern times ate 70 per cent milled rice only after the advent of milling shops, which opened around 1650. These milling shops employed standing mortars (fumiusu) that greatly facilitated the speed and the extent to which the rice could be polished.[50] Medieval sake brewers would have had to rely on a wooden mortar and a large pestle to hand-mill their rice, a laborious method that could not easily yield highly polished rice. In other words, the 'white' rice used for the recipes in the Sake Journal would likely have had more bran and looked browner than modern table rice. The directions for goshu state that the rice must be 'thoroughly steamed', another indication that the white rice used was closer to what is called brown rice today.[51] Still, it was white by the standards of the day.

Besides omitting information about milling rice and fining the sake, the process of adding substances like ash to the sake to clarify the liquid, the recipes in the Sake Journal skip several other crucial steps. In describing the brewing process today, brewers often use the shorthand expression kōji, moto, tsukuri. Kōji making is the process of spreading the kōji mould on steamed rice and helping it propagate through controlling the temperature and manipulating the rice by hand, a process that takes forty to sixty hours. The recipes in the Sake Journal assume readers either know how to create kōji and will factor in the time required to make it, or that they will purchase their kōji ready to use, a legal requirement for brewers in medieval Kyoto, as noted earlier. The Sake Journal's recipes instead focus on how to prepare the 'fermentation starter mash' (moto), creating an environment rich in lactic acid where the kōji can start converting the starches in the rice to sugar needed for fermentation. The medieval recipes call this stage tsukuri, a term that today designates the stage when sake is fermenting – another reminder that premodern brewers did not have a clear understanding of how the ingredients turned into alcohol.

PASTEURIZATION

In addition to the sake recipes, the *Sake Journal* describes methods of pasteurization centuries before Louis Pasteur (1822–1895) experimented with heat to kill bacteria in wine in the 1860s. Premodern sake brewers did not understand the science behind how heat eliminates bacteria, kills yeasts and stops fermentation, but they knew that raising the temperature of sake extended shelf life. Lacking thermometers, medieval brewers relied on sensations of temperature that differed according to the change of season. The *Sake Journal* advised heating the sake in late spring until it was 'warmed for drinking' (approx. 40°C/104°F) but raising the temperature until it was 'hot to the touch' (approx. 60°C/140°F) in the summer.[52] And there are even more precise directions, specifying the 25th day of the fourth, fifth and sixth lunar months as the correct days for pasteurizing. These months, which correspond roughly to May through to July, were early and midsummer,

Yamaoroshi, watercolour by Kiyomi Rath.

a hotter period when sake would have a greater tendency to turn bad. Since even today brewers pasteurize their sake more than once, it is logical that medieval producers set aside specific days to pasteurize their sake and to clean the containers it had been stored in.

The 25th day of the month might have had special significance for medieval sake brewers for several reasons. Buddhists believe there are 25 realms of existence, and there are 25 bodhisattvas working to help humanity transcend suffering. So, the 25th day may have simply been considered lucky. The 25th day of the month was also important for the deity of learning (Tenman Tenjin), the divine form of the ancient statesman and poet Sugawara no Michizane (845–903). In early modern Japan, temple schools closed their doors on the 25th day to honour Tenman Tenjin.[53] It should be remembered that functionaries of Kitano Tenmangu Shrine, where Michizane's spirit was enshrined, held the monopoly on kōji production in medieval Kyoto. Therefore, drawing attention to the 25th day may have been a way for medieval brewers to acknowledge the importance of kōji and, by extension, the power of Kyoto's kōji guilds, which may have been too busy enjoying the day off or involved in ceremonies to sell kōji on those days – thus the brewers turned their attention to pasteurization.

Sake brewing occurred year-round in the medieval period, so it is likely that pasteurization did as well. The *Sake Journal* offers another set of instructions for pasteurization that could be used throughout the year. The medieval process of pasteurization would have helped to stabilize the sake, but it would have also lowered the sake's alcohol content because heating the sake releases alcohol. To avoid this problem, brewers today pasteurize their sake in a contained environment that prevents alcohol from vaporizing, such as by submerging bottled sake in a warm-water bath.

BREWING TOOLS AND TECHNOLOGY

Among the insights one can gain by reading the recipes in the *Sake Journal* is a greater understanding of the tools and technology at the disposal of the medieval brewer, although the specialized terminology is not always clear. For example, some of the recipes call for using a vessel (こか) that could be read as koka, indicating a large wooden bucket, or koga, suggesting a ceramic container. The recipe for Amano sake begins with creating a starter (called a shubo or moto today) in a wooden bucket and then combining it with more ingredients in a ceramic vessel called a kame. As noted earlier, kame were the main containers for medieval brewers and designated a large ceramic vessel with a capacity of 1–3 koku (180–540 litres/47½–142¾ gall.) that had to be partially buried in the ground for stability. Larger vessels were expensive and even more unwieldy, so typical brewers used hundreds of separate one-koku kame in their operations. Since the recipes in the *Sake Journal* call for fashioning a lid for the kame, the ceramic vessels apparently lacked lids, or else the brewers in some instances preferred using lids made of matting that were not airtight. If the brewers reused their mats, then the mats might carry trapped yeasts from previous batches of sake and could thereby serve as a way to introduce these yeasts to a new batch. Recipes in the *Sake Journal* call for initially using 18 litres (4¾ gall.) of rice because this amount was one-tenth of the capacity of the medieval 1-koku kame. Premodern Japan's base-ten system for measuring capacity, which was the normative measurement for cooking and brewing recipes in premodern times, made adjusting the size of recipes relatively easy. So, the measurements in the *Sake Journal* are in terms of capacity, not weight.

Other tools mentioned in the *Sake Journal* include a *zaru*, which usually designates a bamboo colander but in the sake recipes suggests a wicker basket that can hold cooked rice and be submerged in water. A rice cauldron called a *kama*, usually intended for cooking grain or heating water in a home on top of an earthenware, ceramic or metal stove (*kamado*), is also mentioned, as is a 'stirrer' (*neriki*) used to churn the brew. Early modern brewers stirred their sake with long wooden oars called *kai* or *kaibō*, and the medieval stirrer was probably similar. During fermentation, the grains settle at the bottom of the container, and mixing the ferment with the oars releases trapped carbon dioxide and adjusts the temperature.

BREWING IN THE *TAMON'IN DIARY*

The *Sake Journal's* recipes show the prominence of Buddhist temples, and these institutions were at the forefront of brewing technology at the end of the medieval period, as revealed by the *Tamon'in Diary* (*Tamon'in nikki*). The diary is a record kept by three authors from 1478 to 1618 at Tamon'in, a sub-temple of Kōfukuji in Nara. Besides touching on the major events of the day, the record describes life at Tamon'in and the close attention that the monks of that institution paid to brewing, making it one of the most important sources for sake history. For instance, since the dating of the *Sake Journal* is uncertain, *Tamon'in Diary* is the first source to record the word pasteurization (*hi'ire*), in 1568. In the same year, the temple monks describe a sake made by adding ingredients in three stages (*sandan kake*, also called *sandan jikomi*), a refinement of the technique also mentioned in the *Sake Journal* for

increasing the volume brewed by adding the ingredients cumu-
latively over time. The *Sake Journal* describes just one addition of
water, kōji and rice, but the monks of Tamon'in increased this to
three, which would become standard in later centuries.[54] Another
entry for the year 1568 mentions how the monks 'pressed' (jōsō)
their sake, using bags to separate the sake from the lees, a process
the monks did slowly over the course of four days either by hanging the bags and letting the liquid drip out, by squeezing the bags
by hand, or by using a press to force out the liquid.[55]

The monks of Tamon'in brewed sake twice a year, once around
the New Year and again in the summer, and it was the summer
sake that they pasteurized, discovering that doing so extended
the beverage's shelf life in the hottest season of the year. The
monks probably pasteurized their sake several times, although
the process they used remains uncertain. Three separate pasteur-
izations became normative in sake brewing in the early modern
period.[56] Tamon'in's own monks were also consumers of the
temple's sake, often drinking to excess to the point of dying from
alcohol abuse, another fact recorded in the temple's diary. The
temple also used its sake in gift giving and sold it commercially
at the end of the sixteenth century.[57]

The records of the Tamon'in monks first mention *morohaku*
sake in 1576.[58] 'All white sake' – morohaku – featured polished
grain for both the kōji and rice, making the sake more refined
than earlier versions that used brown rice for both or either step.
By the end of the sixteenth century, sake scholars estimate that
all the temple brewers switched to morohaku sake, as seen in
the popularization of the term 'Nara (Nanto) morohaku'.[59] Nanto
referenced both Nara and its temples, and specifically Kōfukuji.

But even as the monks of the Nara region made advances in
brewing, their moment in the sun was beginning to fade. The

last record of sake brewing in the *Tamon'in Diary* was 1618, and other references to Nara temple sake begin to fade after 1650.[60] After the establishment of the Tokugawa shogunate in 1603, temples lost many rights to lands that had supplied them with rice they could use for brewing.[61] The new regime also encouraged religious institutions to move away from commercial businesses, which were to be the sole realm of secular urban craftspeople. Indeed, it was these urban sake makers who adapted the technology of Nara-area temples to develop the commercial sake trade in the early modern period.

HOW TECHNOLOGICAL CHANGES AFFECTED WOMEN BREWERS

The art of brewing changed considerably in the transition from the medieval to the early modern period and those developments diminished the place of women in the sake business. Brewers abandoned using 1-koku ceramic vessels in favour of wooden barrels with much larger capacities, initially up to 10 koku, which allowed them to increase production. Ramping up production created a need for more workers, and a shift away from brewing year-round to winter sake making, described in further detail in Chapter Four, meant these new employees could be seasonal staff. The labourers who were available were male farmers and fishermen seeking employment in the off-season. Typically, workers from the same rural areas would return to the same breweries every year, where they would live for several months while brewing sake. Over time, these labourers organized guilds with masters called tōji who became responsible for all aspects of sake brewing. Women in the households of families who owned breweries probably continued to have an auxiliary role in sake production in the early modern period, but as sake brewing grew in scale the increased physical labour needed in the brewery became the sole job of male seasonal workers. Women continued to brew sake at home up to the twentieth century (and illegally in Japan today), but after the seventeenth century, the title tōji referred to the master brewer, who until only very recently was always a man. This change was not only true for sake but universally in most trades. In the medieval period a 'tradesperson' (*shokunin*) could signify a man or a woman, but in the early modern period the term referred exclusively to men.[62]

'Labourer enjoying sake', netsuke by Doraku, early 19th century, ivory with staining sumi.

THREE
DRINKING IN ANCIENT AND MEDIEVAL JAPAN, 700–1600

There are ample references to foodstuffs in ancient and medieval records, since these were collected as taxes and rents and paid out in salaries and revenues, but in most cases the members of the ruling elite usually only wrote about food and drinking when they had something unusual to say about them. That means that, while we have records of banquets for special celebrations from the ancient through to the medieval periods (700–1600), it is a challenge to reconstruct what people, even the elite, consumed on a daily basis. That is even truer for commoners since the elite who wrote things down cared far less about what their social inferiors ate and drank, except when they viewed them as a societal problem. So, our picture of sake consumption in the ancient and medieval periods depends on when it enters the historical records of the elite, and in those instances sake arrives in the context of ceremony, as an excuse for bad behaviour in courtly literature, or as something gobbled in excess in medieval banquets. Nara-period (710–84) poetry followed Chinese precedents and celebrated sake and intoxication. The effete aristocrats of the Heian period (794–1185) certainly enjoyed and overconsumed alcohol, but they were more reticent in describing all of its graphic effects. However, drinking to excess became more culturally acceptable for the warriors of medieval Japan, where even vomiting was celebrated.

DRINKING IN THE NARA AND HEIAN PERIODS (EIGHTH–TWELFTH CENTURIES)

We have a hard time reconstructing the drinking habits of ordinary folk based on elite documents except in very broad ways. Legal codes of the eighth century organized the population arbitrarily into households, allowing people the rights to agricultural land in return for paying taxes, performing corvee labour and military service. 'Superior households' (jōgo) had seven adult members while 'inferior households' (geko) included just three adults. The number of adults in a household mattered because it determined how much land the household received. Superior households were wealthier than inferior ones, and by extension they had more resources to use to make and purchase sake. By the twelfth century, the term jōgo referred to someone who drank a lot of sake, while a geko was a teetotaller.[1]

One of the crowning literary achievements of the ancient period was *The Collection of Myriad Leaves* (Man'yōshū), Japan's oldest compilation of poetry completed by 759, and it purports to shed some light on the drinking habits of ordinary people. One of the poems, by Yamanoue no Okura (660?–733?), makes passing reference to commoners adding water to leftover lees (kasu) from sake making and drinking that.[2] Presumably, those poor folk could either not afford to make sake or they made the most of what they did produce and even drank the lees. The Man'yōshū also documents 'poetry parties' (*kagai, utagaki*), where commoners met in secluded areas, drank, sang, composed poems and loved freely. For commoners in premodern Japan, sake would have been a delicacy reserved for special occasions such as these poetry parties.[3]

One of the sites of these poetry parties, as mentioned in eighth-century sources such as the *Gazetteer of Hitachi Province* (*Hitachi no kuni fudoki*) as well as in the *Man'yōshū*, was Mount Tsukuba (in modern Ibaraki prefecture), famous for its twin peaks, one gendered as male and the other female. The *Gazetteer* describes how 'people gathered on the sacred mountain to feast and drink.'[4] A famous poem from the *Man'yōshū* does not directly mention drinking, but alcohol consumption set the stage for other night-time activities:

> Climbing Mount Tsukuba on the day of kagai [poetry parties]
> On Mount Tsukuba where eagles dwell,
> Maidens and men, in troops assembling,
> Hold a kagai, vying in poetry;
> I will seek company with others' wives,
> Let others woo my own;
> The gods that dominate this mountain
> Have allowed such freedom since old;
> This day regard us not
> With reproachful eyes,
> Nor say a word of blame.[5]

At the same time that elite literature mentioned these song fests, the imperial court began passing laws in 797 and 798 restricting the night-time gatherings of men and women sharing sake, song and love near the capital.[6] Meanwhile, court nobles adopted their own versions of these gatherings to enjoy dance performances and to compose poetry.

There are some references in the tenth-century *Procedures of the Engi Era* to members of the elite using oakleaves framed in bamboo for drinking sake, as for the enthronement rituals for the emperor, but leaves were too clumsy for daily use. The preferred drinking vessels in ancient and medieval times were unglazed ceramics, Haji or darker Sue ware, two types of ceramics created beginning in the fourth century, the former fired at 800°C (1,472°F) and the latter at 1,200°C (2,192°F).[7]

Besides curtailing poetry parties among the populace, the imperial court several times prohibited farmers, who comprised most of the population, from eating meat and drinking sake, with the earliest prohibitions dating to 644. Ordinary people did not have ready access to meat and sake and only consumed these on special occasions like festivals, so these laws would not have had much of an impact on their daily lives. When the female emperor Jitō (645–703) felt the need to set her country on the right ethical course after heavy rainfall in 691, she too temporarily prohibited aristocrats and officials from consuming meat and sake and ordered temples to recite sutras for the safety of the country.[8] However, most of the subsequent bans against drinking, and there were seven of these from 772 to 811, targeted farmers, exhorting them to avoid drink to facilitate the country's economic and moral recovery from famines, droughts or simply during busy times in the agricultural calendar when farmers ought to be working. A signboard dating from 849, which was rediscovered in Tsubata in Ishikawa prefecture, contains the commands of the district chieftain that set work hours from the hour of the tiger (3–5 a.m.) to the hour of the dog (7–9 p.m.) and prohibited the consumption of fish and sake.[9] The orders can be read as a testament to the ways farmers, even on their long work days, paused for an occasional tipple and the anxiety that that caused the ruling elite, who wanted to see ordinary folk work harder.

The most famous poems about drinking in the Man'yōshū are the thirteen songs in praise of sake by Ōtomo Tabito (665–731). Otomo was a statesman who came from a long line of military commanders and was a confidant of Prince Nagaya, mentioned for his home brewing of sake in Chapter One. His words praising the merits of sake are attributed to the influence of Chinese poetry, in which Tabito was well versed. Ōtomo evokes the 'seven sages of the bamboo grove', a group of Chinese literati from the third century who enjoyed drinking as part of their renouncement of politics. The first three of his sake poems capture their spirit and the thrust of his message that sake was a key to enjoying the good life:

> To turn your thoughts
> to matters of no importance
> it is best
> to drink a single cup
> of cloudy unfiltered sake
> . . .
> Calling sake
> by the name 'sage' –
> how appropriate
> the word chosen
> by the great ancient sages.
> . . .
> In ancient times
> there were seven wise ones.
> What those men too

wanted above all else

seems to have been sake.[10]

Regardless of the restrictions they tried to force on commoners, the members of the imperial court felt it their right to consume sake, and one of the most famous drinking contests in premodern Japan occurred a century after the compilation of the Man'yōshū. Hanawa Hokiichi (1746–1821) included the brief account of this event, *The Record of the Sake Gathering at Teijinoin Detached Palace*, in his massive compilation of many ancient and medieval texts published in 1819, and the work is cited earlier by comic writer Ōta Nanpo (1749–1823) in *The Latter Duck to Water Chronicle*, an illustrated picture scroll about a drinking contest in Edo (Tokyo), in 1815. Ōta saw *The Record of the Sake Gathering at Teijinoin Detached Palace* as the classic example of a drinking party gone wrong:

> In the Engi period [901–923] during the reign of Emperor Daigo [r. 897–930], one can consult *The Record of the Sake Gathering at Teijinoin Detached Palace* and see that there were only eight people invited to attend. Everyone there got so drunk they could not even move. One man collapsed outside the gate. Another man said nothing as he vomited all over the palace floor. The only person who did not cause some kind of harm was the statesman and poet Fujiwara Korehira [876–939]. He won respect and the prize of a swift horse.[11]

The Teijinoin Detached Palace belonged to Emperor Uda (867–931), who had retired from the office of emperor by the time of the contest. For the sake party, the retired emperor prepared twenty large sake cups each for the eight contestants, marking each cup with a fill line to ensure that each vessel contained the same amount of sake. After finishing the sixth cup, most of the participants became disoriented. One left the palace and passed out outside the gate. Another vomited on the floor while others babbled nonsensically. Only Korehira appeared sober, but not even he consumed the twenty cups of sake the retired emperor had prepared. The match was called after the tenth cup.[12]

Such scenes of excessive drinking became typical for the elite of the fifteenth century, but Heian-period literature avoided such crassness to the point that drinking and eating are rarely mentioned. Readers of Murasaki Shikibu's *The Tale of Genji*, written in the early eleventh century, would be hard-pressed to know what the protagonist ate because of a reticence of Heian-period authors to discuss food.[13] The same is true of drink. Sei Shōnagon (c. 966–1017 or 1025), author of a collection of opinion pieces and essays called *The Pillow Book*, wrote of how much she detested seeing men eat.[14] But drunk men were worse, and she included them among her list of 'hateful things':

> I hate the sight of men in their cups who shout, poke their fingers in their mouths, stroke their beards, and pass on the wine [sake] to their neighbours with great cries of 'Have some more! Drink up!' They tremble, shake their heads, twist their faces, and gesticulate like children who are singing, 'We're off to see the Governor.' I have seen really well-bred people behave like this and I find it most distasteful.[15]

The subject of drunk men also appears on Sei Shōnagon's list of 'embarrassing things', which includes 'a man whom one loves gets drunk and keeps repeating himself'.[16] Murasaki Shikibu recorded in her diary how noble women like herself become embarrassed when men see them intoxicated.[17]

The Tale of the Cavern (Utsuho monogatari), a novel completed in the last decades of the tenth century that pre-dates The Tale of Genji, has several scenes with banquets, because the story centres around koto music often performed at these events. Several characters acknowledge the heavy drinking that goes on at these occasions, which the anonymous author chose to refer to only in passing. In one scene, the protagonist, Fujiwara Nakatada, apologizes to Minamoto Nakazumi for his drunken behaviour the other day, and Nakazumi responds that he was too drunk to remember what happened. Nakazumi later pursues Princess Atemiya, and another of her suitors, Minamoto Nakayori, excuses himself to his father-in-law for pining over Atemiya, claiming that he was hung-over for several days after a gathering. His father-in-law, Fujiwara Tadayasu, agrees with Nakayori about the dangers of overdrinking, sharing, 'I have a mind to resign my post in the Imperial Guard, because one can hardly stand the service unless he is a heavy drinker.'[18] While this was a work of fiction, that some members of the ruling elite of the period were heavy drinkers is known from other sources. The death of imperial regent Fujiwara Michitaka (953–995), who passed away around the time of the completion of The Tale of the Cavern, was due to diabetes caused in part by his overdrinking, according to the historical tale The Great Mirror (Ōkagami), completed around 1119.[19] Diabetes was apparently widespread among the Heian aristocracy and Fujiwara Michitaka's family in particular. His brother, the great statesman Fujiwara Michinaga (966–1027), also suffered from the illness.[20]

Tale of Genji author Murasaki Shikibu, like her contemporary Sei Shōnagon, was one of the great poets of the age. Murasaki's protagonist Genji debuts in the novel at a drinking party to celebrate his coming of age at twelve. According to *The Tale of Genji*, Heian-period drinking parties included singing, music performances and poetry composition. In the 'New Wisteria Leaves' chapter of *The Tale of Genji*, His Excellency the chancellor Tō no Chūjō invites Genji's son Yūgiri to his residence to see the wisteria in bloom and celebrate this with music and sake. 'His Excellency soon began to be pretending to be tipsy and boisterously pressed drink on his guests.' The boozy chancellor then started singing about the wisteria trees and passed a cup to Yūgiri, prompting him to give a poetic response. Others drank and tried their best to compose poetic lines, but Murasaki Shikibu records, 'the cup went on round, but the poems tottered drunkenly, and no one managed to do better' than Yūgiri.[21]

Despite the fact that sake-drinking parties often fuelled the composition of poetry in Heian times, the word 'sake' may have become taboo for poets.[22] Sake is only mentioned twelve times and by four different names in the lengthy *The Tale of Genji*.[23] One chapter finds Genji at a flower-viewing party where he dances elegantly, drinks to excess and forces his way into the chambers of the young woman Oborozukiyo at night.[24] Genji's son uses a similar tactic after the aforementioned wisteria drinking party, claiming he is too drunk to return home so that he can beg a room for the night from his host and then sneak out to find the host's daughter.[25] In *The Tale of Genji*, intoxication was both the cause and the excuse for bad behaviour.

SAKE CULTURE IN MEDIEVAL JAPAN

Where Heian-period writers talked around the issue of drunken-ness but rarely addressed it directly, a new celebration of intox-ication can be seen in medieval comic fiction as best revealed in *Essays in Idleness* (*Tsurezuregusa*), composed by the reclusive Kyoto author Yoshida Kenkō (1283–1350) around 1331. Yoshida Kenkō offered biting social commentary and amusing observa-tions. In the very first entry of his collection, he portrayed the ideal person as someone who must be a scholar, a poet, someone who can sing, has good handwriting and some knowledge of courtly ceremony. That individual would be reserved enough at first to refuse sake offered to them, but they would ultimately relent and share a cup or more with friends.[26]

However, with too much drink, 'even dignified men sud-denly turn into lunatics and behave idiotically,' wrote Yoshida.[27] He reminded readers what happened when people drank too much:

A man whose thoughtful manner had seemed attractive laughs and shouts uncontrollably; he chatters interminably, his court cap askew, the cords of his cloak undone, the skirts of his kimono rolled up to his shins, presenting so disreputable a picture that he is unrecognizable as his usual self. A woman . . . clings to a man's hand as he holds a sake cup, and if badly bred she will push appetizers into the mouth of her companion, or her own, a disgusting sight. Some men shout at the top of their lungs, singing and dancing, each to his own tune. Sometimes an old priest, invited at the behest of a distinguished guest, strips to the waist, revealing grimy, sallow skin, and twists his body in

a manner so revolting that even those watching with
amusement are nauseated.[28]

As much as he condemned drunken behaviour, Yoshida Kenkō
also revelled in it. He wrote: 'despite all that I have said, a drinker
is amusing and his offense is pardonable.'[29] People were not themselves when they drank too much and that excused bad behaviour,
which in any case could be hilarious to watch.

In tandem with changing views of sake consumption in
Japanese literature was a shift in governmental approaches
towards sake, moving away from prohibitions and towards efforts
to cultivate sake brewing. As described in the previous chapter,
the shogunate in Kamakura frequently cracked down on home
brewing and alcohol sales in the thirteenth century, but the sake
policies of the subsequent Muromachi warrior government
(1336–1573) located in Kyoto were completely different. Once the
Muromachi shoguns secured their rule, which took them almost
the entirety of the fourteenth century, battling a rival imperial
court at Yoshino in Nara, the shogunate not only quickly realized
the income potential from taxing the burgeoning sake trade, an
idea it usurped from nobles and religious institutions in Kyoto,
but it made sake a key component of political ritual. Sake proved
a powerful tool to forge and maintain vertical and horizontal relationships in medieval society, and drinking copious amounts of
sake became central to elite culture of the fifteenth and sixteenth
centuries. It is no wonder that one prominent Japanese historian
has called this period 'the age of hangovers'.[30]

SHOGUNAL VISITATIONS

Sake served as an important social lubricant in cementing political relationships in the elite culture of late medieval Japan, as seen in the warrior custom of 'visitations' (onari) in which the shogun paid a formal visit to one of his vassals and was lavishly entertained. Some shoguns, like Ashikaga Yoshimochi (1386–1428), paid almost weekly visits to their lords.[31] In 1439 Shogun Ashikaga Yoshinori (1394–1444) visited his vassals every two and a half days.[32]

Shogunal visitations followed precedents set in Heian-period state banquets, which began with a meal in a 'formal setting' (enza) and then proceeded to a 'less formal gathering' (onza).[33] During a visitation, the most ceremonial moment was a drinking ceremony that occurred in an intimate setting in the shuden, the central building of a residential compound where rites were held.[34] The 'ceremonial three rounds of drinks' (shikisankon) took place in a small room shortly after the main guest arrived at the host's mansion. On the right side of the room was a display of felicitous symbols, typically a pheasant and a carp on small-footed tables. On the left side were bows, quivers, armour and other gifts for the guest. Only a few people attended the shikisankon – the host, his sons and the main guest.[35] The host presented the guest with a tray bearing three different-size sake cups stacked on top of one another. The host's son poured the sake into the top cup, which the guest drank and then passed to the host to drink. The same cup was refilled two more times before the parties switched to the next sake cup. Guest and host drank three servings of sake from the two remaining cups for a total of nine cups of sake.

Writing more than a century later, the Portuguese Jesuit João Rodrigues (1561?–1633) described the importance of ritually drinking 'wine' (that is, sake) in this manner:

> Among the Japanese . . . the first and chief courtesy and
> token of interior love and friendship is the [sake cup]
> *sakazuki*; this is to entertain with wine, and two or more
> persons drink alternatively [sic] from the same cup as
> a sign of uniting their hearts into one or their two souls
> into one.[36]

Rodrigues did not, however, suggest that the two people sharing the same cup became equals. The shikisankon reinforced a hierarchical relationship and clarified it to the other competing elements of the Muromachi state. Elite warriors, aristocrats and clerics, who were not direct witnesses to a particular sake ceremony, would understand the rite's significance nonetheless, due to its formulaic nature, frequency and descriptions in the literature of protocols of the period.

Exchanging sake cups fostered a bond between the host and his guest, and the foods served with each round of drink celebrated their shared military heritage. Each round of drinks using a new cup was called a *kon*, and the foods served to accompany the sake came to be referred to as the 'menu' (*kondate*), which is the origin of the Japanese term. However, at the shikisankon, the most symbolically charged 'snacks for sake' (*sakana*) were the ones not meant to be eaten.[37] The *Culinary Text of the Yamanouchi House* (*Yamanouchike ryōrisho*), which dates to the fifteenth century, advises serving five strips of dried abalone, five dried chestnuts and five strips of dried konbu for a shikisankon. All of these foodstuffs could be appreciated visually for their symbolic meanings, but none of them could be consumed as served. Dried abalone (*uchi awabi*) conjured the idea of 'smiting' (*uchi*) one's enemies. Dried chestnuts (*kachiguri*) evoked 'victory' (*kachi*), and the konbu (*kobu*) signified 'happiness' (*yorokobu*). When viewed sequentially the foods became a metaphor for a successful military campaign: defeating enemies, emerging victorious and rejoicing.[38] More rounds of drinks usually followed the shikisankon and foods such as zōni, a hearty soup of rice cakes, vegetables and fowl, was served so that the participants did not have to continue drinking on an empty stomach. For all of its ceremony, and the sparsity of food served, the shikisankon facilitated inebriation and the transition from the atmosphere of formal ceremony to a more relaxed gathering.

The votive powers of these shikisankon snacks came in part from their names but also from their similarities to religious offerings, which highlighted further their ceremonial purpose. The cups and the serving ware used for the shikisankon (as well as for the banquet later) were unglazed ceramics (kawarake), typically Haji ware, which were disposed of after one use, as was the custom for food offerings in religious contexts.[39] Archaeological surveys of medieval warrior residences have uncovered enormous amounts of discarded kawarake. Excavations at the Yanagi Palace Site in Hiraizumi, where the northern Fujiwara family ruled in the twelfth century, have uncovered more than 10 tons of kawarake. Digs at Ichijōdani in Fukui prefecture, the seat of the Asakura warrior house, have yielded 1 ton of sake cups.[40]

After the shikisankon, the party then moved to a larger room in the host's mansion designated the 'meeting place' (kaisho) for a relaxed banquet, which featured more drinking. In 1422 warlord Uesugi Tomokata served Ashikaga Yoshinori 27 rounds of drinks at a banquet. When Shogun Ashikaga Yoshitane (1466–1523) travelled to Yamaguchi in 1500, Ōuchi Yoshioki (1477–1528) hosted a banquet of 25 rounds and served more than 119 foods, not including the inedible snacks for the shikisankon.[41]

The banquet space, the kaisho, was also the event space in a residence, used for informal functions, entertainments, poetry composition and less formal drinking.[42] The host decorated the kaisho with painted screens, hanging paintings and flowers arranged in Chinese bronze and celadon containers, the prototypes of the art of ikebana flower arrangement.[43] In contrast to the formality of the shikisankon, the kaisho was a 'collaborative social setting', according to scholar Matsuoka Shinpei, demarcating 'a space separated from the worldly social order'.[44]

A lengthy course of food and more drinks at the banquet proper might devolve into a more relaxed drinking session called a *sakamori*, which could also refer to a more casual gathering to consume sake.[45] In contrast to the drinking ritual that began the most formal banquets, meant to affirm the hierarchical relationships between the host and the principal guest, the participants in the sakamori drinking session toasted one another – ignoring social, occupational and age boundaries that usually kept them apart.

Sakamori also included impromptu dancing and music, as depicted in 'The Illustrated Debate over Sake and Rice' (*Shuhanron emaki*, hereafter *The Sake and Rice Debate*), one of the best visual representations of late medieval banquet culture. The oldest version of the painting, which dates to before 1569, is in the collection of Japan's Agency for Cultural Affairs.[46]

The Sake and Rice Debate is a picture scroll that includes three speeches: a courtier glorifying sake, a monk preaching temperance and a samurai who agrees with both perspectives and presents a compromise between the two positions. In the first of the four parts of the picture scroll, the protagonists meet in the monk's residence. The courtier, who is described as a 'first-class drinker' and Director of the Sake Brewing Office, Nagamochi,

advocates for sake, and the scene of a drinking party occurs in the second part of the manuscript. Part three is a vegetarian feast at the residence of the 'extreme abstainer from alcohol', the monk Iimuro Ritsushi Kōhan, whose name means 'lover of rice'. The scroll concludes with a scene of a formal banquet in the home of the samurai interlocutor Chūzaemon Taibu Nagahara, who presents a middle position between the two sides, affirming that rice and sake can live in harmony at the same feast. The characters make their speeches advocating their positions, but they do not converse with one another.[47] The early nineteenth-century scholar Hanawa Hokiichi, who included the text of *The Sake and Rice Debate* in a collection of historic documents, compared the text of *The Sake and Rice Debate* to a 'chicken's rib cage – with very little meat on it, but too good to let go to waste'.[48]

In *The Sake and Rice Debate* sake-promoter Nagamochi describes a sakamori sake party in elegant terms:

> For a *sakamori*, stylishly dressed drinkers gather in elegance in a room decorated to shine with gold and silver. There are rare

Drunken vomiting, and drunken dancing, scenes from an early Edo-period (1600–1725) copy of the *Sake and Rice Debate* (*Shuhanron*).

delicacies from the mountains and seas from around the country laid out before them and serving vessels with patterns of autumn leaves along with lacquer drinking vessels inlaid with gold and silver. Monks, laypeople and attractive boys mingle, imbibing and making each other drink.[49]

The thrust of Nagamochi's message is that drinking leads to a long and happy life. He declares:

We all know that the people of ages past said, 'sake is the tonic for longevity and immortality,' and 'sake is the chief cure-all.' Drinking sake refreshes us during the ninety hot days of summer, and consuming warm sake in the dead of winter helps us celebrate the end of the year and the beginning of the next one.

Otoso and *jūbako*, New Year's.

Sake's association with good health and celebration reso-nates in seasonal drinking customs that date to centuries before the composition of *The Sake and Rice Debate*. In the ninth century, aristocrats began the custom of consuming 'sake served with spices' (*otoso*) to celebrate the New Year with the belief that if one person consumes the beverage their household will be healthy; if one household drinks, the entire community will be safe from calamity. Aristocrats in the same period drank sake with chrysanthemum flowers in the ninth lunar month as a tonic for longevity. Both customs, which originated in China, spread to the lower classes in subsequent centuries.[50]

Since sake promotes good health and is essential for refresh-ment and celebrations, Nagamochi explains that it is understand-able why some might consume so much of it. He states that sake is a curative for the fundamental nature of existence, which is suffering, according to Buddhist teachings. Given these circum-stances, he argues, like Yoshida Kenkō did before him, that we ought to excuse drunken misbehaviour such as the scenes of vomiting in *The Sake and Rice Debate*.[51]

VOMITING IS FUNNY

The Sake and Rice Debate shows a reveller on his knees vomiting off the side of a porch with a dog underneath waiting hungrily, while another merrymaker toddles off with the help of his friends. The scene is not meant as a warning sign about the effect of overindulging or a critique of alcohol.[52] We are reminded of Nagamochi's speech suggesting forgiveness for the drunk who consumes too much of a good thing as it is a way to cope with the world of suffering. Not only was puking tolerated in the late medieval period, it became 'all part of the fun' at parties, to quote historian Sakurai Eiji.[53] In fact, there was a specific term for throwing up at drinking parties: 'what came up there' (tōzanoe, tōzae). And there was even a game associated with puking. Anyone who vomited at a party had to host the next gathering.[54] One member of the aristocracy, Regent Nijō Mochimoto (1390–1445), had a talent for vomiting on request at these occasions.[55] Vomiting, in other words, was part of the spectacle of the occasion that made it enjoyable and memorable for the participants, especially those who attended similar gatherings on an almost daily basis, like the shogun. Getting sick provided a bonding experience between the participants as some helped their suffering comrades while others laughed at them, as The Sake and Rice Debate illustrates.

That vomiting was all part of the fun and spectacle of medieval banquets is evident from the diary of Prince Fushimi no Miya Sadafusa (1372–1456), who records numerous occasions of his overconsumption of alcohol. Conversely, the fact that he recorded very little on the days after bingeing suggests that he was too hung-over to write. At one party to entertain the shogun in 1430, Prince Sadafusa vomited on a painted screen he had borrowed. Reading his diary, we can understand how members of the medieval elite drank so much, to the point of becoming sick.[56]

Drinking to excess and even vomiting were not only commonplace at elite parties, but could be seen as ways in which samurai and aristocrats defined their masculinity, both in terms of holding their liquor and losing it publicly, making any event even more memorable. Puking was part of the cultural spectacle of the age, an aesthetic quality called basara, or brashness. Before the tea ceremony became a subdued exercise of quiet contemplation, the basara version of tea, practised in the late fourteenth to mid-fifteenth century, was a drinking contest in a room decorated with Chinese furnishings. Participants brought their own fanciful decorations to display, such as representations of the isles of the immortals, dioramas of festivals, figurines made of vegetables, tiny mountains or painted boxes. Tea tasters tried to guess the locations where the tea was produced. The winners had their choice of the decorations as a prize while the losers were forced to drink sake. Gambling on the outcome of these events was officially prohibited but it continued nonetheless.

Not only was the elite culture brash, but so too was the sake consumed in the medieval period. What sake brewed in the fifteenth century tasted like is an enduring question, but it would have been much rougher than the beverage enjoyed today. Brewed year-round with wild yeasts, medieval sake would have had a gamier flavour profile and a much shorter shelf life than the modern beverage. One wonders if medieval brewing techniques would have always produced something palatable. In other words, the fact that the medieval elite developed customs and games to encourage rapid, continuous and excessive consumption may have been because the taste of sake was not always pleasing and not worth savouring.

MEDIEVAL DRINKING GAMES

Medieval samurai and aristocrats enjoyed drinking games that facilitated rapid intoxication. In contrast to modern drinking games that require the ability to launch a coin or a ping-pong ball into a glass, medieval sake drinking games focused on speed and mental agility. The forerunner of these games, dating at least to the eighth century in Japan, is the 'winding stream party' (*kyokusui no en*), a custom adopted from China. Traditionally held in the third lunar month of the year (April according to the modern calendar), aristocrats gathered in a garden with a winding stream. At the headwaters of the stream someone floated sake cups in the water and challenged each participant to compose a verse by the time the sake cup reached them, otherwise they must drink the cup. Visitors to Kyoto can see a re-enactment of this at Kitano Tenmangu Shrine in March and November.

Another medieval drinking game for the third lunar month was named after the plum flower. Players arranged five sake cups on short stands around a sixth cup to form the shape of a plum flower. The contest was to see how fast a drinker could down all of the cups. A more challenging version of the game played in the seventh lunar month used thirteen cups to evoke the shape of wisteria blossoms.[57]

Speed was also important for the game 'drink like a bush warbler'. Ten contestants sat in a circle with ten sake cups in the middle, taking turns to see who could finish all the cups the fastest. The name of the game came from the fact that the ten cups were arranged to form the petals of two plum flowers, omitting the central cups, as described above. The elite participants would quickly understand the connection between bush warblers and plums because they were frequently paired together in Japanese poetry and painting.[58]

A game called 'drinking ten-times' also used ten sake cups, one for each person sitting in a circle. This time the cups were empty. The oldest person started the game by using a pourer to fill the cup of the person next to them before passing them the pourer. Each participant then filled their neighbour's cup as the pourer made its way around the circle. The challenge was that everything must occur in complete silence. The participants could not even mouth words. If someone spoke, they lost and

Kubo Shunman (1757–1820), *A Winding Stream Party* (*Kyokusui no en*), n.d.,
colour woodblock print, two left sheets of oban triptych.

had to drink all the cups. A variation on this game was to use just five cups.[59]

Other games tested one's ability to drink just the right amount from a shallow sake cup. To win the game 'a single dew-drop', the drinker had to finish all the sake except for one drop, which had to fall from the cup when it was turned upside down. If two drops fell, that meant a loss. And, if no drops fell, the drinker also lost. One can imagine a player shaking their cup to try to get just the right amount of moisture to fall. Another game, 'one character', necessitated leaving a little more sake in the cup, enough to wet a finger and write the character 'one' (一). More challenging yet was the game 'drink a mountain peach', which presented the drinker with a cup of sake with a mountain peach (*yamamomo*; *Myrica rubra*) floating in it. The trick was to bite the 2–3-centimetre (approx. 1 in.) fruit in half while downing the cup of sake.[60]

Other drinking games tested different skills. One, called 'ten varieties of sake', required participants to draw lots and divide up into groups of ten. Each group received three different types of sake and the players had to try to remember how each sake tasted. Then each group received three blind servings of the same sake three times each, randomly. The participants tried to identify which sake they had been served, writing their guesses on a slip of paper. The team with the most correct answers won.[61]

Competition – and drinking – could become heated. At one session at the imperial court in 1478, Shogun Ashikaga Yoshimasa (1436–1490) and his wife Hino Tomiko (1440–1496) participated in a drinking game that lasted from midday to 2 a.m. and then still did not end – the competitors were invited back to compete the following day.[62]

THE INEVITABLE HANGOVER
AND OTHER AFTER-EFFECTS

References to drunkenness can be found in Heian- and Kamakura-period sources, but an account dated to 1416 in *Mansai's Diary* (*Mansai jugō nikki*) is said to be the first reference to a hangover in a historical record. The Buddhist priest Mansai (1378–1435), who was confidant to three shoguns, recorded on the day in question that Shogun Ashikaga Yoshimochi was hung-over.[63] Writing a century earlier and from a literary perspective, author Yoshida Kenkō certainly evoked the pains of being hung-over in *Essays in Idleness*, writing:

Men in the prime of health act like patients afflicted with grave illnesses and collapse unconscious before one's eyes . . . The victim's head aches even the following day, and he lies abed, groaning, unable to eat, unable to recall what happened the day before, as if everything had taken place in a previous incarnation . . . If it were reported that such a custom, unknown among ourselves, existed in some foreign country, we should certainly find it peculiar and even incredible.[64]

The ubiquity and social importance of alcohol took their toll on the ruling elite. The fifth Ashikaga shogun, Ashikaga Yoshikazu (1407–1425), served only three years in office and died young due to his excessive alcohol consumption, and Emperor Shōkō (1401–1428) faced the same illness.[65] Jesuit missionaries who arrived in Japan in the second half of the sixteenth century noted that the ruling elite drank so much at parties that they often became physically ill.[66]

Turning briefly to the other side of *The Sake and Rice Debate*, the advocate for temperance was a monk, but clerics were not uniformly teetotallers in late medieval Japan. 'A wide range of historical sources reveal that drinking sake was prevalent in medieval religious institutions,' indicates Yoshizawa Hajime, a historian of medieval Japanese Buddhism.[67] Despite being officially prohibited from consuming sake in laws articulated in the tenth century and repeated through the twelfth to fourteenth centuries, monastics were also deeply involved in the sake brewing trade, as described in the previous chapter, and some had a reputation for excessive drinking, as told in the quintessential story of a drunk monk in Yoshida Kenkō's *Essays in Idleness*. He recounts an acolyte at Ninnaji Temple in Kyoto who put a pot on his head at a banquet and danced around, much to the amusement of all. Unfortunately, the metal container could only be removed by pulling off the monk's nose and ears.[68] Apart from the prominent examples of some of the ruling elite who died of alchoholism, drinking sake to the point of illness was not a problem that most of the elite worried about in the medieval period, except in the case of the aforementioned monk, who demonstrated that partying too hard could be hazardous to one's health.

FOUR
THE EARLY MODERN SAKE INDUSTRY, 1600–1868

I n 1816 a samurai using the pen name Bun'yo Inshi listed the problems in the city of Edo (Tokyo), citing how the citizens – who numbered 1 million people – downed almost 113.5 million litres (30 million gall.) of sake in a year, a sure sign of the dire state of the times and a waste of rice.[1] Bun'yo's estimates were meant to scandalize his readers, and they were also close to the truth. On a typical year in his lifetime, brewers from around Japan, mostly in the Osaka and Kobe regions where 70–90 per cent of Edo's sake came from, shipped an incredible 700,000 barrels of sake to Edo, each barrel containing 63 litres (16¾ gall.) for a total of 44.1 million litres (11¾ million gall.).[2] Hitting a peak in 1821, Edo received 1.22 million barrels, over 77 million litres (20 million gall.) of sake.[3] Bun'yo decried the wastefulness of Edo's thirst for sake, but it is difficult to determine the amount of rice that was brewed instead of eaten. João Rodrigues, a Portuguese missionary who lived in Japan for almost forty years from 1577 to 1614, estimated that one-third of the rice grown in Japan went to sake making.[4] Other estimates for the early modern period place the amount of rice used for sake at between 15 and 20 per cent.[5]

Rice in the early modern age was not only a foodstuff, but served as a form of currency. The shogunate and regional warlords paid their samurai salaries in rice. These warrior governments recognized that the sake industry's hunger for rice raised the price of the grain, which was a problem in periods of famine, but could also prevent the price of rice from falling in periods of surplus and thus keep samurai salaries high. Consequently, the shogunate frequently took steps to limit or expand the sake industry to affect the supply and price of rice, and those measures directly affected how sake was made. The shogunate also received tax revenues from brewers and that too shaped its policies on sake making.

Just as it is hard to know the percentage of rice dedicated to sake, it is a challenge to guess how much sake was produced in the early modern era. The Japanese government only began keeping national records of economic output after the early modern period ended in 1868. However, six years later, when these records began, sake accounted for 16.8 per cent of the total economic output of all of Japan's industries. That year brewers produced some 612 million litres (161¾ million gall.) of sake.[6]

This chapter charts the remarkable growth of the sake industry over the course of the early modern period – growth that made such productivity possible. The term 'industry' in this context speaks to the scale of some sake enterprises rather than the use of twentieth-century technology. The chapter begins with a brief historical overview followed by a recap of the most important technical advances in medieval sake brewing that formed the basis for the development of the sake industry in the locations of Kōnoike in the seventeenth century, Itami in the eighteenth century and Nada in the early nineteenth century.

POLITICAL AND SOCIAL DEVELOPMENTS AT THE TURN OF THE SEVENTEENTH CENTURY

Breweries in fifteenth-century Kyoto benefited from the policies of the shogunate that encouraged their growth for tax purposes and in order to supply the alcohol that was central to rituals of state and entertaining in the late medieval period. The same breweries had to cope with the fallout when the Muromachi shoguns lost their power. The Ōnin War (1467–77), which devastated Kyoto, was a major turning point in the fortunes of the city and its traditional powerholders. Shoguns kept their titles, but they became the pawns of powerful regional warlords. Much of the population of Kyoto, including the cultured elite, fled the capital and that certainly adversely affected the city breweries, who lost their business in the fighting and their customer base. Temple brewers located outside of Kyoto, such as Shōryakuji, Tamon'in and Asano, helped to fill the gap in the sake supply and became more prominent over the course of the 1500s. When the wars to unify Japan finally concluded in 1600, religious institutions had lost their once considerable landholdings through warrior encroachment, and that meant temples no longer had surplus rice they could use for brewing.

Temple brewers had developed great technical skills creating 'all white' (morohaku) sake that used polished rice for every step; they had also increased the size of their output while maintaining the alcohol level of their sake by stepping up their ingredients, adding them in stages; and they knew how to pasteurize their products. Despite this, however, it was secular

Chirori sake warmer, watercolour by Kiyomi Rath.

entrepreneurs in the early modern period who expanded on those methods. Sake production had always been a way for temples to turn rents paid in kind into a profitable finished good, and with that revenue stream greatly diminished in the early modern period, temples abandoned sake production.

The Tokugawa shogunate also demanded tighter controls over society in response to the social upheavals of the late medieval period. Peasants were to work agricultural lands while living separately in rural areas far from artisans and merchants, who were confined to urban areas – where the military rulers also ordered samurai to live. A shogunal ruling promulgated in 1642 stipulated that the only social group able to produce sake under this new system were urban commoners, and these entrepreneurs were the ones who adapted medieval brewing technology and scaled it up in the early modern period.[7]

After the mid-sixteenth century, sake lost its place as Japan's sole alcoholic beverage. Portuguese, Spanish and other European travellers introduced wine to Japan in limited amounts, and the technology of distilling arrived in the latter half of the 1500s. The Japanese learned to produce shōchū, a distilled beverage that could be made from sugar cane and grain including rice. From the late 1600s, sake brewers discovered that they could also brew shōchū with the lees left over from sake making. When sweet potatoes and white potatoes arrived and became staples in the diet, especially in southern Japan, from the eighteenth century, locals there used those tubers for shōchū making as well.[8] But despite these new beverages, sake remained the dominant drink for the duration of the early modern period.

BUILDING ON LATE MEDIEVAL BREWING KNOW-HOW

Early modern brewers created sake in a manner similar to the sake produced today by building on the technical advances of temple brewers of the sixteenth century. The chief innovation was the development of 'all white' (morohaku) sake, in which polished rice was used for every step in the production. The recipes for medieval sake in the first brewers' manual, the *Sake Journal*, which dates from the mid-fourteenth to late fifteenth century, relied on brown rice or used polished rice in just one of the steps. Early modern brewers made some sake that way, which they called 'partially white' (*katahaku*), signifying the use of polished rice for either the added rice or the kōji, a contrast with the 'all white' type (morohaku) that utilized polished rice for both.[9] Medieval brewers knew that polishing rice improved the flavour. Although they did not understand the technical reasons about how polishing removed the fatty acids in the outer layer of the rice, they knew that sake could be improved even further by brewing it entirely with polished rice.[10]

The journals kept by the monk brewers of Tamon'in make the earliest reference to all-white sake in 1576, and the term morohaku appears as a preferred form of sake in records kept by the imperial court and the banquet menus of prominent warlords in the late sixteenth century. Despite this consumer preference, temple brewers would have had a difficult time making all of their sake entirely with polished rice because technology placed limitations on how well rice could be milled. In the late sixteenth century, the only method for milling rice was to pound it by hand with a large pestle in a mortar, and the level of polishing that resulted was similar to brown rice today.[11] Nevertheless, use of this 'polished' rice was a key innovation that further technological developments would expand on in the early modern period.

Three other innovations documented in medieval records were important for the development of sake in the early modern period. First, early modern brewers pasteurized their sake. The medieval *Sake Journal* advocated pasteurization for summer sake and the monks of Tamon'in only pasteurized sake made in that season. Early modern brewers pasteurized their sake several times, regardless of the time of year they brewed it, and that helped to extend their products' shelf life. Second, early modern brewers developed the process of adding ingredients in stages standardized as the 'three-stage preparation' (*sandan shikomi, sandan jikomi*). Sake can be made, and was made for centuries, just by combining water, steamed rice and rice mouldy with kōji. This works well in small amounts, but adding too many ingredients at once overwhelms the yeast. Medieval brewers did not know of the existence of yeast, but they discovered that if they allowed the sake to rest for a while, they could add more ingredients later. The directions for the sake called goshu in the *Sake Journal* direct the brewer to wait six days and check the sake to see if it is sharp-tasting, a sign that the available sugars have been converted to alcohol, before adding more ingredients. Thus the directions for goshu require adding the ingredients to make the starter and then more in an additional stage. The monks of Tamon'in may not have discovered that ingredients could be added two more times, but they were the ones who first documented using this method in 1586. Their three-stage process supplied them with more sake, which of course made for happier monks who then had more to consume, gift to others and sell. Adding more ingredients required larger brewing vessels, three times the size of the 1-koku pots used in medieval breweries.[12] Making larger containers out of ceramics was both costly and unwieldy. Fortunately, wooden barrels, usually crafted from cedar, proved an easier solution for making large vessels for fermentation and storage, and were sake making's third key innovation in the early modern period. By the end of the early modern period, breweries used barrels with a capacity of 5–5.8 kilolitres (28–32 koku).[13]

Increasing the production volume of sake even further would have tremendous implications for sake's workforce, brewery architecture and other areas that this chapter will explore, including the types of sake made, but for the moment let us consider the implications of the transition from ceramic to wood containers. Wooden barrels, usually made of cedar, made it more challenging to age sake because wood was much more prone to contamination when the sake was kept in it for long periods. This meant a shift away from ageing sake after the seventeenth century, despite a consumer preference of the fifteenth and sixteenth centuries for sake aged several years in ceramic containers.[14] Wooden barrels also changed the flavour profile of sake, giving it a cedar taste. And, since the barrels were only used for a year, there was tremendous demand for cedar from Yoshino in Nara and Akita. Barrel making also became an industry in its own right. In 1769 Mikage Village, part of the Nada sake region described below, had 34 sake brewers and 39 barrel manufacturers.[15]

The high standard for sake brewing among temples in the Nara area prompted imitators. Warlords of the late sixteenth century developed castle towns and gave economic incentives to merchants and artisans to settle there, in part to supply their troops, whom they stationed in these towns, and also to make each warlord's domain more self-sufficient. Peasants submitted their taxes paid in rice to castle towns, providing those urban areas with the raw materials for sake brewing. By the end of the sixteenth century, the castle towns of Fushimi in Kyoto prefecture, Shimabara in Nagasaki prefecture, Karatsu in Saga prefecture and Kagoshima in Kagoshima prefecture had their own breweries serving the local market. These breweries made a variety of sake. However, the 'all white' (morohaku) sake of Nara's temples, made entirely of polished rice, 'was undeniably the best in the land', at least according to sixteenth-century warlord Toyotomi Hideyoshi, the unifier of Japan, and his opinion carried considerable authority.[16]

SHINSHU: THE BEAUJOLAIS NOUVEAU OF THE SEVENTEENTH CENTURY

Before morohaku became the de facto standard for sake in the early modern period, brewers of the seventeenth century focused on 'new sake' (shinshu). New sake was made in the eighth lunar month (September), using the previous year's rice. Brewers in Itami, in modern Hyōgo prefecture, were especially noted for their high-quality new sake, shipped to Edo two months after production, a brew enjoyed for its lingering smell of kōji.[17] Shinshu was brewed with the 'enlightened starter' (bodaimoto) method described in Chapter Two: that is, a portion of the rice used for brewing was steamed and then soaked in water beforehand to induce the production of lactic acid, and that soaking water was used as the basis for the starter (moto) to which the steamed rice and kōji would be added. Lactic acid increased the acidity of the water, killing off harmful bacteria that could interfere with fermentation. Since the water soured in this process, due to the production of lactic acid, bodaimoto was also called the 'pickling starter' (tsukemoto), the 'water starter' (mizu moto) and the 'chrysanthemum starter' (kiku moto) – named after the flower typical for the period when this sake was made.[18]

　　Shinshu was just one type of sake in the brewers' repertoire in the seventeenth century, because the brewing season featured different types of sake in overlapping periods of time. The brewing year started in the seventh or eighth lunar months (August or September) with the production of shinshu using the bodaimoto method and two additional stages of ingredients (nidan kake). At the end of the eighth lunar month, brewers often used a 'simmered starter' (nimoto), signifying that the starter was heated in a cauldron. The trick was to raise the temperature of the starter just enough to facilitate starch to sugar conversion by the kōji, but not to the point that the water would boil and bubble, which would both damage the kōji and kill off the ambient yeasts.[19] Shinshu production lasted until the tenth month (November), when cooler temperatures allowed brewers to add a third stage of more ingredients (sandan shikomi). During this period, they also started producing 'intervening sake' (*aishu*) around the middle of the ninth lunar month through to the tenth month (October and November). In the eleventh lunar month (December), they shifted to 'winter sake' (*kanshu*), which was a morohaku with three stages of ingredients. Production of winter sake shifted to 'spring sake' (*haruzake*) around the second or third lunar month (March or April), and that finished the brewing year around the fifth lunar month (June).[20]

Doburoku was another product of sake brewers and specialized doburoku makers.[21] Today, doburoku is associated either with illegal home brewing or with specialized doburoku sellers, as Chapter Seven describes, but in the early modern period it was legal and a name given to a variety of sake recipes made by professional doburoku makers and sake breweries and at home. The following home-brew recipe for doburoku is typical and comes from the year 1860, from records of the Ishii family in Sannohe in modern Aomori prefecture:

> Use a 360-litre-capacity (2 koku [95 gall.]) barrel. Prepare 14.4 litres [3¾ gall.] of steamed rice. Add to the barrel 41.6 litres [11 gall.] of kōji mixed with 72 litres [19 gall.] of water. Churn this with a stirring paddle. Add the rice to the barrel just after it cools and stir it well. Cover with a lid and let rest. The next day, check to see if the whole of the starter has begun to ferment.
>
> The following day, add 72 litres of water and 41.6 litres of kōji and mix. Quickly cool the day's [14.4 litres of] rice until it is lukewarm to the touch and add it while it is still warm. Add the rice when the starter is also judged to be warm enough. Mix well with the stirring paddle until it reaches body temperature. After three days, bubbles will

start appearing all over, indicating that it is fermenting. When the ferment starts spilling over the edges of the barrel, move the stirrer side to side in the barrel in a cross pattern and put on the lid firmly. About two days later, stir with the paddle, and cool the ferment well by placing it to rest in a cool place with the lid removed. If barley is used, add an additional 0.72 litres [⅕ gall.] of kōji, although 0.9 litres [¼ gall.] is optimal.[22]

Like medieval sake recipes, this one calls for adding one additional stage of ingredients in the same amount, and it uses a vessel with a similar 2-koku capacity as was typical of medieval brewers. The fact that barley could be used as an alternative indicates how locals in Aomori could continue to brew sake even when rice became too expensive or unavailable. No information is provided about how or if the beverage would be pressed. Due to the amount of doburoku produced, the recipe was probably meant for commercial sale. *The Secrets of Pickle Making* (*Tsukemono hidenshū*), an anonymous manuscript in the collection of Tokyo Prefectural Library that dates to the early modern period, contains a more modest recipe for a nigorizake (doburoku) appropriate for the home brewer that uses equal proportions of high-quality rice, water and kōji, 1.8 litres (½ gall.) each, combined in a covered vessel and allowed to ferment for about ten days.[23]

Professional doburoku makers might press their sake to separate the beverage from the dregs, but they did not typically clarify or pasteurize it, and they usually watered down the beverage heavily to make more profit. One survey in Edo in 1837 found 1,863 doburoku producers in the city, the equivalent of one or two for each of the city's wards.[24] Since doburoku was made to be inexpensive, brewers often used rice that had been broken when it was milled and other less expensive rice. Samurai and the wealthy consumed sake, while commoners who might drink sake on festival days chose inexpensive doburoku, called 'white horse' locally in Edo, the rest of the time. Indeed, some scholars assert that doburoku is best thought of as a food and not an alcoholic beverage, providing an essential liquid energy source for hard-working people.[25]

Professional sake brewers also produced their own versions of doburoku. The late seventeenth-century professional brewers' manual *The Idiot's Guide to Sake Brewing* (Dōmō shuzōki) offered readers the option of making a type of doburoku called *nakakumi* (*nakagumi*) if they wanted to produce a sake without pressing it. The sake in this instance was a less expensive variety called 'partially white' (katahaku), signifying the use of only polished rice for either the rice or the kōji.[26] The text directs readers to scoop out the 'middle portion' (nakagumi) of the liquid from the barrel; in other words the upper third or quarter of the brew left clear after the sake lees had settled to the bottom of the barrel. The brewers did not throw out the remaining brew in the barrel; they instead pressed it and perhaps took time to clarify it. Elsewhere in the same text, the author explains how katahaku could be pressed and clarified just like morohaku. In other words, *The Idiot's Guide to Sake Brewing* shows how two beverages could be made from the same recipe, one a doburoku and the other a katahaku sake.[27]

KŌNOIKE AND *THE IDIOT'S GUIDE TO SAKE BREWING*

The first locale that was able to fully capitalize on the methods of Nara brewers was Kōnoike, now part of Itami City in modern Hyōgo prefecture. Kōnoike is associated with a family by the same name who traced their lineage to a former samurai named Shinroku who settled in the area in the late sixteenth century, leaving the life of a warrior behind and taking the name of his new village to become a sake brewer. Shinroku used the techniques of Nara temple brewers to make morohaku sake. From 1599 Shinroku ambitiously began shipping his sake to Edo, which warlord and soon to be shogun Tokugawa Ieyasu (1543–1616) made his headquarters. Shinroku transported his sake across the country on horseback, strapping two 72-litre (19 gall.) barrels on either side of a horse. Although the Kōnoike family made important contributions to sake brewing, as described below, they gave up the business in the late 1600s, moving to Osaka where

Otokoyama sake barrels delivered by cow, photo by Baron Raimund von Stillfried from Stillfried and Andersen, *Views and Costumes of Japan* (Yokohama, *c.* 1877).

they became influential bankers and moneylenders, holding the loans of more than thirty warlords at times. Apparently, loaning money was easier than sake brewing for the Kōnoike.[28]

To counter the acidification of sake as it aged during shipping, Shinroku followed the time-honoured trick of adding ash to his brews. One additional effect of the ash was that, when it was removed, it helped to clarify the sake, improving both the colour and the taste. Kōnoike became famous for this 'pure water morohaku' sake, although earlier brewers probably knew this trick of adding ash with which Kōnoike Shinroku is credited.[29] A different story attributed the discovery that ash purified sake to an incident at Kōnoike in which a frustrated sake worker dumped ash into the sake vat because he was angry with his boss. When his employer opened the vat he made the happy discovery that the cloudy sake had become clear and the taste had improved.[30] Whatever its origins, adding ash became a method used to clarify sake in the early modern period. Brewers added ash to sake in a ratio of one part ash to three parts sake, and then removed it along with the remaining lees the ash had adhered to, leaving the sake clear. Use of ash was prevalent enough that there were specialized sellers in the early modern period who sold finely processed ash made from camellia, oak and evergreen from the Kumano area (in modern Mie prefecture), which they mixed with powdered oyster shell specifically for sake brewing.[31]

We can learn about the style of brewing at Kōnoike and adjacent communities in the seventeenth century from the brewer's manual, *The Idiot's Guide to Sake Brewing*. Despite its modern-sounding name, *The Idiot's Guide to Sake Brewing* was the work of a master brewer who wrote for a select audience of other professionals. Unlike the hundreds of cookbooks and guides to farming published in the early modern period for a wider audience, there were only about half a dozen technical manuals on brewing created and none were published. Completed in 1688, *The Idiot's Guide to Sake Brewing* is the most detailed of these early modern brewing guides. Though unpublished and meant to be kept secret, a relatively large number of transcriptions of *The Idiot's Guide to Sake Brewing* survive, which attests to the fact that the work was disseminated and its information highly valued.[32] Given the author's preference for the Kōnoike style of brewing, it seems they lived or trained in that locale. Little else is known about the author, including their name.

The *Idiot's Guide to Sake Brewing* consists of five volumes, and the author devotes the first one to sake lore, including two stories about the origin of sake in Japan. The first tale is an adaptation of the eighth-century mytho-history *The Chronicles of Japan* (*Nihon shoki*, completed in 720), which tells the story of the storm god Susano'o, who asks for help from two female divinities to slay a dreaded eight-headed monster, Yamata no Orochi. The women brew sake for Susano'o, who entices the beast to drink it, slaying the creature when it is intoxicated. A second story retells the famous *Tale of the Bamboo Cutter* (*Taketori monogatari*), but instead of discovering a baby in a bamboo stump, an old forester finds sake. The first volume also has a long list of poetic synonyms for sake, including 'mad rice' (*kyōpei*), 'fragrant spring' (*kōsen*) and 'sole truth' (*shin'ichi*). The author provides information about the lucky and unlucky days for sake making, stating that the days the astrological calendar called 'dangerous' (*ayabumu*) were actually highly auspicious for brewing, while those marked 'stable' (*osamu*) should be avoided, perhaps because they were not good for fermentation. The author kept an eye on current rice and sake prices and listed them for recent years, and they added a few tips on how to purchase quality rice and make kōji.[33] The volume ends with a description of brewing tools, including a 'standing mortar' polisher (*kara usu, fumiusu*). Up to this period, polishing rice for sake brewing required the use of a mortar and the pounding of rice by hand with a pestle. A standing mortar was a mechanism that allowed the operator to pump their feet to lift and drop a pestle into a mortar. Not only was this method faster and easier, but it also milled the rice better. Conventional mortars produced the modern equivalent of brown rice, but standing mortars could mill rice to the level of modern table rice (about 90 per cent *seimaibuai*, a measure that indicates the amount of grain remaining after polishing).[34] Rice-milling shops employing standing mortars began appearing in major cities from the mid-1650s, making white rice available not just for brewing but for daily consumption.[35] The author of *The Idiot's Guide to Sake Brewing* understood that milling the rice more produced better-tasting, longer-lasting sake.[36]

Volume two of *The Idiot's Guide to Sake Brewing* answers the question of how to create a good fermentation starter. The author provides three recipes, with the first being the medieval 'enlightened starter' (bodaimoto) method that creates lactic acid naturally by soaking cooked rice in water. The second method the author introduced is kimoto, which involves using long, oar-like staffs to churn the starter, a process described later. The third was the 'simmered starter' (nimoto), which calls for heating the starter in a cauldron as described above.

The brewers of Kōnoike were among the pioneers of methods of winter brewing, and the author of *The Idiot's Guide to Sake Brewing* appears to have trained extensively in those techniques, so it makes sense that the entirety of the third volume is devoted to the subject of making sake in the winter. The author describes how the period for winter brewing begins in the eleventh lunar

Mortar and mechanical pestle (*kara usu*, *fumiusu*), operated by standing on the mortar, holding the bar, and using foot power to drive the pestle up and down.

month (December) and lasts for ninety days. Winter brewing, the author noted, was the same as brewing at other times of the year except that it was important that the rice was at a higher temperature when it was added to the starter. The author then describes how to add the ingredients in three stages (*sandan jikomi*) of steadily increasing amounts. The amounts of rice, including the rice infected with kōji, can serve as an example of how brewers increased the size of their mash in the early modern period. The starter stage used 151.2 litres (40 gall.) of rice. The first stage added 234 litres of rice, the second 468 and the last 936 litres (61¾, 123½ and 247¼ gall.).[37] Medieval temple brewers such as Tamon'in, which also added ingredients in stages, used the same amount for each step, but as *The Idiot's Guide to Sake Brewing* shows, early modern brewers discovered that they could double the amounts of ingredients with each stage. That meant early modern brewers could produce eleven times more sake in one batch compared to the monks of Tamon'in while at the same time reducing the proportion of water and kōji used. Making this possible was the switch to larger wooden barrels that were upwards of 20 koku (3,600 litres/950 gall.) in capacity.[38] Sake brewed by this method during the winter produced a sweet flavour profile with a clean aftertaste, according to the author of *The Idiot's Guide to Sake Brewing*.[39] Besides the techniques for winter brewing, volume three describes how to make sake from rice broken during milling and from glutinous rice, the latter usually used to make the sweet liquid flavouring, mirin.[40]

The methods that the Kōnoike had refined for brewing during the winter became standard for early modern breweries, but other regional areas had their styles too, and the author provides details in volume four about techniques in Nara, Itami and Kohama (in modern Hyōgo prefecture). The Nara method, for instance, used one or more additional stages of added ingredients beyond the three stages used in the Kōnoike style, a fourth step that brewers today use largely for flavouring rather than increasing the size of the batch. Volume four also includes recipes for speciality sake such as 'glossy silk' (nerizake, also known as nerinuki), made with glutinous rice, introduced in Chapter Two of this book, as well as instructions for making mirin and for distilling shōchū from leftover sake lees. Brewers added the high-alcohol shōchū to their sake to lengthen shelf life and give their sake a bolder character.

The last volume offers tips and tricks for the various steps of brewing, from how to fix a bad starter to making a sake taste sweeter or drier to pasteurization and shipping. The author explains that sake that has gone bad can be improved by adding wood ash. The alkalinity of the ash balances out acidic and bitter tastes. As noted earlier, ash was also used in the early modern period for fining sake by adding it to the liquid so that it adheres to any remaining solids that could be later removed, giving sake its clarity. *The Idiot's Guide to Sake Brewing* mentions the use of another way of purifying sake called 'removing the dregs' (*oribiki*), which became the standard for the period. Brewers poured sake into a narrow barrel and left it in a cool place, allowing the dregs (*ori*) to settle. The narrow barrel had several holes at various levels on the side in its bottom half. Sake makers first placed a straining bag on the uppermost hole and uncorked it, draining the upper portion of the barrel, which had clearer sake. Then the brewer opened the lower holes to drain off the remainder, which could then be pressed in a sake bag to separate the liquid from the lees, before repeating the oribiki process.[41] *The Idiot's Guide to Sake Brewing* instructed readers to use the oribiki method twice for winter sake, once after it was pressed and then thirty to fifty days later.[42]

THE RISE OF ITAMI AND IKEDA

Kōnoike's rival, Itami, began as a castle town in the mid-sixteenth century and developed its own breweries after the turn of the seventeenth century. Initially, the Tokugawa shogunate controlled Itami directly, using it as a checkpoint for travel, which the shoguns strictly regulated in that period to prevent warlords from moving their armies and to control the flow of goods and people. Itami became a convenient place to store tax payments paid to the shoguns in rice, which provided a ready source of ingredients for local brewers. In 1666, the shogunate granted control of Itami and ten other nearby locales to the Konoe house, a prominent family of aristocrats in Kyoto, providing them with a source of income. This aristocratic connection gave the 36 breweries in Itami access to the market in Kyoto. When, in 1786, Kyoto's city magistrate sought to preserve the monopoly rights of the capital's breweries by preventing even makers from nearby Fushimi from selling their sake in Kyoto, the Konoe family's influence allowed Itami's brewers to sell their products in Kyoto.[43]

Despite access to Kyoto's markets, Itami's brewers shipped most of their sake to Edo, via Osaka. At their peak in the late 1600s, Itami's 36 breweries produced 100,000 koku (18 million litres/4.75 million gall.) of sake yearly and shipped 640,000 barrels to Edo.[44] Where the brewers of Kōnoike had added ash to strengthen their sake for the trip to Edo, those in Itami fortified their brews with shōchū distilled from leftover sake lees, which helped

Shirayuki Brewery, Itami.

Locals line up to fill bottles of water at the outside well at Oimatsu Brewery in Itami. A nearby sign celebrates Itami Morohaku and the sake of Nada.

preserve the sake and contributed to the dry flavour profile that the sake from Itami became famous for.[45] Edo's growing population, which would reach a million by 1700, was Japan's largest sake market, thirsty for the fine sake 'sent down [to it] from the capital region'. By then, the breweries of Kōnoike were shuttered due to the effects of poor harvests and shogunal restrictions. Sake from Itami, meanwhile, became the preferred brand of the shoguns after 1740.[46]

The first person in Japan to make a living from writing fiction, novelist Ihara Saikaku (1642–1693), listed the top varieties of sake in his book *The Eternal Storehouse of Japan* (*Nippon eitaigura*), published in 1688. All of these sake were morohaku, and to the familiar list of the sake of Nara, Kōnoike and Itami, he added Ikeda in modern Osaka prefecture.[47] Ikeda's location on the Inagawa River gave the area's breweries a water source for their sake by tapping into the underground waterways that fed the river, and the same river was a convenient and cost-effective way to ship their products to Osaka Bay and then on to Edo. Ikeda's brewers, who had shipped their sake overland, transitioned to shipping by boat after 1619, capitalizing on a connection with Shogun Ieyasu that began when they supplied arms and sake to the hegemon's armies besieging Osaka Castle in 1614. Generous in victory, the shogun facilitated the brewers of Ikeda in shipping their sake to Edo.[48] By 1657, Ikeda's 42 breweries produced 13,640 koku (2,455,200 litres/648,600 gall.) of sake annually.[49] By the 1660s, specially designed 'barrel boats' carried sake from Ikeda and neighbouring brewing regions to Edo. In that era, it took thirty days for the sake to reach Edo by boat, but enterprising shippers of the mid-nineteenth century managed to shorten the run to just two weeks or less.[50]

Ikeda's sake, such as the brand Manganji Temple, which the townspeople of Edo nicknamed 'Temple', had a reputation for being sweeter compared to the drier sake of Itami and its famous brands, which included Kenbishi, Otokoyama, Oimatsu, Nanatsu Ume and Shirayuki.[51] One of Itami's other claims to fame was its local 'star well' used for brewing. Water 'strong' enough for good sake brewing was said to reflect the stars at night – apparently a virtue of the 'star well' that Itami's brewers used.[52]

WINTER BREWING IN ITAMI:
NIHON SANKAI MEISAN ZUE (1799)

Winter brewing was another characteristic of Itami's sake. *The Idiot's Guide to Sake Brewing* introduces various production methods from summer to winter, but it emphasizes winter production.[53] Winter was the season when the monks of Tamon'in created their finest morohaku, although they did so in very small amounts: about 1 koku (180 litres/47½ gall.).[54] However, given the popularity of 'new sake' in the seventeenth century, brewers may have preferred producing sake at other times of year. After all, sake ferments faster in the summertime, making the brewer's job easier, although sake made too quickly takes on too much of a grainy taste and has a shorter shelf life.[55] Winter produced better sake because it allowed for a longer period of saccharification, the process of kōji breaking down the starch in the rice into sugars needed to feed the yeast, and fermentation, with the cooler temperatures preventing the yeast from becoming overactive.[56] Winter sake could also remain unpasteurized since it kept longer thanks to the colder temperatures inhibiting bacteria that could sour or ruin the sake. To take full advantage of the colder winter temperatures, early modern breweries were designed with a window on the north side, on the second floor, that would let in the cold north winter wind to flow through the building north to south.[57] One of the most striking records of the methods for winter sake brewing in Itami is *The Illustrated Famous Products of Japan from the Mountains and Seas* (Nihon sankai meisan zue), published in 1799, which provides one of the best early modern illustrated sources for understanding the process of sake brewing known as kimoto.[58]

The first image from *The Illustrated Famous Products of Japan from the Mountains and Seas* takes us to the ground floor of a brewery

Washing rice, from *The Illustrated Famous Products of Japan from the Mountains and Seas* (*Nihon sankai meisan zue*; 1799).

in Itami where workers on the left draw water from a well and others in the centre and on the right wash and soak rice. Several workers cooperate in washing the rice in squat wooden 'half tubs' (*hangiri*), rinsing the rice forty or fifty times, for the better-grade sake brewed in the winter in order to remove any bran or other impurities that would affect the taste. Early modern breweries had a rice 'washing place' (*araiba*) near their wells. Larger brewers, such as the one depicted here, could wash 10 koku (1,800 litres/475½ gall.) of rice in a day.[59]

Absent from *The Illustrated Famous Products of Japan from the Mountains and Seas* are scenes of polishing the rice, but that often took place at specialized rice polishers outside of the brewery. The text indicates that using a standing mortar, one person could, in a day, mill four mortars' worth of rice (97.2 litres/25¾ gall.)

meant for the starter or for higher-grade sake or five mortars' worth (121.5 litres/32 gall.) of less polished rice meant to be used later on in the brewing process.[60] Rice milling shops employed seventeen or eighteen standing mortars simultaneously, meaning that they could produce 18 koku (3,240 litres/856 gall.) of polished rice in a day.[61]

The next image takes us to the 'cauldron room' (*kamaya*), where the rice is steamed, cooled and prepared for kōji making. At bottom left, workers tend the fire for the stove (*kamado*), a larger version of a cooking appliance found during the period in homes in urban areas, where it was used in tandem with a cauldron (*kama*) for heating water and simmering foods and a steaming basket (*koshiki*) for preparing rice. Behind them, three workers stir the rice in the giant steaming basket reinforced

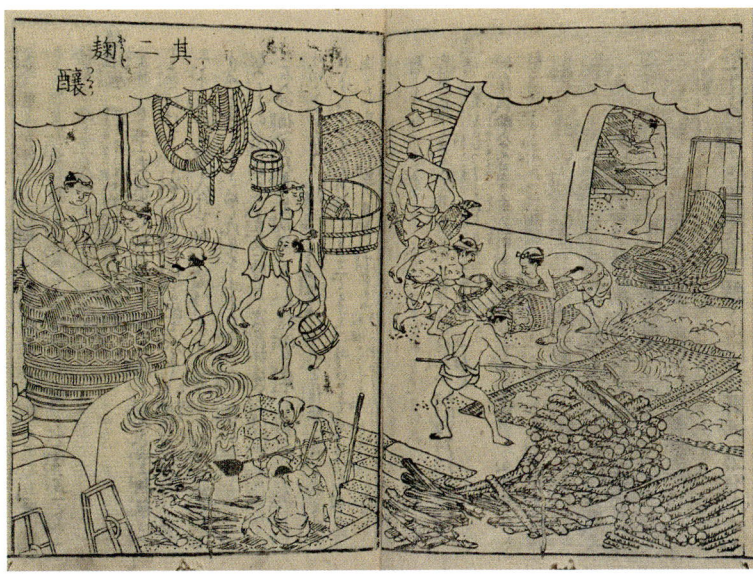

Kōji making, from *The Illustrated Famous Products of Japan from the Mountains and Seas*.

with rope, which they have removed from the top of a cauldron. The top of an adjacent cauldron peeks out from the stovetop on the edge of the left side.

The same image also gives us a glimpse of the room used for kōji making – the kōji muro – through the doorway on the right. In front of the doorway, workers transfer the rice into small buckets then spread it out with wooden rakes on straw mats, where it can cool. After it is cooled, some of this rice will become kōji by being dusted with kōji spores in the kōji room. In contrast to their medieval predecessors in Kyoto forced to purchase their kōji pre-made, brewers in the early modern period cultivated their own kōji for sake brewing, although they might still purchase the spores from speciality producers. According to *The Idiot's Guide to Sake Brewing*, a brewery's kōji room was approximately 20 square metres (215 sq. ft), about the size of a typical Western hotel room, which was believed to be the optimum space for producing kōji for one production run that brewed 8–9 koku (1,440–1,620 litres/380–428 gall.) of sake. Temperature regulation determined the size and dimensions of the kōji room, since a larger room would be too cold for ideal kōji growth. Kōji rooms had removable doors and windows that could be opened to affect the temperature and to allow air to circulate.[62] Note the door propped up against the right side of the kōji room in the image. Typically, it took three days to make kōji.[63] Itami brewers were able to reduce the amount of kōji they used in comparison with the formulas used previously.[64] Using too much kōji affects the taste and colour of the sake, and it reduced the beverage's shelf life.[65]

The next illustration shows workers creating a starter in half barrels where they mix water, rice and kōji-inoculated rice by hand and with oar-like stirrers in a process called 'mountain levelling' (*yama oroshi*), meant to soak and break down a 'mountain'

Moving the starter, from *The Illustrated Famous Products of Japan from the Mountains and Seas.*

of rice to facilitate saccharification so that the starter will grow.[66] In Itami, the rice was stirred once every two hours for three days to mix the ingredients and induce the development of lactic acid in the half barrels. Then the ferment was transferred to larger vessels to raise the temperature of the starter. In the image, workers carry the starter to larger barrels upstairs (glimpsed in the top right corner of the previous illustration), where the starter would begin to ferment after three days. Early modern brewers would not have understood the chemistry – that they were producing natural lactic acid – except that the water would be sour-tasting. Likewise, they would not have known about yeast, but they could see that fermentation was beginning when bubbles started to appear. The colour, taste and fragrance of the starter would also provide clues as to when the starter was developing. When ready, the starter was again divided into smaller vessels for additional stirring with the oars for two to three days in order to lower the temperature.[67] It usually took two to three weeks in the wintertime for the starter to evidence enough bubbles to indicate fermentation in preparation for the next step.[68]

The next image shows the starter resting in the warmer parts of the brewery upstairs covered with matting for a period of time, which enabled the yeast to build up. Then the 'starter was brought down' (moto oroshi) to the ground floor, where it was combined in a larger barrel in preparation for the gradual staged addition of more ingredients.

The last image from The Illustrated Famous Products of Japan from the Mountains and Seas depicts the final process of sake making when brewers press the sake from the lees. In the top right corner,

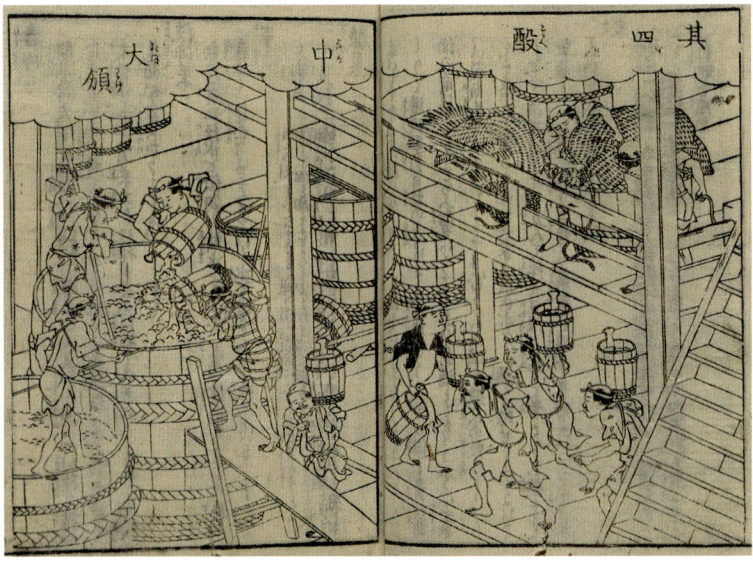

Adding stages of ingredients, from The Illustrated Famous Products of Japan from the Mountains and Seas.

Separating sake from the lees, from *The Illustrated Famous Products of Japan from the Mountains and Seas*.

two workers struggle as they add weights to a lever attached to a giant sake press, nicknamed a 'boat' (*fune*) due to its shape, which contained cloth bags filled with sake and lees. Weight from the press forces the liquid out of the bags, separating it from the lees as shown in the centre of the image. The massive press here could hold three hundred to five hundred bags with a combined volume of 12 koku (2,160 litres/570½ gall.).[69] The left side depicts how finer particles could be removed to clarify the sake by the oribiki method, which allowed the lees to settle at the bottom of a narrow tank from which the brewers could drain the liquid from several vertical taps.

THE TRANSFORMATION OF SAKE INTO AN INDUSTRY

The illustrations from *The Illustrated Famous Products of Japan from the Mountains and Seas* show two factors that helped brewers increase production in the early modern period, laying the groundwork for the industrialization of brewing, defined here as the development of methods to increase production dramatically. Initially in breweries, processing rice – milling, washing and steaming – all occurred in the home of the brewer, typically at the front of the residence in a large room with an area of earthen flooring. As brewers made larger facilities to increase production, they moved rice mills to separate buildings, or they purchased polished rice from subcontractors. Larger operations required new buildings to house their equipment with designated locations in the brewery for specific steps in the brewing process, from washing the rice in the 'washing place' (araiba), steaming it in the 'cauldron room' (kamaya), taking some of it to the kōji room (kōji muro) and moving the starter upstairs to rest, to eventually pressing it in the 'press room' (funaba), all locations shown in *The Illustrated Famous Products of Japan from the Mountains and Seas*.[70] In short, brewery architecture isolated the key steps of sake brewing to optimize them – like a modern factory.

Larger breweries also developed a specialized labour force for each of these steps in brewing. Overseeing the entire operation was the 'master brewer' (tōji), assisted by a 'head brewer' (kashira). Another experienced worker, the taishi or kōjishi, was in charge of kōji making, and another, the motomawari, focused on building the fermentation starter. Both positions required specialized training.[71] Larger breweries might also have someone in charge of the equipment and another person supervising pressing. More experienced workers ranked above newcomers called 'run arounds' (oimawashi), who might start off by helping the person assigned to cook meals for the crew.[72]

Besides needing specialists, large breweries – ones that produced 1,000 koku (180,000 litres/47,550 gall.) annually – required a comparable labour force. A small brewery in Nada that made just 100 koku of sake (18,000 litres/4,755 gall.) required only two or three extra workers to assist the master brewer.[73] But a brewer making 1,000 koku of sake in the hundred-day winter brewing season processed 1.5 metric tonnes of rice, and produced 10 koku (1,800 litres/475½ gall.) of sake per day.[74] According to *The Idiot's Guide to Sake Brewing*, ten people were needed for such an operation. One 1,000-koku brewery in Ikeda employed four times that number of people in 1772, but that may have included workers who polished the rice.[75] Increasing the labour force further allowed brewers to cut the winter brewing period to ninety days by 1850.[76]

THE TŌJI GUILD SYSTEM

The transition to producing more sake in the wintertime required hiring a seasonal workforce that included people with specialized knowledge, and this prompted the development of the tōji guild system. Brewers up to the seventeenth century hired locally, but by the end of the 1600s local labour proved insufficient to meet sake makers' needs.[77] At the same time that brewers sought seasonal workers, those who farmed and fished desired other employments in the months they could not work at their main occupations. A shorter growing season in the provinces around Edo (Tokyo) meant that farmers there could not plant a second crop in the winter like the peasants in southern Japan. Likewise, people who fished in regions like Echigo (modern

Niigata prefecture) could not ply their trade in the winter months. In the late seventeenth century, the shogunate allowed peasants to travel for seasonal work.[78] So groups from these areas and other parts of the country travelled outside of their villages to find seasonal employment, and many found their way into the brewing business. By the late eighteenth century, some of the workers from the greater Edo area made their way to Nada, supplementing other itinerant workers from Yamashiro (Kyoto), Ōmi (Shiga prefecture) and Kii province (modern Wakayama and part of southern Mie prefectures). By the 1830s most of Nada's workers came from Tanba province near Kyoto, and they formed the basis for the Tanba tōji guild.[79] Brewers were contracted to a master brewer (tōji), who had a tendency to hire workers from their own regions, and the guilds that they organized took the names of these regions, such as Harima (modern southwest Hyōgo prefecture), Echigo and Nanbu (Iwate prefecture).[80] The organization of these guilds followed the way villages were organized, with a leader (tōji) supported by head brewers (kashira), instead of village head men. Not every brewery needed a master brewer or a tōji guild, especially if it was smaller in scale or it created simpler recipes like doburoku.[81]

As seen in *The Illustrated Famous Products of Japan from the Mountains and Seas*, brewing in the early modern period was a male vocation. Writing a century before the publication of that text, the comic novelist Ihara Saikaku falsely claimed that breweries prohibited women from entering.[82] However, Saikaku wrote to entertain male readers, and that shaped his representation of women and sexuality. His fiction cannot be taken as fact. Scholars have yet to find any actual prohibitions barring women from breweries in the early modern period.[83] So it is unfortunate that the notion endures in popular media today that women were somehow considered 'impure' or that a taboo prevented them from brewing sake in the early modern period. The story instead lies in the changing face of sake's labour force and the shift to seasonal brewing. Women no doubt continued assisting family-run breweries and played other roles in sake making, but their contributions were not recorded in surviving documents because women's labour is often taken for granted. In the twentieth century women often prepared meals for the brewery workers during the sake-making season, so it is probable they did that in the early modern period as well.[84] Wives in farming and fishing families also managed the household in the months their husbands were away working in breweries, so they too contributed to sake production indirectly. And women brewed doburoku at home to sell or for their own consumption. But as is often the case in history, the stories of these women were never recorded or acknowledged because their labour was taken for granted.

THE BREWING REGULATION (*KABUDAKA*) SYSTEM

What had been a preference for winter brewing became a mandate after 1667 when the shogunate ordered that breweries could only create sake in the wintertime, limiting production from the ninth to the third lunar month (October to April).[85] The shogunate reiterated this ruling in 1670, 1671, 1672 and 1673, and regional warlords promulgated similar laws in their domains.[86] The shogunate's limitations on brewing in the winter was initially an effort to cut sake production in response to poor harvests and to curb consumption among non-samurai, one of many such moralistic sumptuary laws from the military government.

Although *The Illustrated Famous Products of Japan from the Mountains and Seas* provided the general reader with an understanding about how sake could be brewed in the winter, the transfer of these techniques to different regions of Japan proved a challenge. As early as the 1690s, domains in Aizu (Western Fukushima prefecture) and Akita invited master brewers from the Itami area to bring their skills to local breweries, but these enterprises failed.[87] Brewing in the territories around Edo had also long lagged behind the Kansai region, with the people of Edo calling the area's sake 'local bad brew' (*jimawari no akushu*). Even with the backing of the shogunate in 1790, breweries in Musashi near Edo and Shimōsa (modern Chiba prefecture) failed to produce sake that rivalled what was made in Itami and other locales in the Kansai region.[88] The reasons for this failure were not immediately clear, but the brewers of Itami and Nada had certain local advantages that made their sake highly sought after in Edo, as described later.

The initiative of the shogunate in 1790 to promote sake in the Edo area was only one of a series of interventions the warrior government made regarding the sake industry. Previously, in response to the Great Tenmei Famine (1782–8) that devastated northern Japan and led to the deaths of nearly a million people, the shogunate ordered that sake production be cut in half and it later demanded that it be reduced to one-third of previous levels. By 1790 Japan had recovered, and the shogunate tried to promote sake production near Edo to curtail imports from the Kansai area.[89] The warrior government's approach to sake brewing, in other words, was reactive and in response to the country's changing economic conditions. Over the course of the early modern period, the shogunate ordered the reduction of sake 61 times, mostly in response to famines and poor harvests, but its policies were also guided by the recognition that sake brewing was a revenue source.[90]

As noted earlier, the shogunate promulgated rules in the first decades of the seventeenth century restricting sake brewing to urban areas and explicitly forbidding peasants from making and even drinking alcohol. These laws evolved into a system to monitor sake production. In 1657, the shogunate began licensing breweries, providing owners with small wooden plaques that indicated their rights to produce sake and the amount of rice they could use for brewing as measured in units of koku (with 1 koku being 180 litres/47½ gall.). The amount of rice a brewer was allowed for brewing was called their 'level of rice share' (*kabudaka*). Brewers could not legally use more rice than they were allowed, although they could transfer or loan their rights to brew, along with the rights to purchase a set amount of rice, to other brewers. In return for the right to brew sake, sake makers paid a licensing fee to the shogunate. To monitor the system, the shogunate conducted surveys in 1666, 1680 and 1697 to check that breweries followed these restrictions and that their output did not mysteriously exceed the amount of rice they were allowed to use. The most important of these surveys was conducted nationally by the shogunate in 1697, sending its agents to breweries to measure sake that was unfinished, unsold and in barrels against the amount of rice the brewery was allocated.[91] That year the shogunate surveyed 27,251 sake producers with an average level of rice allocated being 33.4 koku (6,012 litres/1,588 gall.) producing 34.6 koku (6,228 litres/1,645¼ gall.) of sake. Brewers in the Kinai region (the provinces around Nara and Kyoto) produced 20 per cent of the sake in Japan that year, followed by makers in the Kansai region at 16.7 per cent, and the Dewa region (Akita and Yamagata prefectures) at 16.7 per cent.[92] The amount of rice each brewery was authorized to purchase, their 'level of rice share' (kabudaka) verified in the 1697 survey, became the frame of reference for

Former Okada residence and sake brewery, built in 1674 in Itami.

shogunal policies that ordered cuts in production in response, for instance, to famines. Theoretically, less rice used for sake meant more rice available to eat. The warrior government also limited sake production as a moral injunction to commoners not to consume too much, but hampering sake sales eroded the government's revenue stream.[93]

Besides paying for licences, in 1697 the shogunate ordered breweries to pay an operation tax based on 50 per cent of the value of the sake that they produced. This amount was the equivalent of what peasants living on shogunal lands paid annually in tribute (tax) to the shogunate. The military government presented this measure as an effort to discourage sake consumption, one of a series of moral pronouncements and sumptuary rules it promulgated as a way to shape society. But brewers opposed this tax, and they were the ones in charge of collecting it. Because sake makers determined how much they should pay by themselves, breweries either under-reported their sales or cut production. Sake makers also passed the cost on to consumers, which raised the price of sake and made the law widely unpopular. Brewers sent 640,000 barrels of sake to Edo in 1697, but the next year, after the tax took effect, they only sent 58,000 barrels. In 1699 only 42,000 barrels arrived in Edo and by 1700 that number fell to just 22,000. The shogunate needed the injection of revenue from the operation tax because its monetary reserves were in decline by the late seventeenth century, but that tax yielded just 1 per cent of the warrior government's budgetary needs, so the shogunate ended the unpopular tax in 1709.[94]

The shogunate also encouraged sake production, such as in the aforementioned example in 1790, as a way to maintain the price of rice, because the value of rice had larger implications for the early modern economy and political system beyond ensuring access to foodstuffs. The warrior government and regional warlords paid their samurai stipends in rice. If the price of rice fell, that made it more difficult for samurai to purchase other commodities when they cashed in their rice-stipends for coins. Although the samurai government disdained commerce and had difficulty understanding supply and demand, it recognized that taking rice off the market such as by turning it into sake kept the price of rice high. Consequently, in the beginning of the eighteenth century when rice became more plentiful in rural areas, the shogunate reversed its previous edict that had prevented peasants from making sake.[95] In the 1754 'free to brew ruling' (*katte tsukuri rei*) it relaxed the restrictions on sake brewing and even allowed sake breweries in rural villages. This led to expansion of sake production in the villages in the Nada area.[96]

THE RISE OF NADA

The brewing powerhouse that grew up in Nada from the mid-eighteenth century had its origin in several small hamlets located between Kobe and Nishinomiya, which came to be known in 1886 as the 'five villages of Nada' (Nada gogō) and grew to include Nishinomiya. Historically, most peasants in this region had very small plots of about an acre (4,047 sq. m), so rather than grow rice, early in the 1600s they turned to cash crops such as silk rearing and rapeseed used for oil. Cash crops, however, required fertilizers, such as sardines, which became increasingly expensive over time, prompting the more entrepreneurial and wealthier residents of the Nada area to try sake brewing.[97] Nada's brewers had an official allocation (kabudaka) of just 840 koku in 1665, but that grew to 1,200 koku by 1684 (151,200 and 216,000 litres/39,943 and 57,060 gall.). However, the real growth in Nada's breweries came after the mid-eighteenth century with the shogunate's laws encouraging breweries in rural areas.[98] Nada's rise from the 1750s required additional labour. Since the early 1700s, workers from the Tanba area had worked seasonally in Nada, and the Tanba tōji guild system developed in Nada by the early nineteenth century.[99]

Most of the breweries that make Nada famous today were established around the turn of the eighteenth century, and the number of brewers and the size of their operations increased steadily over the course of that century. Mikage, one of the Nada villages, had six breweries in 1716, a number that tripled by 1769 and became thirty breweries by 1785. Sake gave rise to related businesses such as rice brokers, and there were ten of these in Mikage as well as eighteen barrel makers, and eighteen enterprises that transported sake by boat. Nada's growth can also be

Katsushika Hokusai, *The Waterwheel at Onden*, from the series 'Thirty-Six Views of Mount Fuji', *c.* 1830–32, colour woodblock print.

measured in the amount of sake the region sent to Edo. By 1786, Nada's 321,000 barrels of sake accounted for 41 per cent of all the sake sent to Edo. If we include nearby areas recognized as Nada today, that number becomes 55 per cent.[100]

Several factors contributed to Nada's rapid growth, and one of these was the early adoption of waterwheels to mill rice after 1750. By 1788 Nada had 65 waterwheel-driven mills. Nada could power its mills with the rivers flowing off the nearby Rokkō Mountains. Itami, in contrast, did not have this geographical advantage and did not switch to waterwheels until 1804.[101] Polishing rice by hand was both time and labour intensive to the point that there was often a shortage of rice millers, which increased the cost of polished rice. A polishing shop might have seventeen or eighteen standing mortars, mentioned earlier, but it could not compete with a waterwheel that typically had forty separate mortars producing twice as much rice in a day as a milling shop.[102] Waterwheels not only solved the labour shortage problem and lowered the cost of polished rice, but milled rice to an even greater extent than could be done by a standing mortar, improving the polishing rate (seimaibuai), the amount of the rice grain remaining after polishing, from 92 per cent with a standing mill to 86 per cent with a waterwheel.[103] By the 1780s, improvements in water-mill design lowered the polishing rate to 80 per cent, and by then Nada had more than two hundred waterwheels milling rice.[104]

Improvements in rice polishing did not find their way to a list of reasons that one brewer from Nada explained around the year 1850 were causes for the popularity of the sake in his area. The brewer cited instead the well water from Nishinomiya; rice from Settsu province (today part of Hyōgo prefecture and the northern part of Osaka prefecture); the fragrant cedar woods of Yoshino in Nara used for the barrels for brewing and shipping sake; brewery methods adopted from Itami; cool winds from the Rokkō Mountains; and warm winds from the Sea of Japan.[105] Notwithstanding Nada's location, which put it closer to the coast and so made shipping from there easier than from Itami, of all these factors, the well water from Nishinomiya was the most important in the area's rise to prominence for sake brewing. Breweries in other parts of Japan used Yoshino cedar, Settsu rice and the winter brewing methods developed in Itami.

Breweries in Nishinomiya can be traced to the first decades of the seventeenth century and their number grew to 58 by 1666. However, Nishinomiya's rise to prominence as a sake brewing area came two centuries later, although it remained much in the shadow of Nada.[106] As Nada's fortune's grew, Nishinomiya's fell. There were 82 breweries in Nishinomiya in 1724, but just 33 by 1770.[107] In 1821, Edo imported a record 1.2 million barrels of sake,

Kikumasamune Sake Brewery, Nada, now a museum.

and 60 per cent of it came from Nada compared to just 7 per cent from Nishinomiya.[108]

Nishinomiya remained famous for its water, which was later nicknamed 'shrine water' (miyamizu), referencing the local Nishinomiya Shrine. The special properties of this water were allegedly discovered by a member of the sake-brewing Yamamura family around 1840, but there may be more fiction than fact in that story.[109] According to the tale, the Yamamura family owned two breweries, one in Nada and the other in Nishinomiya. Try as they might, the Nada brewery was never as good as the Nishinomiya location until the brewer thought to take water from Nishinomiya to Nada. That solved the problem in Nada, and thereafter Yamamura vowed to use only Nishinomiya water in both locations. Unbeknownst to anyone at the time was that the hard water from Nishinomiya had a very low iron content and it was high in potassium and phosphoric acid. Water with high iron content used for sake brewing will darken the brew's colour and negatively affect its taste and smell. The mineral content of Nishinomiya's water was well suited to promoting the growth of kōji, dissolving sugars, fermentation and creating dry sake. Thus drawing on Nishinomiya's waters gave birth in the nineteenth century to a cottage industry of water sellers to Nada breweries, and gave the region a distinct advantage over rival areas.[110]

THE SPREAD OF WINTER BREWING

What happened in Nada did not stay in Nada. In the last decades of the early modern period, master brewers from Nada were invited to teach their skills in the provinces around Kyoto, Edo and in the northwest part of Honshu, the modern provinces of Niigata and Kanazawa, and elsewhere. Brewers from the Echigo Guild, who had mastered Nada's methods, brought those skills to smaller breweries in the provinces around Edo early in the first decades of the nineteenth century. By the end of the early modern period in 1868, the techniques of Nada had spread throughout Japan.[111]

Kyoto had been brewing morohaku sake from the early seventeenth century, but its breweries were on a smaller scale and remained technologically less advanced compared to sake makers in Itami and Nada. Kyoto's flat topography made using waterwheels for milling more difficult than in Nada, placing another limitation on the breweries there.[112] Near Kyoto, brewers in Fushimi did not begin using waterwheel-driven mills until the Meiji period (1868–1912).[113] One of the ways that Kyoto's breweries survived was by producing for the local market and prohibiting the imports of sake from other areas. Kyoto and nearby vicinities had 626 breweries in 1697 and nearby Fushimi 66.[114] Kyoto's brewers successfully lobbied shogunal officials to prohibit sales of sake from other areas in rulings promulgated in 1698 then repeated in 1701, 1772, 1783 and 1826, which indicates that local sake merchants often required a reminder that they could not buy outside brands. While the small neighbourhood breweries of Kyoto gave beautiful names to their brands, some of which were said to have been coined by high-ranking aristocrats, outside of the capital, the reputation of Kyoto's sake was that it was too sweet.[115] Kyoto sake was consumed locally so it did not have to be fortified with shōchū, which made the sake of Itami and Nada drier tasting.

Contemporary records make it difficult to know the exact number of breweries in Japan by the end of the early modern period except to extrapolate backwards from records that the Meiji government began keeping in 1876. Based on these sources, sake scholar Suzuki Yoshiyuki sets the number of breweries in 1868 to 30,000, which would be 3,000 more than the numbers in the shogunate's famous 1697 survey.[116]

Although the number of breweries did not grow much in 170 years of the early modern period, this chapter has shown how sake, the beverage, changed, evolving from a drink made almost year-round on a small scale with a few workers to one produced by a large and specialized male seasonal labour force in just a few months using polished rice and sometimes fortified with distilled alcohol. That sake was an important revenue source for the government remained constant, as it had since the early fifteenth century, and that role would take on even greater importance in the modern period.

Painted sake barrels (*kazaridaru*) displayed at the entrance to the Meiji Shrine in Tokyo.

FIVE
THE RISE OF NIHONSHU, 1868-1989

I n the early seventeenth century the word 'sake' included a variety of alcoholic beverages, from the 'new sake' produced in the late summer to the 'all white' (morohaku) of the winter, but these drinks used similar recipes, ingredients and production methods. Over the course of the early modern period (1600–1868) shogunal laws, changing consumer preferences and the move towards employing a large seasonal workforce to increase production narrowed sake to the 'all white' version brewed in the wintertime. Producers and home brewers still made other types of sake including doburoku, an inexpensive beverage that was typically unfiltered, unpasteurized and heavily watered down when sold. The distinction between sake and doburoku became clearer in the Meiji period (1868–1912) when the central government outlawed both doburoku and home brewing in 1899.

Prohibiting home brewing was just the first step in the national government's efforts to reshape sake, resulting in a beverage remarkably different from its early modern predecessor and the drink legally defined as sake (seishu) in Japan today. The modern beverage that developed under government policies in the twentieth century was 'Japanese sake' (Nihonshu), a term coined along with similar words such as 'Japanese cuisine' (Nihon ryōri), 'Japanese dress' (wafuku) and 'Japanese confectionery' (wagashi) in the late nineteenth century as a way to demarcate domestic products from new foreign imports.[1] 'Japanese sake' was an improved beverage that benefited from government-sponsored research such as at the National Research Institute of Brewing (NRIB) founded in Tokyo in 1904. Nihonshu included additives illegal in brewing today, such as salicylic acid, used as a preservative from 1903 to 1969.[2] Applied topically, salicylic acid is considered safe to treat dandruff, warts and acne, but ingesting it can cause headaches, indigestion, seizures and even cardiac arrest.[3]

Besides the inclusion of dangerous additives, much of the sake made between 1943 and 1989 was an engineered beverage no longer consisting solely of rice, water and kōji, but composed of two-thirds brewers' alcohol, sweeteners and flavourings such as monosodium glutamate (MSG). One cannot call a beverage 'sake' when only a third of the alcohol in it has derived from rice, according to Nishimura Takaharu, sake brewer and former member of the board of directors of the Japan Sake and Shochu Makers Association.[4] This chapter examines how a drink that in 1868 was made from rice, water and kōji transformed into an engineered beverage that contained two-thirds artificial ingredients and at times unsafe additives. To call this drink a national beverage, Nihonshu, is fitting because it was the product of national government policies, specifically those of the Ministry of Finance, which prioritized the drink as a revenue source rather than showing concern for the quality of the beverage, the health of consumers or the long-term viability of the brewing industry. The rise of Nihonshu, a word that became even more widely used beginning in the 1960s, brought short-term financial benefit to larger breweries when they made engineered sake, but it cheapened the sake brand and contributed to the beverage's decline in the post-war period relative to beer.

MEIJI TAXES AND THE PROHIBITION OF HOME BREWING

The fall of the Tokugawa shogunate, and the transition to a new form of government with the emperor as figurehead in the Meiji Restoration in 1868, was less of an immediate rupture to society than the changes that came afterwards, and the same was true for the sake industry. There were no protracted wars of Restoration, so it was unfortunate that Fushimi, a brewing hub near Kyoto, lost several breweries from fires in the brief battles that did take place. Instead of a revolution, the Meiji leaders, all of whom were former samurai, sought to establish a modern system of government, and they began by eliminating dated practices of the past while looking outside of Japan for inspiration and technology. The Meiji government's trial-and-error approach to modernizing society was evident in their evolving policies regarding sake as the regime attempted to determine how to maximize the beverage's potential as a source of tax revenue to fund the ambitious goals of developing Japan.

In 1868, the year of its founding, the Meiji government began taxing breweries, charging both sake and doburoku makers 20 gold coins (ryō) for every 100 koku (18,000 litres/4,755 gall.) of product they produced. To put this in perspective, 20 gold coins was enough to buy a (0.18-litre/just over ⅓ U.S. pint) serving of sake for 2,708 people in 1864.[5] This was a steep tax for the period, but since it was based on self-reported amounts, many brewers, especially doburoku makers, neglected to pay at all or the full amount, and the government did not have the means to enforce payments.[6]

In 1871, the Meiji regime revised the brewing laws to allow anyone to make sake using as much rice as they wanted, abolishing the old limits the Tokugawa shogunate had placed on production. However, sake brewing required purchasing a licence that cost 10 ryō as well as an annual payment of 5 ryō. Sake makers also had to pay an ad valorem tax of 5 per cent on sales.[7] Doburoku makers paid 5 ryō for their licences plus 1 ryō annually and 3 per cent on sales, and the government declared that doburoku makers had to use substandard or damaged rice.[8]

In 1872, of the 3.1 million koku (558,000 kl/147,408,000 gall.) of alcohol produced in Japan, 95.5 per cent of it was sake, 3.6 per cent was doburoku, while shōchū, wine and beer was a paltry 0.7 per cent.[9] That year, Tokyo had one or two doburoku makers per ward, most of which were in Fukagawa, the capital's historic downtown area and site of its grain markets. Typical doburoku makers produced at most 20 koku (3,600 litres/950 gall.) each.[10] Sake brewing, meanwhile, was Japan's largest manufacturing sector in value in 1874, accounting for 16.8 per cent of the value of goods produced nationally, exceeding even textiles. Unlike other products, sake was made entirely for the domestic market. In 1874, Japan's major brewing centres were Nada, Nishinomiya, Aichi, Niigata, Tochigi and Kyoto City. Fushimi, Akita and Hiroshima had yet to become major players.[11]

In 1875, the Meiji regime again modified the tax laws so that sake makers had to pay 10 yen for a licence, 10 yen more for yearly renewals and 10 per cent on their production. Since doburoku makers had not been paying their share of taxes, the government stopped taxing them, which prompted many sake breweries to shift to making doburoku.[12] A survey of the 4,500 doburoku makers three years later found on average they produced around 14 koku annually compared to the 27,000 sake brewers who produced 187 koku on average (2,520 and 33,660 litres/666 and 8,892 gall.).[13] By 1875 sake production grew to 5 million koku (900,000 kilolitres/ 237,751,000 gall.).[14]

The Meiji government continued to revise its tax policies to raise revenue from brewers. The short-lived tax holiday for doburoku makers ended in 1877 when they had to pay 5 yen in taxes and 5 per cent of sales, a quarter of what sake brewers had to pay. The following year, the Meiji government replaced the ad valorem tax with a specific tax calculated on production. Sake brewers paid 1 yen for every koku (180 litres/47½ gall.) they produced and doburoku makers 30 *zeni* (a zeni was one-hundredth of a yen) for the same amount. These fees were standardized in 1880 with breweries and doburoku makers each having to pay 30 yen annually and a tax of 2 yen for every koku they produced.[15] Tokyo's doburoku makers fell in numbers after 1881 but collectively they still made more by volume than rival sake brewers in the city.[16] Tokyo consumers continued the early modern preference of favouring sake imported from Nada over the product of local brewers.

While professional doburoku makers who made their product in quantity for sale faced new taxes in 1877, many people still made the beverage at home; but after 1882 home brewers had to purchase home-brew licences for 80 zeni at their local government office. The licence allowed lay people to brew up to 1 koku of sake or doburoku annually.[17] As a point of comparison, 80 zeni was enough to purchase 32 (0.18 litre, 6.14 u.s. fluid oz) servings of sake in 1881 or the same amount of soy sauce.[18] This made purchasing a home-brewing licence cost-effective even if one only made 1 koku of sake yearly, especially considering that the fine for brewing without a licence ran between 3 and 30 yen.[19]

Many people took advantage of the home-brewing system in various ways. In the northern Tōhoku region, some 65 per cent of farmers bought home-brew licences, and it is likely that some produced for commercial sales.[20] In fact, the government recognized that families were pooling individual 1-koku licences to produce more for sale, so the government revised the law in 1882 to stipulate that the 1-koku allotment was per household, not per person.[21] The number of home brewers who purchased licences nationally increased steadily, reaching 67,000 in 1883, 73,000 in 1886 and over a million in 1895. Collectively, home brewers produced 1 million koku, about a quarter of sake production in 1895, although the official numbers for both sake and doburoku were under-reported to avoid paying taxes. In the same year professional doburoku sellers made just 270,000 koku.[22] By comparison in 1881, there were 27,000 sake brewers making 5.2 million koku of sake. With an average of 150 koku of sake produced, mid- and small-level sake brewers remained the norm.[23]

Licensed home brewing became a victim of its own success. In 1883, the year that the numbers of home brewers started increasing, the amount of sake produced fell from 5 million koku to 3 million koku.[24] By 1895, 13.6 per cent of households nationally held licences for home brewing with the highest numbers found in the Tōhoku region in the north of Japan and Kyushu. Doburoku production in Iwate, Miyagi and Akita was on a par with sake in 1886, and producers made nine times more doburoku than sake in Kagoshima that year.[25] From 1881 to 1886, 11,721 sake breweries, some 44 per cent of total number in Japan, went out of business.[26]

Konohanano Doburoku Brewery, Asakusa, an establishment that has revived the tradition of urban doburoku brewing in Tokyo.

Viewing the proliferation of home brewing as the cause of sake's decline (and not problems in the economy or high taxes on breweries), in 1886 the Japanese government prohibited home brewing of sake and enacted a graduated tax on home brewing of doburoku based on the assessed financial resources of brewers, in an effort to clamp down on home brewers who were selling their products. Producers whom the government considered to be from a lower economic level paid 2 yen in taxes to be able to make 1 koku of doburoku by household annually. The taxes for middle-level makers ranged between 3 and 8 yen to be able to make the same amount. Anyone the government considered wealthy could not make doburoku at all.[27] By arbitrarily targeting brewers with capital reserves, the government effectively ended commercial sales of doburoku by small shops, inns and restaurants that had been making the drink and selling it.[28] Less than half a per cent of shrines in Japan made their own sake and doburoku for festivals, and these needed licences after 1896 and they could not brew more than 7 kilolitres (1,849 gall.) annually.[29] In 1899 the Meiji government completely eliminated home brewing and that seems to have benefited the sake industry. The number of sake breweries grew by 4,100 from the years 1897 to 1900.[30] Commercial makers of doburoku in Tokyo disappeared, while home brewers went, and remained, underground.[31]

Competition from home brewing was only one reason breweries closed in the late nineteenth century, and not the most critical. The Japanese economy suffered in the early 1880s, with commodity prices falling as much as 50 per cent due to global pressures and government fiscal policies that cut spending in an effort to curb inflation. At least a tenth of Japan's farmland changed hands as indebted farmers had to sell their lands. Japan's economy recovered by 1890, but millions suffered financially in the 1880s.[32]

Affecting the sake industry directly and more significantly were taxes on sake, which breweries, not consumers, had to pay.[33] In the five years after the Sino-Japanese War (1894–5), which effectively gave Japan control over Korea and Manchuria, the Japanese government raised taxes on sake three times. In 1883, brewers had to report their land, buildings and savings to the government, and these records show that many rural brewers had taken out mortgages on land as they tried to expand production.[34] In 1886, sake was assessed at 4 yen per koku produced, but that amount became 15 yen per koku by 1901. In 1894, sake amounted to 16 per cent of the government's total tax revenues, but by 1900 sake contributed 35 per cent of government revenue. Sake, in other words, financed the expansion of Japan's military from an army of 200,000 troops in 1894 to 600,000 in 1900.[35]

Brewers sold their sake in the late summertime, but the government required that they pay taxes quarterly, which meant that they owed taxes before they had earned any revenue from sales. Breweries also had to pay taxes on sake that went bad during production and that they could not sell. Since brewers were taxed on the amount of sake they produced, some opted for making thicker sake with a higher alcohol content without much water added. They would water this sake down after it had been assessed for taxes. This practice continued until 1940, when the government set the legal limits for the amount of alcohol in sake.[36] Other producers simply under-reported the amount of sake they made, although the government's tax agency, the Ministry of Finance, created detailed manuals for its agents to allow them to ascertain how much breweries actually produced.[37] As much as the Ministry of Finance aided brewers by sharing technical information, as described below, the same know-how helped tax agents to audit brewers more successfully.

For many breweries, especially smaller producers, high taxes made their production unsustainable. The old brewers in the northern and southern areas of Kyoto City (Kamigyō and Shimogyō) went out of business in the early twentieth century.[38]

Kawamura, a small brewery in Osaka, which produced around 100 koku a year in 1887, paid almost as much in taxes (42 per cent) as it did for rice (44 per cent), leaving little margin for profit. One bad batch of sake could spell financial ruin for any small brewery, and many rural sake breweries went bankrupt.[39] In 1880, there were 25,480 brewers and 52 per cent of these made less than 100 koku, but by 1908, the number of brewers had fallen to 10,804.[40]

The government continued increasing taxes on breweries in the first years of the twentieth century as a way to finance war with Russia (1904–5). In 1896, brewers paid 7 yen per koku of sake they made but that amount had more than doubled by 1904 and became 20 yen by 1908. Japan's brewing industry contributed 40 per cent of the government's revenues in 1904, down from 47 per cent in 1901, an amount that included beer and shōchū makers, but sake brewers paid 92 per cent of these taxes.[41] In sum, Meiji-period taxes on sake brewers helped finance Japan's modernization and development into a modern military power with overseas colonies. Home brewing, however, did not disappear after it became illegal in 1899. In fact, in the years the government raised taxes on sake it also caught more home brewers who were producing inexpensive doburoku to meet local demands.[42]

THE RISE OF FUSHIMI

When Japan began keeping records of sake brewing production nationally in 1878 the area with the largest number of breweries was Ishikawa (including Toyama and Fukui prefectures) with 1,468 breweries. Second was Hyōgo with 1,179. Third was Shimane (including Tottori) with 1,173, Nagano fourth with 1,019 and Niigata fifth with 1,011. But the region with the highest concentration of breweries was Hyōgo prefecture. Of the 167 breweries in 1878 that produced 1,000–2,000 koku (180,000–360,000 litres/47,550–95,100 gall.) annually, 42 per cent were in Hyōgo. The same prefecture boasted 31 breweries that made between 2,000–3,400 koku yearly, 81 per cent of the total category in this group. All of the breweries making over 3,500 koku a year were in Hyōgo, concentrated in Nada.[43] Besides being able to pay higher tax rates and having a reputation for making fine sake that dated to the eighteenth and early nineteenth centuries, the brewers of Itami and Nada were able to capitalize on railway transportation of sake that began in 1887 to sell their sake nationally even more effectively.[44]

These numbers, which built on the legacy of brewing in the early modern period, did not include Fushimi, which only became

Gekkeikan Ōkura Sake Brewery, Fushimi.

a major sake centre in the Meiji period. Located 10 kilometres south of Kyoto and an important transportation hub between Kyoto and Osaka via river traffic, there were thirty sake brewers in Fushimi at the beginning of the Meiji period producing 9,000 koku annually, but by the end of Meiji in 1912, Fushimi's output had more than quadrupled and included 21 brewers producing more than 1,000 koku each. Fushimi developed a reputation for more 'feminine' sake – gentle, refined, rich and full-bodied – compared to the drier, 'masculine' sake of Nada.[45] Thick and sweet sake became especially popular from the 1910s to the mid-1930s, and Fushimi's Gekkeikan Brewery made their brand sweeter by using more highly polished rice and adding glutinous rice in an additional fourth stage to the conventional three-stage (*sandan jikomi*) sake brewing process.[46]

Ōkura Shoten, the brewery that became Gekkeikan, began producing sake in 1637, and it grew to become Fushimi's largest sake maker in 1788, making 172 koku (30,960 litres/8,179 gall.) that year.[47] But the brewery's take-off to become a national brand was under the eleventh head of the family, Ōkura Tsunekichi (1874–1950), who changed the company's name to 'laurel wreath' (*gekkeikan*) in 1905. Ōkura's family brewery had escaped the damage that other Fushimi breweries suffered in the brief wars of the Meiji Restoration. But located outside the traditional sake stronghold of Nada, Gekkeikan initially had difficulty breaking into the national market. Gekkeikan enjoyed a surge of popularity after the Russo-Japanese War when a national hero from that conflict, famous for the capture of Port Arthur, General Nogi Maresuke (1849–1912), declared, 'the laurel wreath (*gekkeikan*) goes to the true victor.'[48]

Much of Gekkeikan's national success was due to it numerous innovations. Gekkeikan was the first brewery to break with using traditional barrels to sell sake in bottles, opening a factory for glass bottles in 1909 and offering bottled sake for sale in 1911. Before this, consumers brought their own containers to sake sellers for filling. Gekkeikan advertised its bottled sake as 'sanitary, harmless and made without preservatives', a reference to the salicylic acid that many brewers used. Gekkeikan also bypassed traditional networks of sake middlemen in Tokyo to enter into a distribution agreement with the upmarket grocer and distributor Meidiya (Meijiya), founded by Mitsubishi in 1885. Gekkeikan's sales in Tokyo took off from 1915.[49] Meidiya also marketed Kirin beer, one of the leading brands in that period and throughout the twentieth century.

Besides revolutionizing sake consumption, glass bottles were easier to pasteurize than wood containers because they could be bathed in warm water and did not trap bacteria like wood. Brewers in Nada and Sakai soon switched to glass bottles.[50] Manufacturing of glass bottles for Nada's breweries began in

Prior to the advent of glass bottles, sake shops lent customers refillable porcelain containers; these with a capacity of 7.2 litres (4 shō) are from Fuku Bijin Brewery, Saijō Hiroshima.

The back side of this ceramic container has the name of the Fujii Sake Shop with their address and phone number, and a reference number (a 32) written above; Fuku Bijin Brewery, Saijō Hiroshima.

earnest in 1918 with the Tokunaga Glass company in Tenmayoriki machi in Osaka.[51]

Wooden barrels were not only used in shipping sake to sellers, but were important in sake production. Indeed, the ability to make giant wooden barrels with upwards of a 5,400-litre capacity (1,427 gall.) was what had allowed the sake industry to increase production in the early modern period. New cypress barrels contained natural preservatives preventing spoilage (*hiochi*), but after years of use they could become prone to produce lactic acid bacteria called *hiochikin*, which turns sake cloudy, foul smelling and undrinkable. Spoilage was a dire problem for breweries, which could lose 20–30 per cent of their production from sake turning bad, and consecutive batches of spoiled sake could bankrupt a brewery. The cypress favoured for sake barrels became more expensive after the 1923 Kanto earthquake when it was needed for building construction, so many brewers made the switch to bottles and copper brewing tanks. Use of copper, aluminium and metal containers inhibited spoilage, but those metals leached out and contaminated the sake. Copper was also expensive. Nada brewers pioneered use of 12-koku capacity enamel tanks in 1927 and introduced a 33-koku capacity tank soon after (2,160 and 5,940 litres/570½ and 1,570 gall.). In 1927, Gekkeikan constructed its 'Shōwa Brewery', a two-storey ferro-concrete and climate-controlled facility where in 1930 it began using enamel brewing tanks.[52] Enamel tanks, which became more widely used from the 1920s, were an important step towards year-round brewing, realized after the Second World War.[53]

Despite its advances, Fushimi lagged behind Nada when it came to polishing rice. Most brewers at the beginning of the Meiji period still relied on standing pedal mortars (*fumiusu*) to mill rice, which polished the grain manually to the level of modern table rice (around 90 per cent seimaibuai). The waterwheels used in Nada from the mid-eighteenth century polished to a rate of 80 per cent seimaibuai. Around 1887, as Fushimi and other regions began adopting waterwheels, brewers in Nada and Nishinomiya shifted to steam-driven polishers, which could polish to 70 per cent seimaibuai.[54] However, early steam-driven mills polished rice unevenly and made the rice wet. The first electric polishers imported from the United States in 1897 were also not well suited to Japanese sake rice. Fushimi switched to electric polishers in the Taishō period (1912–26), but electric rice polishing remained problematic until 1929, which brought the debut of a vertical milling machine from the Satake corporation that made polishing rice below 60 per cent seimaibuai possible.[55] Even after this innovation, many regional brewers – those outside of Nada – continued to use ordinary table rice. Some brewers chose

Enamel sake tanks sunk into the floor, Saijō Tsuru Brewery, Saijō Hiroshima.

speciality 'sake rice' that had larger kernels with higher concentrations of starch, using varieties such as Omachi, a strain of rice from Okayama, isolated in the mid-nineteenth century. However, Omachi was difficult to grow because it was susceptible to insect damage. Strides were made in the Meiji period to produce rice suitable for sake brewing. In 1923, scientists at the Hyōgo Prefectural Agricultural Station began crossing different strains of rice and yielded the variety Yamada Nishiki in 1936, which today is the rice of choice for most sake brewers.[56]

Gekkeikan also expanded abroad, supporting Japan's colonial efforts in Manchuria and Korea in the early decades of the twentieth century. The Japanese government allowed brewers to produce sake tax-free in Japanese population centres in Manchuria; larger brewers in Nada and Fushimi opened breweries to serve those areas. Gekkeikan established a brewery in Fushun in Manchuria (modern Liaoning province) where it produced 'Manchu Gekkeikan' using local rice. Gekkeikan also produced sake in Korea for the Korean market, but Manchuria was where sake companies began experimenting with making artificial sake, as described later.[57]

EFFORTS TO IMPROVE SAKE

The Meiji period witnessed drastic changes to the economy, society and governance as the national government sought to modernize, and that extended to the sake industry, which was a major source of the government's revenue. Significantly, it was the Ministry of Finance, as opposed to the Ministry of Agriculture or another government agency, which took the lead in efforts to improve sake, which speaks to the drink's economic importance for tax revenues. Judging from the manuals it created for internal use to assess taxes on breweries, the staff of the Ministry of Finance not only developed expertise in sake production, but sought to reshape sake making by publicizing existing proprietary knowledge from breweries in the Nada area and by introducing scientific brewing techniques. However, the first government-sponsored scientists who turned their attention to sake brewing were not well acquainted with the beverage. Their efforts to apply Western brewing methods for beer to sake failed.[58]

The Meiji government hired thousands of foreign experts as advisers in the late nineteenth century and these included scientists who focused on sake. The Englishman Robert William Atkinson (1850–1929) came to Japan in 1874 and became a professor at Tokyo Imperial University. Although not a specialist in brewing, Atkinson turned his attention to the problem of pasteurization and spoilage (hiochi). In the early decades of the Meiji period, breweries typically used a steel vessel with a varnished interior for pasteurizing sake, but they would then return the pasteurized sake to their original wood barrels for storage, where the beverage could be easily recontaminated. Atkinson advised brewers to use new barrels for storing sake after pasteurization, and he helped invent a piping system that moved sake from its original barrel to the pasteurization vessel to another barrel for storage, although few breweries used this new invention initially. German adviser Oskar Korschelt (1853–1940), hired as a professor of medicine at Tokyo Imperial University, initially told the Japanese to make sake from barley instead of rice. But he later played an influential role in sake brewing, advocating for using salicylic acid as a preservative for sake. Korschelt argued that salicylic acid, which was invented in Germany in 1853, could replace the need to pasteurize sake entirely. Yet when sake breweries eventually adopted using the compound, they used salicylic acid in conjunction with pasteurization. Japan's government recognized the dangers of salicylic acid early, and the Ministry of the Interior banned its use in foods in 1900. However, with permission from the Ministry of Finance, brewers continued to add salicylic acid to sake until 1969.[59]

In 1896, the Ministry of Finance established a Department of Appraisal for the sake industry charged with overseeing brewery taxes and working to improve sake. One of its members, Yabe Kikuji (1868–1936), was the first to isolate sake yeast in 1897, a discovery that confirmed that yeast, not kōji, was the reason sake fermented. When the Ministry of Finance founded the National Research Institute of Brewing (NRIB, Nihon Shuzō Shikenjo) in Takinogawa, Tokyo, in 1904, many of the staff were from the Department of Appraisal.[60] The Takinogawa facility featured a brick building able to produce 1,000 koku of sake yearly with a cooling system imported from Germany.[61] The main goal of the NRIB was to improve the quality of sake, thereby increasing the government's tax revenues.[62] One of the earliest projects of the institute was to continue Yabe's work and collect ambient yeast from breweries around the country. The NRIB isolated sixty yeasts in 1906 and marketed the best of these to brewers, each with a numerical designation beginning with Yeast Number One collected from Sakura Masamune Brewery in Hyōgo prefecture.[63]

The NRIB also developed innovations in the fermentation starter, inventing the methods known today as *yamahai* and *sokujō*. In a traditional method of making the starter called kimoto, such as in the example of Itami morohaku described in the previous chapter, brewers add rice, water and kōji into half barrels, and after a period of soaking, they churn the mixture with oar-like stirrers in a long process involving considerable manpower over three days. The descriptive name for churning the starter is 'levelling the mountain' (*yama oroshi*), because the brewers mash a figurative hillock of rice into a paste to break down the rice and encourage saccharification and the development of lactic acid. Brewers then move the starter to a larger barrel for two to three days with more mixing before returning it to half barrels to adjust the temperature. This method required time, intense labour and ample space for all the barrels. In 1909, NRIB staff member Kagi Kinichirō abbreviated the kimoto method by eliminating the laborious churning of the sake in the half barrels. His method came to be called 'stopping the yama oroshi' (*yamahai*). He combined water and kōji and allowed the starter to rest for several hours before the rice was added. In seven to eight hours, the rice absorbs the water and begins to float. The brewer then stirs the starter and lets it rest. In four to five days bubbles appear, indicating that it has begun to ferment. Thus, even without grinding the starter with oars, the yamahai starter showed improvements in saccharification and the rice broke down readily.[64] The yamahai method was possible because brewers were able to use more highly polished rice and no longer needed to grind harder grains in the starter as they had in the past.

However, it was the sokujō method, which the NRIB popularized towards the end of the Meiji period, that became the industry standard, a process innovated in 1899 by Eda Kamajirō (1872–1957). Eda was a university professor who worked first for the Ministry of Finance before taking a position at the NRIB in 1909. All preceding methods of building the starter, from medieval bodaimoto to early modern kimoto, relied on the development of natural lactic acid produced when boiled or steamed rice soaks in water over time. Lactic acid increases the acidity of the starter, inhibiting bacterial contamination and providing an environment conducive to the yeast growing. For his 'quick starter' (sokujō), Eda added lactic acid directly to the starter along with yeast, alleviating the need to develop it naturally.[65] Like the yamahai method, the quick starter dispensed with grinding the ferment in half barrels, and it was also more foolproof in producing a viable starter in four to five days, one that showed even more efficiency in breaking down the rice and transforming starches to sugars. The sokujō method worked regardless of whether the brewer used hard water typical of Nada's breweries or softer water such as from Hiroshima or Fushimi. By the mid-1920s, most brewers had switched to using either the yamahai or the quick starter method.[66]

Although the research of the NRIB provided many watershed advances to brewing, sake makers themselves also took steps to improve their products. Many brewers looked to Nada for guidance, inviting tōji from Nada to their local breweries and creating publications to disseminate technical information. Miura Senzaburō (1847–1908), who opened a sake brewery in Hiroshima in 1878, made multiple trips to Nada to study brewing methods, and he took steps to secure better quality rice, more finely polished, for his brewery in Hiroshima City. Hiroshima's sake history dates to the seventeenth century in the area's castle towns and urban centres, but Hiroshima's sake did not become nationally famous until the twentieth century, when its brewers began winning awards in competitions sponsored by the NRIB starting in 1907. Miura is owed credit for the achievements of Hiroshima's sake because he shared his knowledge of brewing techniques with area tōji. By 1925, of the 378 tōji in Hiroshima prefecture, 299 were his former disciples. One of the secrets of Hiroshima sake was polishing rice at a low seimaibuai to give it a fruity bouquet reminiscent of apples and bananas, an aroma called *ginjō*, giving rise to sake called *ginjōshu* by the early 1920s. It helped that the Satake vertical rice mill, which made polishing rice to 60 per cent seimaibuai possible, was a local Hiroshima invention. Miura also discovered that brewing at a lower temperature helped to compensate for using the soft water of the Hiroshima area, which lacked the mineral content of the hard water of Nada and meant that it took longer for the starter to develop. Ginjōshu began as sake meant to impress judges in competitions, but in the 1930s brewers in Nada, Akita and Saga prefectures began marketing ginjōshu.[67] Today ginjōshu designates a category of premium sake,

A local resident draws water from the brewery well outside Hakubotan Brewery in Saijō Hiroshima. Founded in 1675, Hakubotan is one of the oldest breweries in Hiroshima.

as Chapter Seven describes, and many in the sake world consider Miura to be the 'father of ginjō'.[68]

Kumamoto's sake owed its improvements to its own local 'sake god', Nojiro Kin'ichi (1876–1964). Nojiro grew up in a family of soy-sauce makers in Shimane prefecture, but he moved to Tokyo to study before taking a job in the tax office in Kumamoto in Kyushu. Kumamoto was long famous for its 'red sake' (*akazake*), which derived its colour from ash added to control the acidity and stabilize the beverage. Nojiro assisted local brewers in transitioning towards making seishu, and he eventually established a research station in conjunction with local sake makers. One of his innovations was developing a way to ventilate kōji-making rooms to assist kōji respiration and growth, but more important was his isolation of a yeast in 1953 that made fermentation possible at a lower temperature, a necessary advancement for improving ginjō sake, and a yeast widely used for that purpose today.[69]

SAKE'S DARK VALLEY

Before the Second World War, sake production peaked in 1919 at 6.18 million koku, but with the global economic decline in the 1920s, the 1923 Great Kanto Earthquake, and Japan's mobilization for war, production struggled to reach 5 million koku (900,000 kilolitres/237,751,000 gall.).[70] Sake was still the drink of choice in the 1920s, although it was losing ground to beer among younger consumers due to the aggressive marketing of beer companies, which included newspaper advertising, posters, hot-air balloons, cars bearing the logos of beer brands and even beer-bottle shaped automobiles used for publicity.[71] Beer companies had an advantage over sake brewers because there were only four brands of beer available, compared to the 9,587 breweries competing with each other for market share.[72] Beer won the battle of the beverages during the Second World War thanks in large part to policies of the Japanese government.

As Japan mobilized for war in the late 1930s, government policies towards alcohol were shaped by the need to manage resources. Ingredients for sake and beer could both be used for food, but rice was considered much more of a national staple than wheat and barley. In 1937, the government began limiting the amount of rice that could be used for brewing, mandating that brewers cut their rice use by half the next year. In 1938, the National General Mobilization Law limited the availability of polished rice for the general population and placed price controls on brown rice. In 1939, the Ministry of Finance fixed prices for sake as it did for other key consumer goods including miso, soy sauce and fish, and in the same year it established the Greater Japan Alcohol Sales Company to manage all sake sales throughout Japan. By then Japanese department stores had taken rice off their dining room menus. Cuts in production and fixed prices meant that sake sellers began watering down sake, leading critics to call it 'goldfish sake' – suggesting that the beverage had so little alcohol that fish could live in it.[73]

In 1943, the Japanese government took complete control of the production of alcohol. It nationalized the beer brewing industry, making a single brand available to consumers with ration tickets. It was beer, not sake, that the government viewed as key to Japan's war effort. Sake production during the war was one-seventh of its pre-war peak, while beer brewing continued at one-third of its production level before the war.[74] Making beer available to consumers was seen as key to morale at home, and the armed forces supplied troops with beer on Japan's front lines until the very end of the war.[75] These government initiatives introduced more consumers to beer and help explain the rise in popularity of that beverage in the post-war era. Sake fared very differently. In 1943, the Ministry of Finance ordered half of Japan's breweries to close and half of the brewery labour force to be transferred to work in industries supporting the war effort. Fushimi's more than seventy breweries became thirty-four, and the sake makers who remained reduced their production volume by 46.2 per cent.[76] Bombing also reduced the number of sake breweries to 3,178 by 1945.[77]

Two more wartime initiatives had a lasting impact on the sake industry: the implementation of a ranking system in 1943 and the creation of artificial sake. Though sake production was curtailed, the government still derived tax revenues from the drink, and in 1943 the Ministry of Finance established a scheme that taxed sake according to four different ranks. The ministry later reduced these to two ranks, first and second, with a higher 'special class' on top. These ratings had nothing to do with the quality of the sake but were instead based on the amount of alcohol (ABV) and the concentration of 'extract', a measurement of non-volatile substances like glucose. There was not much difference between the grades, and the ranking system reflected old biases, with sake from Nada and Fushimi given 'special' status, or first rank, and other regional sake earning second-rank status by default. Although rankings were based on samples taken at the brewery, those could be doctored to achieve the desired results.[78] In effect, breweries simply paid higher taxes to earn a special or first-class ranking for their sake. Special-class ratings cost five times more than second-class ratings, and a first-class rating was 2.5 times more. Many brewers simply refused or could not afford to pay higher taxes for the higher rankings. The ranking scheme was misleading to consumers because sake ranked 'special' or first class was not necessarily of higher quality than second-rank sake. Yet the classification system continued until 1989.[79]

Experiments in developing artificial sake began in Manchuria when breweries faced shortages of rice in 1939 and warfare cut shipments of rice from Korea. Breweries initially tested the use of local upland rice and foxtail millet (awa) for sake making, but without success. In 1941, sake makers began adding alcohol made from sugar to the main fermentation mash to boost output, but just adding alcohol and water did not produce a beverage that tasted like sake. Sugars, lactic acid and amino acids like MSG were also needed to give the beverage a sake-like taste. The NRIB continued these experiments the following year, as did 55 breweries in Japan. Soon the rest of Japan's breweries adopted what was considered the optimum ratio of 10 koku of steamed rice to 5 koku of brewer's alcohol at 30 per cent ABV along with sugars and flavourings.[80]

Brewers had been adding distilled alcohol to sake as early as the seventeenth century, and the Ministry of Finance had relaxed the laws concerning the ingredients that could be included in sake in 1940 and 1949, allowing the use of malt sugar, glucose, amino acids like monosodium glutamate, mineral salts and flavourings – permitting the resulting beverage to be called 'sake' as long as the artificial ingredients did not exceed half of the content. Traditionally, 10 koku of white rice produces 15 koku of sake watered to 17 koku, but adding alcohol and other ingredients increased the output to 42 koku of sake – actually 52 koku when it was watered down further for sale.[81] In other words, with the added ingredients, brewers could triple the amount of sake they produced, so this engineered beverage was called 'three times more sake' (sanzōshu or sanbaijōshu). In 1953, 59.3 per cent of sake

used this method.[82] Sanzōshu production continued into the
period of Japan's recovery from the Second World War to the era
of high-speed economic growth in the mid-1960s, the 1970s and
on into the 1980s. Production of sanzōshu increased to the point
that, from the mid-1950s to the mid-1970s, sake made just with
rice and without added alcohol (jummaishu) disappeared from the
market.[83] Some brands of Japanese whisky and shōchū were also
little more than alcohol, water and artificial flavourings in this
period.[84]

Reflecting on the proliferation of this engineered beverage,
sake historian Yoshida Hajime wrote:

> Adding alcohol was in some ways an unavoidable measure
> for a [wartime] period that would be hard to conceive of
> today when there was a rice shortage. I can understand that.
> However, when Japan entered a period of rice surplus [in the
> 1960s], the sake industry continued to concentrate on just
> increasing production, and for a long time they were unable
> to supply consumers with sake that did not contain salicylic
> acid. So, word spread of the bad reputation of 'artificial sake
> containing salicylic acid' and people forgot about sake that
> truly tasted good.

Yoshida, and other sake scholars, agree that the bad reputation
that sake developed from sanzōshu was a key reason why consumers, especially young people, turned away from sake in the
post-war era.[85]

The beer industry capitalized on sake's misfortune. Japan's
beer makers were major corporations with ample capital to inv-
est during the post-war era in rebuilding factories, ramping up
production and advertising. The beer industry was also quicker

to revive after the Second World War since barley was in greater supply than the staple rice needed for sake. Beer brewers returned to pre-war production levels by 1951, but it took sake makers another decade to do the same.[86] That beer makers promoted lager beer as a 'clean' alcoholic beverage appealed especially to younger drinkers and women. In 1959, beer surpassed sake in sales as the most popular alcoholic beverage in Japan.[87] The increased Westernization of the diet from the mid-1960s did not necessarily contribute to the continued decline of sake consumption relative to beer. However, the fact that beer could just as easily as sake complement Japanese foods like tempura, and that Japan completely lacked any tradition of pairing sake with certain foods comparable to wine and European cuisines, meant that beer could easily replace sake as the drink of choice for almost any meal in Japan. Today, it is typical in Japan to hear customers begin their orders at a restaurant saying, 'I'll have beer first' (*toriaezu bīru*), and this phrase dates from the era when beer became the country's most popular beverage after 1959, which is around the time that revellers began saying 'kanpai' with beer instead of toasting each other with sake at the start of a party.[88]

Sake production increased up to 1973, but beer production grew at twice the pace. In retrospect, bad-tasting sanzōshu was to blame.[89] Nishimura Takaharu (b. 1945), an executive for the three-hundred-year-old Sawanotsuru Brewery in Nada, and a former director of the Japan Sake Brewers Association, identified sanzōshu as one of the chief reasons why, by 2011, sake's market share among alcoholic beverages in Japan was just 6.7 per cent, about where it remains today. Sake scholar Gautier Roussille calls the same engineered drink sake's 'original sin'.[90]

Nishimura identified another important reason for reductions in the consumption of sake, namely the practice of 'barrel

buying' (*tarugai, okegai*). The post-war era did see some technological developments, with improved rice steamers in 1955, automated kōji makers in 1956, a new sake press in 1963 and stainless
steel tanks in 1965 – all innovations that made year-round brewing possible in the mid-1960s. Yet, the success of sanzōshu offered little incentive to make improvements in more traditional
methods of sake brewing during this period.[91] Gekkeikan began
brewing year-round in 1962 and the major Nada brewers soon
followed.[92] But the large breweries in Nada and Fushimi could
not keep pace with demand in the 1960s, so they purchased sake
from smaller producers, blended the sake with their own products, and repackaged the drink under their own brand names.

This 'barrel buying' system allowed larger makers to sell
more sake. Conversely, 'selling barrels' provided an easy market
for smaller breweries who could offload their products to larger
breweries without paying any taxes. Around 1969, taxes amounted
to 20–50 per cent of the retail price of sake, a cost that still had
to be paid by the brewery.[93] In 1961, 32 per cent of the sake sold
went through barrel buying to other brewers. In 1966, 41.6 per
cent of sake brewers 'sold their barrels' to other breweries.[94]
By 1973 some 50–80 per cent of the sake made by large brewers
originated from other producers through barrel buying.[95] Sake
journalist Funase Shunsuke estimated the amount of sake that
major brewers bought from other producers and sold under
their own label around this time, and he found that the rates
were 82.7 per cent for Kenbishi, 75 per cent for Sho Chiku Bai
and 67.3 per cent for Gekkeikan.[96] An article in the *Asahi Shimbun*
newspaper in January 1981, based on tax agency records, concurred
with this number for Gekkeikan and added that the rates for the
Hakutsuru Brewery stood at 62.9 per cent and for Nihon Sakari
at 55.9 per cent.[97] Popular criticism of this practice helped curtail

it and contributed to the 'local sake' movement of the 1980s described in Chapter Seven.[98]

By the mid-1960s the winter beverage of the 1860s was made year-round and sake in general was easier than ever before to make and sell on a large scale. Year-round brewing demanded a change in sake's labour force from seasonal to permanent work. In the era of Japan's high-speed economic growth in the 1960s and 1970s, the long, intense hours of working as a brewer and the years needed to become a tōji were far less appealing to young people, who enjoyed more occupational choices. As of June 2022 entry-level workers in the sake industry earned the equivalent of U.S. $950 per month with a median salary for workers reaching only $1,641 monthly. According to the same survey of 59 sake workers from 29 prefectures, nearly 56 per cent worked more than nine and a half hours a day during the brewing season, and 88 per cent reported that they could not take a day off during that period.[99] With younger people opting for other careers, older tōji could not find successors. In 1934, there were 63,000 brewery workers, typically with 8.5 per brewery. But in 1973, the number of workers declined to 20,000 and fell to 12,287 in 1983.[100] The number of seasonal tōji also declined. In 1986, 74 per cent of tōji worked seasonally, but that number was just shy of 16 per cent in 2016.[101]

In response to changes in sake's labour force, brewery owners promoted automation to boost production. A business profile of the modernization of one of the five largest sake makers in Nada compiled in 1969–70 described an enterprise with 'traditional' facilities and an automated factory. The company brewed half of its sake in the traditional plants, the other half in the factory, and purchased two-thirds of the sake sold under its brand name through 'barrel buying'. The traditional facility employed seasonal workers for 150 days a year with work days that began at 5 a.m.

Hakutsuru Brewery, Nada.

and lasted until 4 p.m., with separate night shifts. In the automated factory the employees worked for three hundred days of the year under the supervision of a chemical engineer, not a tōji, and the work day lasted from 8 a.m. to 5 p.m. The factory workers were generally more educated than those in the traditional facilities, with 60 per cent having attended high school compared to just 10 per cent of the workers in the traditional facility. The brewery recruited its factory employees based on the results of a competitive exam, rather than the traditional apprentice system. However, the factory foremen came from the ranks of the traditional workers, and their 'old customs seem to be obstacles to the smooth operation of the modern factory', according to the study's authors.[102]

The scope of the brewing industry also changed over the course of the twentieth century. In 1902, there were 12,496 breweries producing over 3.2 million koku (576,000 kilolitres/ 152,163,100 gall.) of sake. By 1968 the number of breweries fell by more than two-thirds to 3,582, but these manufacturers produced twice as much sake as their predecessors in 1902, some 6.9 million koku.[103] Larger sake brewers sold as much sake as they could produce and more, but by 1970 half of Japan's sake brewers were operating near a deficit, which explains why smaller breweries sold sake to larger producers and why both made artificial sake.[104] Sake production peaked in 1973 at 9.81 million koku, but thereafter production levels and the number of breweries declined so that by 2016 Japan's 1,615 breweries made just shy of 3 million koku of sake.

Though coined in the late nineteenth century, the word 'Japanese sake', Nihonshu, came into more widespread use in the early 1960s at the time that artificial sake (sanzōshu) dominated the marketplace and beer had become the nation's alcoholic beverage of choice.[105] 'Nihonshu, the sake that ought to represent the country of Japan, became predominantly sanzōshu in the period of the war and post-war,' explains sociologist Hashimoto Kenji. He continued, 'the national brand controlled the market and was brewed with a middle-of-the-road taste geared to consumers around the country.'[106] Calling this drink 'Japanese sake' draws attention to the fact that it developed with the national government's direction through the Tax Agency, which favoured increased production over the health of the consumer, the sustainability of smaller makers, and the long-term fitness of the sake industry. Of course, the Ministry of Finance and other government agencies did not compel sake brewers to use salicylic acid or to make sanzōshu, but both were legal and tacitly if not directly encouraged to sustain taxes on sake. Whether it was called Nihonshu, seishu or sake, the modern beverage of the post-war era diverged from sake's premodern roots as a rice-based alcoholic drink. Thankfully, early modern methods of production did not disappear in the twentieth century, and the sake produced in the 1990s was a very different product, allowing the words Nihonshu, sake and seishu to take on more positive connotations once again.

銘
酒
諏方盛

通い徳利

'Commuter vessel' (*kayoi tokkuri*) from the modern era bearing the name Suwamori, the former name of Aumont Sake Brewery, Shibata City, Niigata.

SIX
A BRIEF HISTORY OF IZAKAYA

With roots in the fifteenth century, *izakaya*, drinking places that serve food, have in this century become a global phenomenon. A survey of sake consumption from early modern times to the present is beyond the scope of a single book, but izakaya provide an appropriate lens to examine a popular and important aspect of sake culture over time. Whether in Japan, New York, Taipei or London, the izakaya, literally 'an establishment to sit and drink sake', offers one of the most enjoyable places to enjoy sake, or another beverage, and usually a variety of good food.

BREW SHOPS (SAKAYA)

The history of this casual and fun atmosphere for eating and drinking can be traced back more than six hundred years to medieval 'brew shops' (sakaya) that made and sold sake, as Chapter Two described. A typical sakaya of the fifteenth century used hundreds of ceramic vessels to brew and store sake. To keep their sake pots safe from falling over, brewers sank the 250-litre (66 gall.) vessels into the earth to give them stability. Since the sake pots could not be moved, customers who wanted to buy sake had to visit the sakaya and bring their own containers to fill, a practice that lasted until the early twentieth century when breweries began selling sake in bottles.

Early modern (1600–1868) sake sellers provided customers with containers, small flasks (*tokkuri*) with a capacity of 5 *gō* (0.9 litres/¼ gall.) and larger vessels containing 1 *shō* (1.8 litres/ ½ gall.) of sake, which became the traditional standard size for sake bottles in Japan (*isshōbin*) in the twentieth century. Early modern sake sellers advertised the name and the location of the shop on their containers and sometimes also included a reference number, rather like a library book, so that customers would return the vessels, dubbed 'poor person's bottles' (*binbō tokkuri*) and 'commuter vessels' (*kayoi tokkuri*) in the Meiji period (1868–1912). Mino Takada ware (Gifu prefecture), Tanba Tachigui ware (Hyōgo prefecture), Arita ware (Saga prefecture) and Hasami ware (Nagasaki prefecture) were the typical ceramic styles for 'poor person's tokkuri'. At home or in izakaya, people preferred smaller tokkuri for pouring. Tokkuri with a capacity of 2.5 *gō* (450 millilitres/ 1 pint) were the standard size used in Edo, as revealed in archaeological discoveries from the residences of commoners and samurai.[1] A standard size for tokkuri in Japanese restaurants today is smaller, just 180 millilitres (just over ⅓ pint).

Sakaya were not just places to buy sake to take away, but they became convenient places to sample, and evidence of 'standing bars' (*tachinomi*) where customers stood and drank date to the fifteenth century in Kyoto.[2] With over three hundred sakaya in early fifteenth-century Kyoto, competition for the local market must have been fierce. It is easy to imagine some of the brewery owners offering free samples or serving 'snacks for sake' (*sakana*) like pickled vegetables or salt-preserved seafood (*shiokara*) to lure customers and make them thirsty. These tactics would have encouraged customers to stand around drinking and eating in the sakaya, and over time, these became standing bars and neighbourhood hangouts.

By the seventeenth century, with the shogunate's strict laws controlling brewing, sakaya sold but did not produce their own sake, especially in Edo where locals preferred the sake of the Kansai region. Edo's sake retailers purchased from brokers who bought their sake from wholesalers (*ton'ya*) who specialized in the sake of different regions of Japan. Some wholesalers began as branch stores for brewers in the Kansai region. By the end of the seventeenth century, when wholesalers formed their own guild, there were 120 ton'ya that specialized in sake from the Kansai region.[3]

Although they no longer made their own sake, early modern sakaya still advertised their products, like breweries, by hanging a large ball made of cedar branches outside their shops. This ball, called the *sakabayashi*, changed colour from green to brown as an indication of the progression of the brewing season. Any shop that brewed, sold or served sake used sakabayashi to advertise. By the mid-eighteenth century there were more than 2,000 sakaya in Edo.[4] A survey of sake sellers from that era found that larger sakaya sold sake by the barrel or in smaller units of shō. For mid-level sellers, most of their business was in units of shō. At the bottom were ordinary shops whose business was entirely in servings of shō, so this group was also called *shō-zakaya*. The illustration overleaf shows the interior of one of these small sellers in the mid-nineteenth century.[5]

SEATED SAKE

Although food stands and standing bars still exist today and were typical of eating and drinking spots that cater to labourers in cities in the first half of the twentieth century, sitting down is certainly more comfortable than standing. The first reference to a 'seated sake seller' (*izake*) dates to the end of the 1600s.[6] 'Seated sake sellers' were part of the diverse landscape of places to dine out and drink that emerged in seventeenth-century Edo, which included food stands, eateries and inns.[7] At the higher end in the late seventeenth century in Edo were posh 'tea houses' and auxiliary establishments that served food and entertained with courtesans in the city's licensed quarter in Yoshiwara, but there were many less expensive restaurants that sold hearty dishes of grains and vegetables as well as food stands and peddlers that offered inexpensive bowls of soba or wheat noodles. Some food stands paired warm sake with boiled foods like the gelatinous devil's tongue (*konnyaku*) made from the root of the *Amorphophallus konjac* plant, taro or fried tofu.[8]

Eating out might seem like an extravagance, but it was often less expensive and a much more convenient option than cooking at home in early modern Edo. Edo's commoners lived in small dwellings where the kitchen was in a narrow space just inside the entrance. Tucked into this area was a small stove able to prepare rice or simmer foods but not do both tasks well simultaneously. So, the people of Edo and other cities usually cooked rice only once a day and reheated it for their other meals. These conditions gave opportunities to entrepreneurs. 'Simmered food shops' (*niuriya*) sold inexpensive side dishes such as grilled fish, boiled vegetables and stewed greens for customers to take home and eat. Many of these shops conveniently charged the same price for

A small volume sake seller from the book *Ogonsui daijin sakazuki* (1854) by Tamenaga Shusui. The shopkeeper hefts a large barrel of Kenbishi brand sake. In the background are smaller barrels with funnels and masu measuring cups on the top. The masu cups wait for the seller to use them to measure sake to fill the ceramic tokkuri bottles on the floor in back for sales to customers.

their foods, which gave rise to their nickname, 'four copper coin shops' (shimon'ya).

Unlike the strict laws controlling sake brewing in the early modern period, there were no laws or taxes for selling sake retail or in restaurants, which meant that there was brisk competition among purveyors of alcohol.[9] The only laws affecting sellers were for those operating after dark, to try to prevent their portable braziers and oil lamps from causing fires. In the wake of the Meireki Fire of 1657, which damaged Edo Castle, destroyed four hundred urban wards and killed 100,000 people, Edo's city

Detail from *Picture Scroll of Early Modern Artisans* (*Kinsei shokunin zukushi ekotoba*) by Kuwagata Keisei, early 19th century. A 'four copper coin shop' (*shimon'ya*) on the far right competes with a stand selling tempura on the far left. Customers enjoy squid from the middle stand. Standing while eating remained a common practice in inexpensive restaurants into the 20th century.

magistrates prohibited food vendors, including niuriya, from operating after 6 p.m. and banned food peddlers. The shogunate repeated these prohibitions in 1662, 1670, 1671 and 1686, indicating that the night-time businesses were in fact flourishing. Finally, in 1699, the city's magistrates relented and allowed evening sales – except on exceptionally windy nights.[10]

Around the year 1750, 'seated sake shops' and 'simmered food shops' combined into a new business model, the 'simmered food seated sake shop' (*niuri izakaya*), a cumbersome term even in Japanese that was soon shortened to izakaya, a variation of the term izake. Izakaya's rise to popularity in the mid-eighteenth

century coincided with the shogunate's relaxation of laws controlling sake brewing that allowed new breweries to open even in
rural areas and lowered the price of sake.[11] The first reference to
an izakaya appears in a petition made to an urban magistrate on
behalf of two men who sought in 1749 to open an izakaya and
other eateries on the grounds of Tomioka Hachimangu Shrine
in Fukagawa, Edo, on the pretext of providing funds to repair a
shrine structure that had been destroyed in a rainstorm. Apparently, the scheme worked because the shrine rebuilt its lost building in 1752 using the revenue from these establishments.[12]

An image from the book A Tale of Hazakurahime in the Fourth
Month (Hazakurahime uzuki monogatari), dating from 1814, shows
an izakaya that provides both takeaway and dining-in services.
On the left side, fish and an octopus hang over large platters of

An izakaya from *A Tale of Hazakurahime in the Fourth Month* (*Hazakurahime
uzuki monogatari*; 1814) by Bisanjin.

simmered foods to catch the attention of passersby, while on the right side customers lounge on benches and the raised interior of the establishment enjoying sake and side dishes.

Early modern izakaya lacked chairs and tables. Customers sat on long benches or on the raised floor of the establishment, as in the image.[13] Meiji-period izakaya added empty barrels for seats. Previously, sake sellers would not hold on to used barrels since they were too valuable. They sold them to dealers who re-sold the barrels to soy sauce makers.[14] Western-style chairs and tables were not a standard feature of izakaya until the mid-1920s.[15]

The image from the book *A Tale of Hazakurahime in the Fourth Month* shows customers drinking from a new type of serving vessel, small cups called *choko*. Choko were produced in the kilns of Arita in modern Saga prefecture and elsewhere and popular-ized in Edo around the time that izakaya appeared in the mid-eighteenth century.[16] The drinkers pour their sake from ceramic containers called *chirori*, also used to heat sake. In Kyoto and Osaka, drinkers warmed and served their sake in kettles called *chōshi*, a vessel reserved only for special occasions in Edo. Kyoto and Osaka drinkers also favoured the traditional shallow sake cups (*sakazuki*) used in prior centuries. Custom dictated consuming warm sake from the ninth day of the ninth lunar month to the third day of the third lunar month (October through to April).[17] During the months for drinking sake at room temperature, smaller tokkuri were used in izakaya, a custom that has continued to this day.

The only women in the scene in *A Tale of Hazakurahime in the Fourth Month* are the two servers. Izakaya were male spaces, because women other than waitresses or entertainers generally did not drink in public from the early modern period through to the twentieth century. Edo's population growth in the seventeenth

Tokkuri and choko, watercolour by Kiyomi Rath.

century was largely of men, due to the influx of samurai whose lords needed them to build and staff mansions in the city. Samurai left their families in their home domains while they lived with their lords, who spent alternate years in Edo, a scheme that kept the regional warlords under the watchful eye of the shogunate and reduced the financial resources of the lords, who had to

Sake flask used for warming and pouring hot sake,
1650–90, glazed porcelain.

maintain mansions in the city and travel back and forth to their home provinces in alternate years.

The influx of male samurai meant that at times Edo's male population was twice that of women, and male samurai constituted half of the city's population of 1 million by the eighteenth century.[18] Thus Edo's entertainments catered to men. The famous gambler Shimon Tatsugorō (1800?–1875) exclaimed, 'I want my sake hot; my side dish to be sashimi; and the server to be a beautiful woman,' a sentiment that most of his male peers would probably agree with.[19] Even after Edo's population reached more of a parity of men and women, izakaya and other drinking and eating establishments in general remained masculine spaces. In the early twentieth century 'bluestocking' feminists made a point of drinking in male enclaves in Tokyo such as Yoshiwara as a way to advocate for women's rights, but female customers were not a typical site in izakaya until the 1970s, as described below.[20]

Early modern izakaya did not use menus; instead the owners wrote the names of the foods they served on the wall, a custom that many izakaya continue to this day. And, rather than advertise sake by brand name, early modern izakaya sold sake at different grades. Customers ordered by indicating how much they wanted at what price. 'I'll take 3 gō [0.54 litres/1 pint] for 24 coins,' would be a typical order.[21] Izakaya also sold less expensive locally made doburoku, known in Edo as 'white horse' (shirouma).

To accompany sake, izakaya offered foods reflecting the establishment's historical roots in shops that specialized in boiled dishes such as simmered beans and vegetables slowly stewed in soy sauce (nishime). Other typical dishes included tofu grilled with a sweet glaze (dengaku), grain dishes cooked with vegetables, soups and simmered fish. Like all early modern homes, izakaya lacked ovens to prepare baked goods. Most izakaya dishes were finger foods, but some prepared *nabeyaki*, a stew with fowl or fish flavoured with miso and served in a pot that was meant to be shared. Pickles (*tsukemono*), or sometimes simply a dollop of salty miso, were enough to accompany the sake in some establishments.[22]

With frequent changes in the value of early modern currency, it is almost impossible to provide modern equivalents for prices, but food historian Nagayama Hisao drew some conclusions by comparing prices against the cost of rice historically. Nagayama estimated that a gō (0.18 litre) serving of sake at a standing izakaya in the early modern era cost the equivalent of 152 yen in 1982, which would be 202 yen ($1.33) in 2023 prices, while a small chōshi container of sake was 228 yen (306 yen, $2.15 in 2023). In terms of food, an octopus leg, sardines, simmered konnyaku and a serving of simmered beans were 76 yen, his conversion of the standard 4 copper coins charged for these dishes. Grilled tofu was 95 yen and soup made from whale 304 yen. These prices should be taken with a pinch of salt, but they can provide a sense of relative cost.[23]

With their affordable prices, izakaya drew customers from the working classes, and they were often a rough crowd, as one disciple of the poet Matsuo Bashō (1644–1694) explained in a haiku:

Going out to drink	*Nomi ni iku*
The izakaya is rowdy	*izake no are no*
There will be a fight	*hito sawagi*[24]

Izakaya patrons included low- and middle-ranking samurai, shopkeepers, peddlers, palanquin carriers and servants. Some izakaya catered to late-night revellers, selling soup made from leftover

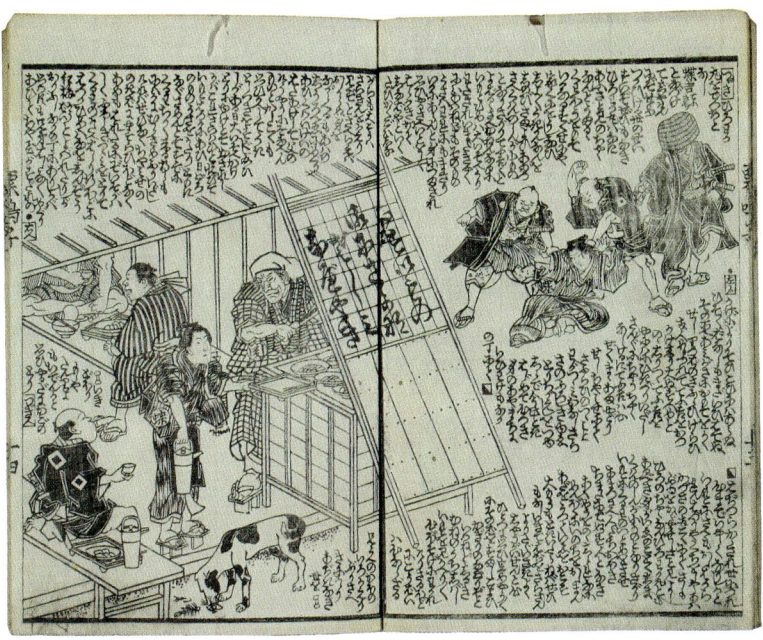

An izakaya advertises 'soups, side dishes, sashimi, and stews (*nabeyaki*)'
on a sign in front of the cook from the book *Keisei awa no naruko* (1851)
by Rakutei Saiba.

tofu-lees along with sake to the customers of the licensed quarters.
Other izakaya offered foods like boiled tofu as well as sake for a
working man's breakfast.[25]

Besides the hanging cypress ball, another advertising tactic
that developed in the late nineteenth century was a shop curtain
made of multiple strands of rope (*nawa noren*). The rope curtain
kept flies away from the customers inside and provided some
privacy while at the same time letting in the breeze and allowing the delicious aromas of simmered foods to waft outside to
entice new customers. Noodle shops, restaurants that specialized
in grilled eel, and similar establishments used rope curtains, but

the device had become synonymous with izakaya by the turn of the twentieth century.[26] An 1811 survey found 7,603 food sellers and restaurants in Edo and of these 2,374 were shops selling simmered foods, including izakaya, compared to just 217 sushi restaurants and 718 udon and soba noodle shops.[27] With a population of 1 million, in Edo there was an izakaya for every 553 people, a similar proportion of izakaya to population as Tokyo in 2006.[28]

The maturity of Edo's izakaya restaurant market is demonstrated by the development of speciality izakaya in the mid-nineteenth century. 'Potato izakaya' (*imozakaya*) served potatoes slowly cooked in broth until the liquid disappeared – a dish called *nikorobashi*, and one often found on izakaya menus from the early 1800s. There was also a resurgence in popularity of standing bars (*tateba, tachinomi*) by the beginning of the Meiji period in 1868. Like today, these featured inexpensive sake and foods. 'Have a little tipple' (*chotto ippai*) became another catchphrase for izakaya in the second half of the nineteenth century. A potato izakaya that became famous for its inexpensive food was 'Three Penny House' (Sanpuntei), a reference to a small coin valued at one-tenth of a copper coin (mon). The first Sanpuntei opened in Fukiyachō in Edo in 1849, and imitators soon started shops by the same name in other parts of the city.[29]

IZAKAYA IN MODERN JAPAN

The description of izakaya at the turn of the twentieth century that author Hirade Kōjirō (1869–1911) included in his book *A History of the Customs of Tokyo* (*Tōkyō fūzokushi*) shows the continuity of those establishments in the transition to the modern period. Hirade cited a survey from 1897 that found 4,470 eateries in the city of Tokyo and 476 'places to drink sake' (*meishuten*). He had praised the capital's Western and Japanese restaurants, but he took a dim view of izakaya identified by their trademark 'rope curtains'. Hirade wrote,

> these are places where people of the lower classes
> like rickshaw pullers pay to get drunk on a cup of cheap
> doburoku (*nakagumi*) . . . They sit in a row on empty barrels
> and have side dishes like boiled octopus legs and sardines
> doused with vinegar, drinking like whales and eating
> like horses.[30]

Hirade lamented how they wasted their money on alcohol while forgetting their wives and families.

Because they catered to the lower class, izakaya did not feature in the restaurant reviews that became part of the culinary literature of the early twentieth century, although they remained an important part of the nation's dining-out scene. *Culinary Magazine* (*Kuidōraku*), Japan's first gourmet magazine, which launched in 1905, five years later than the first Michelin Guide in France, gravitated towards high cuisine and Western restaurants, even gesturing at Western readers by including an English-language table of contents for each issue. The inspiration for the gourmet magazine came from one of the bestselling books of the early twentieth century by Murai Gensai (1863–1927), a work serialized in a newspaper in 1903. Murai was a teetotaller who advertised his culinary novel by telling customers to purchase it instead of alcohol. Murai even penned a diatribe against drinking titled *Pleasures of Sake* (*Sake dōraku*) in 1902 that described how family life could be destroyed by alcohol.[31] Murai's dislike of dining out and of traditional indigenous methods of cooking were also factors that steered him, his readers and his imitators away from izakaya.

That izakaya were the antithesis of fine dining is told in one of the first dining-out guides to Tokyo, *A Walker's Guide to Dining Well in Tokyo* (*Tōkyō meibutsu tabearuki*), published in 1929. Meant to serve as a publication for white-collar 'salarymen' on where to eat lunch and entertain, the book, by writers from Tokyo's *Jiji shimpō* newspaper, was as much about the modern experience of eating in restaurants as the food. The authors claimed that the inspiration for their book was a story told by the famous comedian Sanyūtei Enshō IV (1846–1904), a tale of two connoisseurs going for a walk while debating the best spots to eat. Each place the walkers find they decide not to enter, commenting on the pros and cons of the establishment in detail. They even stroll past Yaozen, long one of the most famous traditional Japanese restaurants in the city. The pair realize too late that they have reached the outskirts of the city, but rather than turn around and walk back, they enter a lonely izakaya, taking a seat on barrels. They order grilled tofu, potatoes and konnyaku, standard fare for an izakaya, but the antithesis of any gourmet meal. Rather than being disappointed, they toast each other on their great culinary discovery, and passing through the rope curtain on the way out they decide to return to the same place the next day.[32]

Despite this nod to tradition, *A Walker's Guide to Dining Well in Tokyo* and similar eating guides focused on modern eating establishments such as department store dining rooms, diners (*shokudo*) and Western-style cafes where alcohol was served, all places where men could not only dine well but ogle the female waiting staff and the few women customers dining at department store restaurants.[33] Izakaya remained male spots for serious drinking, not lunch spots or places to enjoy high-quality fare.

Another author famous for his eating guides was Matsuzaki Tenmin (1878–1934), who did include izakaya in his *Walker's Guide to Dining in Tokyo* (*Tōkyō tabearuki*), published in 1931. Matsuzaki estimated that there were 16,000 restaurants in the capital and 25,000 more in the surrounding area. In the same way that the characters in Sanyūtei's comedic story had to hike to the outskirts of the city to discover an izakaya, Matsuzaki locates izakaya on the city's less-developed periphery, as if they were a throwback to earlier modes of dining. He explained,

> there are not many izakaya, those establishments repre-
> sentative of the term rope-curtain, in the core of the city.
> Karoku and Suehiro in the Ginza and Nadaya in Nihonbashi
> are sake-bars (*sakaba*) that do not offer light foods and
> emphasize drinking the highest quality sake from Nada.

However, Matsuzaki observed that Nadaya and Suehiro have also started serving food and stews (*nabemono*) to appeal to customers.

Interior of a small izakaya, Hachinohe, Aomori prefecture.

Rather than provide a variety of different brands of sake, these izakaya sold just one brand. Karoku sold Kikumasamune and Suehiro sold Sakura Masamune, both from Nada. Karoku attracted famous clients such as the mayor of Tokyo, authors and journalists, and anyone in their fifties or sixties ought to drink there and enjoy their fatty tuna marinated in Kikumasamune sake, according to Matsuzaki. Matsuzaki confessed that he often got blind drunk there.[34] Drunken customers taking up space and not leaving had likely been a problem for izakaya owners from the beginning, but the custom of serving a small plate of food as a seating charge called to'oshi or tsukidashi dates to Matsuzaki's time in the mid-1930s.[35] Recently, some izakaya have stopped the custom, responding to customer complaints about it.[36]

Izakaya, along with the rest of Japan's 25,600 dining and drinking establishments, were ordered to close in 1944 due to the Second World War. In their place, the government established 'people's bars' (kokumin sakaba) in the major cities. The bars opened once a week after 6 p.m. for a brief time and sold customers either 'a bottle of beer, a shot of whisky, or a few cups of cheap sake'.[37] Gritty drinking spots (nomiya) were a feature of the black markets that appeared around Shinjuku and other Tokyo train stations like Shibuya, Shinbashi, Yūrakuchō, Kanda, Ueno and Ikebukuro in the immediate post-war period.[38] The government had cleared these areas as firebreaks in 1943, and the open spaces were perfect for hawkers and impromptu eateries. The alcoholic beverages initially available at these sites were not sake or even doburoku. One was kasutori shōchū, a beverage that sounds like it is made from leftover lees (kasu) from sake or doburoku but was in fact brewed from any viable means for making distilled alcohol, like potatoes or barley with flavourings added. More dangerous was the beverage called 'bomb' (bakudan), made from toxic methyl alcohol (methanol) used for fuel. Consuming methanol can cause blindness and death. Bomb killed several people, including the well-known author of proletarian literature Takeda Rintarō (1904–1946) and novelist Oguri Mushitarō (1901–1946).[39]

Drinking spots were a prominent feature of post-war black markets. At the east exit of Ikebukuro station 43.4 per cent of the vendors sold alcohol. In Yūrakuchō three hundred bars and izakaya each sold 18 litres (4¾ gall.) of alcohol daily. During these hard times, drinkers wanted every drop they paid for, so barmen placed plates under glasses to catch any spills, a custom that continues in many izakaya. To accompany booze were the quintessential foods of the post-war period: ramen noodles and grilled *horumon*. This word derived from the English word hormone in the 1920s, suggesting something healthy. In black markets it referred to inexpensive beef and pork entrails that were also sold as 'grilled chicken' (*yakitori*).[40]

The most prominent restaurants in the post-war era outside of the black markets were ones that catered to men, serving them alcohol after work, and these included the first chain izakaya such as New Tokyo (*Nyū Tōkyō*), founded by Mori Shintarō in 1937. Mori's izakaya chain borrowed many concepts from Western-style beer halls, the first of which opened in Ginza in 1934, as part of a scheme by the president of the Nippon Beer Company, makers of the brand Ebisu, to advertise its beer. Mori opened his own Ebisu beer hall in Shinjuku Tokyo, then established New Tokyo izakaya in Yūrakuchō in a building called the White Palace. The ground floor of the White Palace was a German-style beer hall; the floor above offered beer and Japanese food; and the second floor had tatami rooms where the beef hot pot dish sukiyaki was served. There was a cafe on the third floor, along with the company office, and a room for parties on the fourth

Small izakaya built under the train tracks in Kobe.

floor that included an outdoor terrace. By 1956, when the company moved its headquarters to Yokohama, there were one hundred izakaya with the New Tokyo name in and around Tokyo
and the founder was hailed as the 'father of beer halls in Japan'.[41]

　　Yokohama in 1956 was also where Yamada Tomikatsu (1920–
2001), founder of the chain izakaya Yōrō no Taki, moved his
company headquarters from Nagano prefecture. In 1933 thirteen-
year-old Yamada left his family – who raised silkworms in Nishi-
gori Village (now Matsumoto City) in Nagano prefecture – for
Osaka, where, with only an elementary school education, he found
work as a stevedore, often eating at the curry rice shops and other
blue-collar eateries that catered to port labourers. Five years later
he returned home and used his savings to open the Fuji Diner,

learning the fundamentals of cooking and restaurant management from nearby restaurateurs. Yamada's personal skills and inexpensive food made his restaurant profitable. But he lost all of his wealth and property during the Second World War, not due to bombs, but because he had to pay a fine for trafficking in black-market goods. Surviving the war, he managed to revive his business, and obtaining a licence to sell liquor in 1951, he opened the first 'Longevity Falls' (Yōrō no Taki) izakaya in Matsumoto City that year, named after a famous waterfall in Gifu prefecture that, according to legend, once produced sake that healed the ill parents of a loyal son. His izakaya became famous for its simmered foods and Yamada sold franchise rights. Within five years the number of branches grew to 130 shops in Nagano prefecture alone. When he moved the company to Yokohama in 1956, prompted by having to pay a 2 million yen fine for tax evasion in Nagano, Yamada changed his name to Kinoshita Tōkichirō, the birth name of Toyotomi Hideyoshi, the warlord who unified Japan in 1590. He also revamped his principal business under the name 'Popular Drinking Spot (*taishū sakaba*) Yōrō no Taki'. In these new establishments, Yamada focused on selling alcohol and foods like yakitori, simmered dishes and sashimi that were less complicated to make and did not require professional chefs. His chain spread to Tokyo and grew to 32 locations in 1961, reaching 100 by 1965.[42]

Chain izakaya, like other chain restaurants, have standardized decor and menus, and they use training manuals to show staff how to prepare and serve food. They also rely on central kitchens, which prepare foods for franchise operations, reducing cost and deskilling food preparation. Central kitchens and training manuals allow chain izakaya to employ part-time workers as cooks instead of professional chefs.[43] Knowing how to cook is not necessary for owning and operating an izakaya, according to the 1996 book *Of Course People without Money Should Start a Business!* (*Kane no nai hito koso shōbai o yare!*), written to encourage readers to open their own Daikichi yakitori izakaya franchise. The author explained:

> Someone who has never once cooked rice. Someone who cannot cook at all. That guy is good enough for a yakitori business. Not just izakaya but any business is about dealing with people, so specialized knowledge does not carry much weight.

Daikichi's narrow menu of about thirty items, most of which are variations on grilled meat, and the typical layout of its small restaurants, focusing on counter seating, make preparing and serving food easier than larger restaurants with more extensive menus. Data in the same text showed that only 42 per cent of Daikichi izakaya owners had any professional experience cooking or operating a restaurant: 28 per cent were former white-collar workers.[44]

The number of chain izakaya quadrupled from the years 1988 to 2018. Cookdoor, a website for restaurants operated by the Tōken Corporation, a major real estate and construction firm, lists a total of 34,408 izakaya, including yakitori restaurants, as of November 2023. According to this website there are 162 branches of Tengu and 376 for Yōrō no Taki, but the top three chains are Uotami with 575 outlets, Yakitori Daikichi with 539 and Torikizoku with 506 shops; the last two are yakitori chains.[45] Today it is a challenge to find an independent izakaya that is not part of a chain in a major city, prompting some observers to worry about the future of independent izakaya.[46]

While izakaya traditionally targeted middle-aged men, iza-kaya chains – especially since the 1970s – have tried to cultivate young people and women as their customers by offering lighter foods, low alcohol drinks and even special 'ladies only' drinking nights.[47] Dining out in general, and izakaya especially, remained male-dominated spaces until the 1970s, with the exception of department-store dining rooms before the Second World War and beer gardens in the 1950s.[48] However, the number of women drinking in public grew steadily in the post-war period. An annual survey by Japan's national broadcaster (NHK) asked respondents whether they had drunk alcohol at least once in the year.

Branch of the chain izakaya Sakanaya Dōjō in Niigata City.

In 1954, women responded positively at a rate of just 13 per cent and men at 68 per cent. By 1976, the number of women claiming to drink alcohol rose to 53 per cent compared to men at 85 per cent. Thereafter the number of women who admitted to drinking climbed steadily to 61 per cent in 1984 and 63 per cent in 2013. Younger women had an even higher propensity to claim to drink, sometimes at even higher rates than men. In 2006, 90 per cent of women in their twenties reported drinking compared to 84 per cent of men. By 2013, drinking rates reached gender parity with 84 per cent of men and women in their twenties reporting drinking alcohol.[49] The survey is probably as much a measure of the social acceptability of drinking than of the actual prevalence of it, so it can be interpreted as showing the gradual decline in the taboo against women drinking in public.

The rise in drinking rates for women coincided with the increased popularity of women and families dining out in the 1970s, which came with the introduction of fast-food restaurant chains such as Kentucky Fried Chicken (1970), Mister Donut (1971) and McDonald's (1971) as well as the debut of family restaurant chains like Skylark (1970) and Friendly's (1977). A new generation of women's magazines also appeared in the same period that catered to a growing audience of 'office ladies' and unmarried working women aged eighteen to twenty-four, informing them of new foods and fashionable places to dine. Where earlier women's magazines had discussed food in terms of recipes mothers could make for their families, the new periodicals *An'an*, established in 1970, and *Non-no*, founded in 1971, were written in the conversational language of younger readers and emphasized eating out as entertainment and an escape from household chores.[50]

The chain izakaya Tengu, founded in Western Ikebukuro in Tokyo in 1969 by Iida Tamotsu, targeted female customers and influenced other chains. Inspired by his travels in Europe and with his father in the retail liquor trade, Iida transformed the floor above a branch of his izakaya in Kanda into a Western-style pub with brick walls where he served wine, scotch and imported German beer to accompany Western foods. Discovering that patrons wanted to order Japanese food from the restaurant below, he eventually combined the Japanese and Western menus, and served wines from California, Italy and Germany. The modern interior and eclectic food and drink offerings that paired Japanese foods with imported beverages appealed to younger customers and women especially, setting a format for his popular chain of izakaya and inspiring imitators in the 1970s.[51]

An'an and Non-no encouraged younger women to try Western foods like pizza, which arrived with the Shakey's chain in 1973, which the magazines introduced to readers as 'Italian okonomiyaki', a savoury Japanese pancake made with cabbage, flour and egg binding and other ingredients. The women's magazine Hanako, which debuted in 1988, also encouraged its young women readers to explore dining-out options that had been male preserves. With the magazine's encouragement, so-called 'geezer gals' (oyaji gyaru) ventured into off-track betting parlours and other male spaces, including izakaya.[52] As izakaya have spread globally from New York City in the 1990s to Taiwan, Seoul and Hong Kong a decade later, they have become feminized 'safe zones' for women, allowing them to enjoy light foods and low-alcohol beverages in comfortable surroundings different from domestic male-dominated drinking spots.[53]

Besides introducing new consumers to Western foods and beverages, izakaya played an important role in the 'local sake' (jizake) movement in Japan from the mid-1970s and the craft sake movement abroad from the 1990s.[54] 'Local sake', as described in the next chapter, were brands from Niigata, Kōchi and elsewhere that were ranked lower than the sake made by the major producers of Nada and Fushimi, but were nonetheless heralded as outstanding by sake journalists, who pointed out the inconsistencies in the current sake ranking system, where major brewers could simply pay to have their sake ranked higher. 'Local sake' makers, especially those that made 'all rice sake' (junmaishu) without added alcohol, eschewed these rankings as well as the problems associated with the cheaper sake sold by major brands, which if they were not comprised largely of brewers' alcohol and flavourings then were at least a blend of the products of multiple smaller brewers, obtained by 'barrel buying'. The father of the founder of the Tengu chain was a sake wholesaler in Nihonbashi in Tokyo, which helps to explain why the chain was not only the first to serve wine, but an early promoter of 'local sake' in the late 1970s. Besides chains, other izakaya that promoted jizake from the late 1970s advertised themselves as Japanese 'sake bars', 'noted sake brand izakaya' and 'local sake izakaya'.[55]

Today, the decor of many izakaya, whether they are within Japan or elsewhere, evoke the origins of izakaya in early modern Japan, but izakaya have succeeded as a global form of restaurant because of their flexibility as a space to enjoy food and alcohol, without limiting the types of foods or drinks served. Izakaya are as likely to have modern interiors and serve pizza as they are to offer Chinese dumplings or sashimi in a Japanese setting. A recent study of izakaya outside of Japan compares them to Irish pubs, which reflect local expectations of these spaces as much, if not more, than their historical origins. 'The global izakaya is a cultural form that borrows eclectically from the original Japanese drinking culture while accruing new associations outside of Japan,' according to that study's authors.[56] Globally, izakaya have introduced new customers to sake and many izakaya have it as their mission to promote the beverage. But izakaya as a phenomenon are larger than the beverage that was their former focus. At one time it was sake that lured men to izakaya. Today men and women might enter and leave without drinking a drop of Japan's national alcoholic beverage.

The chimneys of the breweries of Saijō Hiroshima in the dawn light,
watercolour by Kiyomi Rath.

SEVEN
THE QUEST FOR 'REAL SAKE', 1970-2020

In 1973 sake production peaked at an all-time high of 1.8 million kilolitres (475,500,700 gall.), but many smaller makers, who made up the majority of the roughly 3,000 breweries, were struggling to make a profit. Sake was also facing a public relations problem that journalist and consumer advocate Funase Shunsuke called the 'six sins', defined in his words by 'sake that would make you feel like vomiting if you drank it'. The first sin was the prevalence of 'three times more sake' (sanzōshu), a beverage made with alcohol and other ingredients that tripled the volume of the drink produced with rice, water and kōji alone. Chapter Five examined how this sake recipe that debuted in the Second World War became dominant in the post-war period. The next three sins were the additives used to make sanzōshu, namely brewer's alcohol, sweeteners (glucose, malt sugar and corn syrup) and some twenty artificial flavourings including monosodium glutamate (MSG) and succinic acid, which contributes sour and umami tastes. The fifth sin was 'barrel buying' (tarugai), where larger producers bought sake from smaller breweries, blended it and sold it under their own label. The final sin was the official ranking system introduced in 1943 that graded sake from Nada and Fushimi as 'special' and 'first class', while relegating the products of 'regional' breweries to 'second rank' by default, simply because the makers would not pay higher taxes for the top ratings. Funase and the organization he represented, the Consumers Union of Japan (Nihon Shohisha Renmei), embarked on a campaign in 1975 'toward real sake', which became the title of the organization's 1981 bestselling book about sake. Writing in retrospect in 2005, Funase credited the consumers' movements for changes in the sake industry including the disappearance of sanzōshu, ultimately phased out in 2006, and a reduction in the amount of barrel buying and artificial ingredients.[1] The tax agency also discontinued the problematic rating system in 1989 and established a new one in 1992.

At the same time that critics catalogued sake's sins, they presented alternatives in home-made doburoku and 'local sake' (jizake). Despite being outlawed in 1899, the cloudy beverage doburoku and home brewing never disappeared, and a campaign to legalize home brewing gained momentum in the 1980s, changing the image of doburoku from a dubious illegal beverage into an example of authentic and natural rural handicraft, qualities that also became associated with legal 'local sake', a term used to signify sake from brewers outside of the major sake producers of Nara and Fushimi. Sake journalists from the late 1960s onwards pointed out the disconnection between the official rankings and the quality of local sake, giving rise to the 'local sake boom' in the 1970s and 1980s that highlighted brands from Niigata and other prefectures. The growing interest in doburoku and local sake were also part of the rise in popularity and commodification of rural food culture in the 1980s, when heirloom vegetables and

other products from the countryside and coasts became delicacies used in fine dining to create a local cuisine and to attract
domestic tourists.

THE ATTEMPTED DOBUROKU REVIVAL

In the 1980s, one of the most important challenges to the sake
industry and tax laws came from the advocates of doburoku.
Doburoku became more prominent in the 1980s, but it also had
never disappeared, even after it was made illegal in 1899. Folklorists surveying food culture in Japan's rural hinterland in 1941
found that 44 of 85 localities studied across Japan produced
doburoku from rice, foxtail millet, barnyard millet or a blend of
rice and barley. Wartime necessity may have prompted use of a
variety of grains to make doburoku, but the examples of non-rice
doburoku also testify to the fact that sake could be made from
other grains besides rice, which was always in short supply in
mountainous regions.[2]

Illegal brewing continued into the post-war period. In 1955,
the Tax Administration Board of the Ministry of Finance estimated that over 203 million litres (53½ million gall.) of illegal liquor,
including sake and doburoku, were produced in the 1954 fiscal
year, with rural villages in the Tōhoku region responsible for over
151 million litres (40 million gall.). These totals actually marked
a decline compared to 1950, when an estimated 451 million litres
(119 million gall.) of illicit booze were produced.[3] In 1959 tax agents
discovered a home-brewing operation when they encountered
several drunken horses that had either willingly consumed the
brew or had been forced to do so by moonshiners in an effort to
hide the evidence.[4] Three years later, in 1962, the *Japan Times* newspaper ran a story describing illicit doburoku brewing as 'a national

pastime' according to the tax officials cited, who estimated annual production of doburoku at 144 million litres (38 million gall.), enough to fill bottles that would stretch 30,000 kilometres (18,640 mi.), the equivalent of two and a half trips to Hawaii. The Tōhoku region was again the top doburoku producer, followed by Hiroshima and the Kanto area. The tax agents warned, without any evidence, of 'third country nationals' producing dangerous brews 'causing deformities and hereditary abnormalities', who operated in cities. But the real reason cited for the persistence of doburoku was 'the secretiveness of the village folk' and the lack of special agents to root out moonshiners.[5]

Casting doburoku as dangerous, foreign and backward gave reasons to ban it, but another home-made alcoholic beverage raised questions about the rationale for laws prohibiting home brewing. In 1961, a government official responsible for making policy statements from the prime minister's cabinet wondered aloud in a prominent financial newspaper, the *Nihon Keizai Shimbun* (*Nikkei*), why it was legal to make 'plum wine' (*umeshu*) at home given the law prohibiting home brewing. Umeshu is a blend of distilled alcohol with apricots and sugar. To the extent that sake might be called an 'old man's drink', umeshu is a grandmother's beverage, something the women of the house sip when they have sore throats or to beat the heat in the summer. If American apple pie or British fish and chips were beverages, umeshu would be the equivalent for the wholesome, home-made, motherly image the drink evokes. Was the official floating the idea of prohibiting home-made umeshu or merely pointing out an inconsistency in Japanese law? The following year, the National Tax Agency clarified that producing umeshu at home was legal as long as the maker only combined ingredients and did not ferment them. In 1971, the Tax Agency clarified further that combining alcohol with apricots to produce umeshu at home was legal, but rice, barley and millet could not be added, and the alcohol used could only be distilled alcohol, not wine or sake.[6] In trying to clarify the law, the Tax Agency walked a very fine line, because mixing ingredients to make umeshu was a similar process to making doburoku, with just two differences. First, umeshu and doburoku used different ingredients, albeit all of them were not only legal but readily available. Second, doburoku required fermentation, but fermentation, it could be argued, was only allowing nature to take its course, waiting while ambient yeasts consumed sugar to produce alcohol. Making doburoku, then, was no different to cooking, according to some of its advocates. Why then was making umeshu legal but doburoku illegal? Several doburoku advocates asked that question repeatedly.

Rather than being illicit and dangerous, doburoku ought to be understood as a natural, comforting beverage that was an expression of Japanese cultural heritage, argued Sakaguchi Kin'ichirō (1897–1994), a professor at Tokyo University nicknamed 'Professor Sake' for his expertise in fermentation and kōji. In his 1964 book *Japanese Alcohol*, Sakaguchi called for a revival of doburoku as a seasonal and local pleasure:

> As a consumer, I would like to imagine a day when there are local sake makers in Japan who work to produce distinctive local sake ideally suited to the local foods and environment that could be enjoyed throughout the country. There would also be sake makers like that who during the winter brewing season could even make a lively, somehow sweet, but still tangy with alcohol, warm beverage called 'doburoku' . . .
> It is regrettable that one is not able to sample that drink at all today.[7]

Sakaguchi's view not only represented an indirect critique of the major brands of sake, but reflected a change in attitudes about rural areas in the 1960s. Before the Second World War, rural areas might be storehouses of tradition, but that made them backward in the eyes of the people who did not live in them and for many of the folklorists and other scholars who studied rural Japan. But against increased urbanization and modernization brought by Japan's post-war 'economic miracle', a new appreciation and anxiety developed in the 1960s about what was being lost in the countryside. The focal point for aspirations to recover the rural past was the 'home town' (furusato), a scenic rural place in Japan that tourists could visit where traditions supposedly endured. Food writers introduced 'home-town' recipes that evoked authenticity and motherly love, providing language to advertisers who used the term 'home town' to sell processed foods like instant noodles.[8] Sakaguchi's depiction of doburoku as small-scale, authentic and harmonizing with nature was part of a reimagining and romanticization of rural Japan. He not only helped to popularize doburoku, but established the foundation for the new appreciation of 'local sake' (jizake) that blossomed in the 1980s.[9]

In the same year Sakaguchi called for a revival of doburoku, one sake maker found a way to reproduce the flavour profile of the drink and its characteristic unfiltered look. Cloudy sake was so firmly associated with doburoku that the government prohibited the production of all unfiltered sake in 1899, but in 1964, sake brewer Masuda Tokube'e Shoten in Fushimi, makers of the Tsuki no Katsura brand sake, followed these laws and filtered their sake but used a coarser filter, resulting in a cloudy drink that fitted the legal definitions of sake. After more than half a century, cloudy sake, dubbed nigorizake, a different way of pronouncing the same Japanese characters for doburoku, was legal again.[10]

An article in March 1973 in the monthly *Modern Farming* (*Gendai nōgyō*) took up the question, 'Why Is Doburoku Making Bad?' This rhetorical gesture allowed the authors to explain that doburoku was an example of agrarian culture and self-sufficiency, something well known to the readers of this publication – meant for residents of rural Japan, particularly farmers. The article was also a launching point for a monthly column in *Modern Farming* that lasted for three years, showcasing how farmers in various parts of Japan home-brewed. The series featured quaint illustrations and handwritten text with charming portraits of the anonymous brewers by illustrator Kaihara Hiroshi, who put a human face to the hitherto secretive world of doburoku. Many examples of the recipes were variations of the basic doburoku recipe in which rice, kōji and water were combined simultaneously, but some methods were more complicated and followed the same techniques as sake brewing of adding the ingredients in stages. One home brewer in Iwate prefecture showed how to make doburoku from barnyard millet (hie) and foxtail millet (awa). Readers could also learn how to brew doburoku from long grain rice from Southeast Asia or from leftover mochi rice cakes. A contributor from Kumamoto prefecture shared how he was able to make doburoku in the wintertime by the traditional method of burying his sake pot in a pile of cow manure, which naturally heated the ferment. The series, which included instructions for making brandy, wine and beer, made clear that many 'village folks' were creatively continuing traditions of home brewing despite it being illegal. The publisher, the Rural Culture Association of Japan (Nōsan Gyoson Bunka Kyōkai), compiled these articles into two bestselling books: *Make, Taste and Share: A National Treasury of Doburoku* (*Tsukuru, nomu, mawaru: Shokoku doburoku hōten*, 1989) and *An Illustrated and Annotated Global*

Treasury of Home-Made Alcohol (*Zukai bunshū: Sekai tezukuri sake hōten,* 1998).[11]

Celebrating regional brewing methods was part of the Rural Culture Association's larger programme to document and publicize rural traditions in the 1980s. The association published a fifty-volume series of books, *Collected Writings on Japanese Foodways* (1984–93), intended to recover the traditional foodways of Japan's 47 prefectures by using oral interviews to reconstruct the diet of the decades before the Second World War. The series was highly influential for the way it celebrated regional cuisines, offering inspiration to farmers and entrepreneurs who could monetize this heritage by selling local heirloom vegetables and other regional delicacies. In 1987 officials, chefs and local producers in Kyoto designated a range of produce as 'traditional Kyoto vegetables' and the city of Kanazawa in Ichikawa prefecture designated their local vegetables ten years later. Used in cooking, traditional local vegetables became ways to craft an authentic local cuisine and other food products marketed to tourists, a boon to farmers, chefs and rural communities.[12]

If doburoku retained the authenticity and naturalness that sake had lost, it was hard to explain why it was illegal, pondered a writer in the *Japan Times* in 1981. 'To make these [alcoholic] drinks at home offers the possibility of being able to enjoy products free from additives, as well as "local" flavour.' The writer continued, 'basic to all of this is the question of whether the Japanese are entitled to enjoy the true and the natural, or must be content with the artificial and the commercial.'[13] Other commentators agreed that by preventing farmers from making doburoku, not only did that jeopardize rural heritage, it might prompt them to turn away from natural foods and consume processed foods instead. After all, doburoku was not just a beverage, but an

Narazuke, Kyoto.

ingredient used in recipes. Doburoku lees were used for pickling and in miso soup.[14]

One of the most well-known pickles using the lees leftover from sake or doburoku making is 'Nara pickles', *Narazuke*, famous in Nara but made throughout Japan as in the following recipe from Yamanashi prefecture, which calls for sake lees (kasu) and shōchū, although home-made versions of these beverages could easily be used instead.

NARAZUKE

Ingredients: oriental pickling melon (uri), salt, sake kasu, sugar, shōchū

The recipe usually calls for oriental pickling melon, but it is fine to use any vegetable available in a farm home. Salt the winter melon and other summer vegetables using salt that is roughly 2 per cent of the amount of vegetables used and set these salted vegetables aside until the cooler autumn season. To make the narazuke, prepare a fermenting medium of sake lees by thoroughly mixing together the lees with sugar, shōchū and a little salt. Place this in a cool storage area. Contact a sake maker in advance to order the sake kasu and shōchū so that you will have those on hand. In early autumn [the last ten days of October] take out the salted vegetables you set aside and place them in an ample amount of water for one or two days to remove the salt. Then dry them in the shade for one or two days until the moisture is gone.

Wipe the vegetables well with a dry cloth and take out the sake kasu that you had left to sit in a cool place. Spread the lees on the bottom of a container, arrange some vegetables within it, then add more layers of sake kasu and vegetables. Be sure to add a little more sake lees on the top. Wipe the edges of the container clean with a dry cloth. Make the top of the pickles level and place a covering made of washi paper firmly on top so that it covers the interior of the container. Place more washi paper to cover the top of the vessel.

Within a month these will taste delicious if they are left in a cool place in a storage area. People concerned about the smell should omit the step of washing the pickles to remove the salt – use the kasu to remove the salt instead.[15]

The recipe above calls for commercial sake, but the editors of *Modern Farming* referred to that beverage as 'fake'. Kaihara Hiroshi, who illustrated the series of articles with recipes for doburoku in that magazine, explained,

> the 'three-times more sake' (*sanbaijōshu*) and sake with alcohol that is the sake of today is no longer authentic sake, and I for one do not like it at all. We live in a time when sake is no longer something that people care for.[16]

The editors of *Modern Farming* concurred: 'The sake that is sold today is not sake, but synthetic. This synthetic alcoholic beverage uses chemically produced alcohol instead of fermented alcohol, and it includes sugars, succinic acid, flavourings and colourings.' The editors estimated that only 1.2 per cent of the sake produced was made wholly from rice (junmaishu) – the rest was 'fake sake'. Drinking only 'fake sake' meant that consumers no longer knew the taste of real sake, and sake was no longer a beverage made of indigenous rice but produced instead from imported corn syrup from Southeast Asia and Brazil. Legalizing home brewing would help solve these problems, revitalizing the sake industry just as home brewing had improved the alcoholic beverage market in other countries, the editors of *Modern Farming* opined.[17]

The essay by the editors of *Modern Farming* castigating commercial sake and extolling home brewing appeared in the book *Let's Make Doburoku* (*Doburoku o tsukurō*), published in 1981. The book's editor, Maeda Toshihiko (1909–1993), became a leading voice for legalizing home brewing. Maeda was a writer and former village mayor who from the 1970s became prominent in the protest movement against the usurpation of farmlands for the construction of Narita International Airport, a struggle waged by local farmers, leftist political parties and student organizations from the late 1960s to the early 1980s. Maeda's opposition to strong-arm government policies dates to the 1930s when, as a member of the Japan Communist Party (JCP), he was imprisoned from 1932 to 1938 under the Peace Preservation Law, used by Japan's 'Thought Police' to jail socialists and anyone viewed as challenging private property or the government. After the war, Maeda left the JCP and served as mayor in Miyako town in Kyushu from 1948 to 1953. He also wrote a newsletter that circulated to several thousand people and later published a book based on that newsletter. In 1977 he moved to Shibayama district in Chiba prefecture, to a dwelling built by volunteers, in order to be closer to Narita Airport and so able to support groups opposed to its construction, becoming the sage-like mentor to one organization called the Farmer-Worker Solidarity Hut.[18] That sake laws were historically used in Japan to fund the military gave further reason for Maeda and others on the Left to seek their repeal in the age of protest against government overreach and militarism.

Maeda called for the legalization of home brewing in *Let's Make Doburoku*. In the introduction he explained that home brewing was both a constitutional right and central to Japanese culture.[19] Other contributors to the book included Kobayashi Takasuke, a law professor at Aoyama Gakuin University, who elaborated on the legal argument that prohibitions against home brewing were multiple violations of people's rights to property and the pursuit of happiness guaranteed by the post-war constitution. Maeda argued that the Japanese needed to relearn how to make things. He called for a cultural revolution in which Japanese people produced what they consumed, contending that the Japanese should make their own alcohol, tofu, miso and eventually their own home-made sausage and bacon. Maeda asserted that

Japan could not claim to have a food culture unless people actually made foods themselves.[20] Being a maker was empowering. Sake brewers never become alcoholics, Maeda claimed, and he shared a story about an alcoholic colleague who cured himself after he started home brewing. Maeda thus sought to turn a passive consumer culture into a politically active maker culture. Besides essays advocating for the legalization of home brewing, his book contained recipes for sake, shōchū and wine as well as versions of doburoku made from rice, foxtail millet and barnyard millet.[21]

For Maeda, doburoku was a good place to begin the cultural revolution of making because it was an easy beverage to produce even for beginners, as exemplified in his volume by a recipe from Akita prefecture, 'where doburoku was king'. The parenthetical observations are in the original.

AN EASY WAY TO MAKE DOBUROKU

Place 5.4 litres (3 shō) [1½ gall.] of well-polished rice in a barrel and add 7.2 litres of water (4 shō) [2 gall.] and allow to rest for about three days. At the same time take about two-rice bowls' worth of leftover cooked rice and place it inside a clean bag in the centre of the rice in the barrel. Stir once per day, roughly squeezing the bag. After three days a sweet fermenting smell will appear (and also a smell like sake). The water that has that sake smell is the *moto* (also called a *shubo*. This is the starter for the sake. The aroma indicates that natural ambient yeast has begun to grow in the water). In Akita prefecture, we call this 'soured starter' (*kusare moto*). The aforementioned steps are the basic preparations for brewing.

Save the water and put it aside (but you no longer need the rice in the bag). Remove the rice with a colander, mound it together and steam it. (Use your fingers to mound the rice together. The rice does not have to be any more pressed together than that.) After steaming it, spread out the rice on a straw mat and let it cool to 30–35 degrees (body temperature). When it has cooled, add 3.6 litres (2 shō) [1 gall.] of kōji and mix. (If the rice is too warm, the kōji will die.)

Add the rice and kōji to a container with an 18-litre (1 to) [4¾-gall.] capacity, then add the 'soured starter'. Make a lid out of newspaper so that dust and other contaminants cannot get inside. Bubbling (fermentation) will begin in about three days, so stir it and monitor the level of the liquid. It is better if the liquid does not rise above the level of the rice. If there is too much water, it will bubble prematurely, and it will quickly take on a sour taste. After ten days, it will become doburoku.[22]

The recipe yields 14.4 litres (3¾ gall.) of doburoku in ten days, but the directions suggest waiting an additional five or six days to taste whether the brew is ready or not. 'The alcohol will initially taste sweet and then gradually become drier tasting. The recipe is ready when the taste mellows out.'[23]

Several aspects of this doburoku recipe call to mind the medieval beverages in the *Sake Journal* examined in Chapter Two. 'Soured starter' is a variation of the medieval 'enlightened starter' (bodaimoto). Both develop lactic acid by soaking rice in water for several days. Both the doburoku recipe and medieval sake required fashioning impromptu lids for the containers, which were not airtight but were instead meant to keep out contaminants while releasing carbon dioxide produced in fermentation. And both recipes rely on ambient yeast, although a note to the instructions for the doburoku suggests adding two teaspoons of commercial yeast for a 'foolproof recipe'. A variation on this recipe in *Let's Make Doburoku* adds hops to the starter to make a 'flower starter' (*hana moto*). Both methods were ideal for amateur brewers, according to the text.[24]

To demonstrate how easy it was to make doburoku, and to advocate for the right to home brew as well as raise money for his group protesting against Narita Airport, on 20 December 1981 Maeda hosted a doburoku party for activists near his home in Shibayama, where he served his own home-made doburoku.[25] He invited politicians and even the head of the National Tax Agency, receiving in response a warning from the Tax Agency that he could face a fine of 100,000 yen and five years in prison if he followed through with his plans. Maeda claimed that laws prohibiting home brewing were a violation of his constitutional rights and he held his doburoku party anyway.[26] The following day, Tax Agency officials guarded by one hundred riot police raided Maeda's home, confiscated his home-brewing equipment and fined him 23,000 yen (about u.s. $213 in 2024).[27] Maeda refused to pay and sought a trial contesting the legality of the prohibition against home brewing. He also held another 'doburoku party' in Tokyo with supporters on 16 May 1982. Appealing against the penalty to the Chiba Prefecture District Court, Maeda argued that Article 13 of Japan's constitution, which ensured 'the right to pursue happiness', gave him the freedom to brew and that home brewing was no different from cooking. However, in 1986 the district court found Maeda guilty of brewing without a licence and fined him 300,000 yen (about $2,500 in 2024).[28] Maeda appealed against the verdict to the Tokyo High Court, which upheld the lower court's decision on 29 September 1986. He then brought the case to the Supreme Court to inform the public of the 'stupidity of the Liquor

Tax Law', but the court ruled against him on 14 December 1989. The court's presiding judge, Sato Tetsuro, declared that legalizing home brewing would reduce government revenues from liquor taxes, and the court upheld the lower court's decision.[29] Tax revenues ultimately trumped people's freedom to brew.

Home brewing remains illegal in Japan, but in 2003 the government revised the tax laws granting licences to specific locales to allow inns, restaurants and other businesses within them to produce a minimum of 6 kilolitres (1,585 gall.) of doburoku annually. This rule made commercial doburoku-making possible, but effectively prohibited private individuals from home brewing due to production volume requirements set beyond the means of a typical home brewer. Farm households that used their own rice for doburoku making were allowed an exception to this rule. Today, there are more than a hundred 'doburoku districts' where doburoku is made and can be purchased, and similar regional approvals for wine and liquor were permitted in 2008.[30] In 2019, the National Tax Agency also allowed 'special sake brewing zones', enabling existing breweries to expand production as long as they offer classes on sake making to entice tourists to visit.[31]

Doburoku districts were one of several policies from the national government, particularly the Ministry of Agriculture, Forestry and Fisheries (MAFF), to promote and spur the local economies of rural areas premised on the recognition that 'local foods', including local alcohol, can draw tourists to remote areas. Many of these local products are sold at 'roadside stations' (michinoeki), a concept that developed in the 1990s to encourage cultural attractions and the sales of local products at upmarket highway rest stops. The promotion of local foods also dovetailed with the successful campaign in 2013 to gain Intangible Cultural Heritage status for 'Japan's traditional dietary cultures' (washoku), with the

United Nations Educational, Scientific and Cultural Organization (UNESCO). According to its official definition, washoku 'favours the consumption of various natural, locally sourced ingredients such as rice, fish, vegetables and edible wild plants'. The doburoku districts concept supports this valorization and commercialization of local food culture while at the same time prohibiting local people from producing alcohol for their personal enjoyment.[32]

Today, the legal version of doburoku, nigorizake, has become arguably one of the most approachable beverages for the non-sake drinker, as seen in the ways that major brewers offer nigori in fruit flavours marketed to appeal to new customers, as the next chapter describes. Nigorizake has become a gateway to sake in the same way that the California roll, made of avocado, artificial crab, cucumber and mayonnaise, functions for sushi. How ironic, then, that this traditional home-made beverage remains illegal in Japan. One wonders how many more consumers might take a greater interest in sake if they were allowed to drink and make doburoku freely.

THE LOCAL SAKE MOVEMENT

The doburoku campaign of the 1980s coincided with the 'local sake' (jizake) movement and both critiqued the dominant practices in the world of sake. Where doburoku fans touted their beverage's authenticity and naturalness compared to commercial sake, local sake advocates pointed out how the ranking system supported the major breweries of Nada and Fushimi while downgrading the 'local' sake from other regions that actually tasted better. 'Local sake', in other words, long had a pejorative meaning, but that was soon to change. Beginning in the late 1960s, journalists began criticizing the ranking system for sake, explaining that it was not based on quality but rather the fact that major brewers had paid two-and-a-half times more taxes to have their sake ranked 'first rank' instead of 'second', and five times more for a 'special class' ranking.[33] Of the 2,400 brewers, 93 per cent were small or mid-size and did not make any first-class sake.[34] But, due to the prevalence of barrel-buying, major brewers, which only made 20 per cent of the sake they sold, purchased 'second rank' sake from smaller breweries, which they blended and resold as their own 'first rank' sake; that made the ranking system a 'fraud' according to its critics. The National Tax Agency ignored the practice of repackaging lower-ranked sake as first and special class due to the higher revenues from those sake. People who consumed special ranked sake were basically drinking the cost of the taxes, according to the Consumers' Union of Japan, which petitioned the Ministry of Finance to end the sake ranking system in 1981.[35]

In place of national brands with first and special rankings, local sake advocates like the Consumers' Union of Japan celebrated 'all rice sake' (junmaishu), a sake made only with rice, kōji and water and without added alcohol. Junmaishu is a legal category for sake today, but the term was not widely used in the early 1980s, even among sake sellers. In the 1980s only 1 per cent of the sake produced was junmaishu.[36] Major brands such as Kikumasamune, Ōzeki and Sho Chiku Bai derived 45 per cent of their alcohol artificially, not from rice. Local sake proponents explained that if Japan's brewers used only domestic rice, that would not only improve the taste of sake but help Japan's rice farmers. Consequently, the Consumers' Union urged buyers to ignore major brands advertising on television, buy junmaishu from brands they have never heard of, and serve that sake chilled instead of hot.[37]

Sake writer Inagaki Masami's influential book *Choose Real Sake* (*Honmono no Nihonshu erabi*), published in 1977, was said to have been inspired by his trying junmaishu for the first time in a restaurant in Kyoto in 1974.[38] After this revelation, Inagaki's writings helped to popularize the 'local' brands Koshi no Kanbai (Niigata prefecture), Nishi no Seki (Oita), Hakutaka (Hyōgo), Shōtoku (Kyoto), Umenishiki (Ehime), Hatsumago (Yamagata), Kamo Izumi (Hiroshima) and Urakasumi (Miyagi), all brands that became stars in the local sake boom.[39]

Koshi no Kanbai was a particular darling of fans of local sake. Writer Sasaki Hisako introduced the brand from Niigata in the magazine *Sake* in 1967, in an article that many see as marking the beginning of the local sake movement.[40] The Consumers' Union highlighted that the makers of Koshi no Kanbai, Ishimoto Shuzō, only produced about 500 kilolitres (132,000 gall.) annually in order to maintain the quality of their product. Established in 1907, the third-generation owner of Ishimoto Shuzō, Ishimoto

Varieties of Koshi no Kanbai sake.

One of Kamo Izumi's breweries in Saijō, Hiroshima.

Seigo, had insisted in the post-war era on making sake when other brewers were producing sake with added alcohol. Ishimoto used a blend of local Kinmon Nishiki and Yamada Nishiki rice polished to a seimaibuai of 50–60 per cent and he relied on word of mouth rather than advertising to spread the quality of his product.[41]

Searching for ways to sing the praise of Koshi no Kanbai so that non-sake drinkers would understand, one writer in the

Asahi Shimbun newspaper described it as a sake with the charisma of Johnnie Walker Black, a globally famous brand of single malt scotch.[42] Besides Koshi no Kanbai, the same author spotlighted the brands Koro (Kumamoto), Nishi no Seki (Oita), Gohashi (Yamaguchi), Toyonoaki (Shimane), Kamikoro (Okayama), Kamo Izumi (Hiroshima), Umenishiki (Ehime), Hakushika (Hyōgo), Goshun (Osaka), Tamanohikari (Kyoto), Okina (Mie), Michisakari (Gifu), Wakatake Onikoroshi (Shizuoka), Kikuhime (Ishikawa), Tateyama (Toyama), Masumi (Nagano), Setchūbai and Hakkaisan (Niigata), Iwanoi (Chiba), Hitori Musume (Ibaraki), Urakasumi (Miyagi), Suehiro (Fukushima), Ōyama (Yamagata) and Denshu (Aomori).[43]

Writer Tomiko Shirakigawa explained the appeal of local sake in the *Japan Times* in 1981:

> Local sake has its own personality and taste, different for each brand and decidedly different from those of the national brands. Besides, buying and drinking a local brand affords a feeling of discovery which by nature cannot be provided by a national brand. Local sake aficionados can tell you that there are even some brands which are exceedingly rare, and to be able to buy a bottle of such sake is itself an experience they relish.[44]

Despite being highly sought after by some sake connoisseurs, regional brewers initially had difficulty convincing retailers to stock their sake due to the control exercised by wholesalers who marketed the major brands. Attempts by smaller brewers to sell directly to liquor stores were often met by the wholesalers boycotting their products.[45] However, in 1996, four years after the ranking system for sake ended, jizake was available in convenience stores and a single glass in an izakaya of a famous local sake could cost 1,000 yen (1,258 yen/U.S. $8.42 in 2023 prices).[46] To give the appearance of similar craftsmanship, major makers like Gekkei-kan began adding the names of their tōji to their sake bottles in the 1980s.[47]

The new system of ranking, called the 'special-designation sake' (tokutei meishōshu) system, established in 1992, was based on polishing rate and differentiated junmaishu from sake with added alcohol:

Added Alcohol Sake	Brewed with Rice Alone	Polishing Rate (Seimaibuai)
Daiginjō	Junmai Daiginjō	At least 50%
Ginjō	Junmai Ginjō	At least 60%
Honjōzō	Junmaishu	At least 70%
Futsūshu	n/a	No minimum

Sake rankings

Besides these labels, some sake can be labelled as 'special' (tokubetsu) if it has a minimum seimaibuai of 60 per cent, like a ginjō; uses sake rice and not table rice; and has some other characteristics that a brewer wants to call attention to in their product line.[48]

Brewers could no longer sell 'three times more sake' (sanzō-shu) as a sake, but they could still use brewers' alcohol, glucose, malt sugar and amino acids as long as they were no more than 50 per cent of the sake categorized as table sake (futsūshu). Most table sake available in convenience stores and supermarkets is not even labelled as futsūshu, and it is sold for less than 1,000 yen ($6.90) in 900-millilitre (2 pint) cardboard packages resembling milk containers. Brewers' alcohol can only comprise 10 per cent

Variety of sake sold in milk carton packaging.

of ginjōshu and honjōzō sake, and at least 15 per cent of the rice used must be kōji. Although the amount of sake classified as premium (junmaishu, ginjō and daiginjō) has been increasing since the year 2000, as of 2020, 57 per cent of the sake produced in Japan remains futsūshu, which has no minimum polishing rate.[49]

Brewers and sake advocates make the case that futsūshu does not designate bad sake, and the practice of adding alcohol to a premium sake is meant to enhance the flavour and bouquet instead of being a way to simply produce more of it. Certainly, different types of sake serve different markets and purposes. A table sake in a cardboard container could be ideal for cooking or a cheap buzz. A connoisseur might prefer, and can afford, a *junmai daiginjō*. And, there is clearly a market for futsūshu. The output of the major brewery regions of Kyoto and Hyōgo, which collectively produced 48.5 per cent of the sake made in Japan, is mostly in table sake: 83.5 per cent for Kyoto and 79.1 per cent for Hyōgo.[50]

The new ranking system led to a decrease in barrel buying: just 11.6 per cent of the sake sold by major brands in 2012 came from other producers compared to the early 1970s, when the amount was 80 per cent.[51] With a new system based on milling rates, breweries could no longer just pay money to have their sake ranked highly. More companies also switched to junmaishu, but critics found some of the breweries did not have great success, often producing junmaishu that was too intense tasting and had a heavy aftertaste, due to the fact that the breweries were too long accustomed to making sake with added alcohol. Junmaishu requires stricter control of the temperature and fermentation process.[52]

Junmaishu received a further boost in 1995 when the Japanese government ended the system that had, since the Second World War, controlled the sale and distribution of rice. This change allowed free distribution of rice, and sake brewers could buy rice from farmers or grow their own rice.[53] A few brewers had taken steps to purchase rice from farmers much earlier. The brewery Fukumitsuya, founded in Kanazawa in 1625, makers of Fukumasamune, through special arrangements began purchasing

Yamada Nishiki rice directly from farmers in Sakamoto, Hyōgo prefecture, from 1960, and from 1986 they sourced all of their Yamada Nishiki that way as well and purchased other speciality sake rice from other places.[54] After December 2015 all sake made in Japan had to use domestic rice. Besides junmaishu, Japan saw a ginjō boom in the 1990s, with a shift from 'crisp and dry sake' towards sake with a flowery bouquet and a balance of sweetness and acidity.[55] The old methods of making starters, kimoto and yamahai, also saw a revival in the 2000s.[56]

Despite the celebration of local brands, it took consumers time to get used to the new ranking system, and criticism of the 'sins' of the major sake brands, which amounted to half of sake's market, hurt the image of sake. In 2011 sake accounted for only 6.7 per cent of the alcohol sold in Japan. Sake suffered from a negative stereotype of causing drunkenness and hangovers, and of 'smelling like old men', an image that sake brewers are still working to change.[57]

In 1992, it could be said that quality replaced quantity in the measures of how Japan's Tax Agency ranked and taxed sake, although most of the sake produced in Japan remains table sake with almost twice as much futsūshu – when made in 2020, for example – as junmaishu. Sake was much improved in Japan, but production in the year 2000 was less than 30 per cent of sake's peak in 1973. Sake is also produced in fewer breweries, their numbers falling from 3,000 in 1975 to 2,152 in the year 2000, 1,615 by 2016, and reaching 1,150 by 2023. With the number of breweries plummeting, the National Tax Agency is reluctant to license new operations except for those shipping their products solely overseas. The inability to obtain a licence prompted at least one aspiring Japanese sake maker, Atsuo Sakurai, to move to the United States to open the Arizona Sake Brewery in 2017.[58] But in Japan, in 2020, sake occupies 5.3 per cent of the market in terms of sales. In other words, the Japanese drink four times as much beer as they do their 'traditional alcoholic beverage', sake.[59] Perhaps rising consumption outside of Japan, as in the United States, will spur younger consumers to take another look at sake.

EIGHT
SAKE IN NORTH AMERICA, 1908–TODAY

At the same time that promoters of doburoku and local sake were attempting to reshape the domestic sake market in Japan in the 1980s, several of Japan's major brewers sought expansion overseas. Breweries in East Asia, California and Hawaii opened to serve Japanese immigrant communities in the early twentieth century, but the new enterprises of the 1980s coincided with the upswing in popularity of Japanese culture and sushi in the United States, representing an initiative to turn sake into a beverage that appealed to 'Caucasians', to use the language of the day.

What can be called the California sake rush of the 1980s laid the foundation for the American craft sake movement of the 2000s, which today is just as vibrant in Brooklyn, New York, Nashville or Minneapolis as it is on America's West Coast. As of March 2025, twenty breweries belong to the Sake Brewers Association of North America (SBANA), adding more diversity and options to the sake made outside of Japan.[1] Most of these smaller craft breweries were the creations of home brewers and were established from around 2020. Besides working to improve their skill levels in a young industry and find traction for their products, one of the major challenges for American brewers remains how to increase market share in a country where in 2023 sake represented just 0.2 per cent of alcoholic beverage sales, notwithstanding the fact that sake imports to the United States more than doubled in volume from 2012 to 2022 from 14 million litres to 36 million litres (3¾–9½ mill. gall.).[2]

After touching on early breweries opened outside of Japan to serve immigrant populations in Taiwan, Hawaii and California, this chapter profiles several of the major brewers in the United States before introducing half a dozen craft brewers. Sake is entering an exciting period in the United States, an era that master sake brewer Brandon Doughan of Brooklyn Kura compares to the Wild West or the early days of beer.[3] Although developments in the United States will surely foreshadow the popularization and domestication of sake in other countries, the American craft brewing scene now is hard to generalize, so the approach of this chapter is to have brewers themselves describe what they are doing in a country where some sake makers are trying to produce Japanese sake in the United States and others are trying to invent American sake. Initially Japanese companies wanted to produce their products in the United States largely because it was less expensive; more recently brewers, both the major Japanese firms and smaller craft producers, are aiming to create a sake suited for Americans, whether that means introducing flavoured sake to introduce the drink to the uninitiated, making their beverages slightly more acidic to pair better with bolder-tasting American foods, or opening brewpubs as a way to introduce their products to customers by evoking the familiar atmosphere of a beer or wine bar. Sake brewing has more than a century of history in the

United States, but the most exciting historical moment for sake is the present.

SAKE ABROAD FOR THE JAPANESE

Japanese breweries opened operations in colonial Manchuria and Korea to serve Japanese colonists, as Chapter Five described, and the same was true in Taiwan, which Japan annexed in 1895. Before the Japanese arrived, the indigenous population of Taiwan brewed alcohol from foxtail millet, and Chinese immigrants to Taiwan made distilled alcohol from potatoes and sugar cane, but the tropical climate made sake brewing a challenge. Taiwan's earliest sake brewers during the period of Japanese colonization adapted their methods to fit the tropical climate. They used an enlightened starter (bodaimoto), long a favourite for summer brewing. They also developed the ferment in two rather than three stages (*nidan* instead of *sandan* shikomi), and they followed a shorter brewing season that lasted just from December to March. These practices changed when Abe Kōnosuke (1869–1927) financed the construction of a factory for the Nihon Hōjō Sake Brewing Company in Taipei in 1913. Abe, who went on to open Taiwan's first beer company in 1919, constructed a two-storey brick building for his factory with an ammonia-based cooling system so that it could produce sake year-round, a major achievement for the period. The brewery used local rice and rice from Kyushu polished to 85–90 per cent seimaibuai with an American mill. Despite its profitability, with an upswing in demand during the First World War, operations ceased in 1920 when the factory became contaminated with microbes.[4]

Hawaii's first brewery, The Honolulu Japanese Sake Brewing Company (Honoruru Nihonshu Shuzōgaisha), was established by Sumida Tajiro in 1908, and it began selling sake the same year. Sumida faced similar challenges with adapting to the local climate as brewers in Taiwan, which he likewise solved by installing an ammonia-cooled refrigerator in his plant. The Honolulu Brewing Company, known locally as the Mountain Brewery, produced 6,000 koku (just over 1 million litres/264,000 gall.) annually up to the era of prohibition in 1918, after which the company put its cooling units to use to make ice commercially. The company restarted in 1933 as a brewery under the direction of Tajiro's brother, Daizo (1887–1961), who constructed a new brewery able to produce 10,000 koku annually. The renamed Honolulu Sake Brewery and Ice Company was one of four operations producing sake in Hawaii before the Second World War. The war put an end to all of these businesses and forced Daizo into internment in New Mexico. By then, his brother Tajiro had already returned to Japan. During the war the United States Army took over use of the ice-making facilities and cooling rooms, and the company switched to making soy sauce. The company resumed sake production in 1947 using California rice. Takara Shuzō's American subsidiary, Takara USA, purchased the Honolulu Brewery in 1986 and continued production until 1992.[5]

The earliest sake brewery in the United States was the Japan Brewing Company of Berkeley, California, which opened in 1902. Before prohibition, the Japan Brewing Company was one of seven California sake breweries in operation. Sake brewing quickly revived in California after prohibition ended in December 1933, with new facilities opening in 1934 in Loomis, Los Angeles, Oakland, San Francisco, San Jose and Watsonville. But the Second World War closed these operations, sending the Japanese population of these cities to internment camps and prohibiting the production of sake by government order in 1942.[6]

A JAPANESE PRODUCT MADE IN THE USA

In contrast to the breweries established before the Second War that served the Japanese populations in the United States, the 1980s saw the rise of Japanese brewers establishing operations to produce their existing brands for the developing North American sake market. As an alcoholic beverage, sake's appeal may have needed far less translation and demystification than sushi and sashimi, which were also becoming prominent in that decade. In 1984, half of Japan's sake exports went to the United States.[7] In the late 1980s, America's 3,000 Japanese restaurants were the sales point for 80 per cent of the sake sold in the United States, and Los Angeles and the San Francisco Bay area had the largest concentrations of these restaurants.[8] In December 1981 a reporter for the *Mainichi Shimbun* newspaper took note of the sake craze at American sushi restaurants in New York City where Americans were drinking sake hot, cold and mixed into cocktails. What really stood out to the reporter was the high quality of the sake served – the journalist lamented that a similar junmai sake produced by Gekkeikan in the United States was unavailable in Japan at a time when artificial sake (sanzōshu) dominated the market.[9] U.S. consumption of sake doubled between 1985 and 1990.[10]

Beginning in the 1970s, the American press pointed to the increasing interest in sake in the United States while at the same time remarking that the number of sake drinkers was falling in Japan. To explain the ramifications of the Japanese turning away from sake, which writers described as a beverage once celebrated as 'the drink of the gods', columnists asked readers to imagine that 'the Germans were abandoning beer and the French were swearing off wine.'[11] While the Japanese were switching to beer and whisky, in America 'the traditional rice wine is selling very well in Southern California – to Caucasians,' explained *Los Angeles Times* writer Martin Rossman in April 1972.[12] The 'Caucasian market' would only grow in the next decades as more white consumers began eating sushi and becoming increasingly familiar with Japanese culture from the power of Japan Inc., a moniker for Japan at the time, coined in light of the influx of Japanese electronics and automobiles, the popularity of the samurai films of Kurosawa Akira, and the 1980 television show *Shōgun*, an adaptation of James Clavell's 1975 bestselling novel.

Restaurants were gateways to sake for American customers, but that did not mean that the restaurant staff knew how to present the beverage. Fred Eckhardt, a leading expert on home brewing and the author of a book on the history of sake brewing in America, complained in 1992 about the 'infernal' machines at restaurants that served sake 'hot as tea'. The sake-heaters 'keep sake much too hot over long periods of time', ruining the beverage. Eckhardt hoped the 'much abused' practice would soon end.[13] Several of the craft brewers I have spoken with still complain about how hot sake in a restaurant often gives newcomers to sake the wrong impression of the beverage.

The brewery that started the California sake boom of the 1980s was the Numano Sake Company, founded in a remodelled dairy plant in Berkeley as a joint venture of Rice Mills Incorporated of San Francisco and Numano International Company. Take Numano, the company president, had started importing sake to the United States in 1963, but he realized that it would be less expensive to brew Stateside. Numano, called by some 'the father of United States sake', began trial production in the Berkeley plant in 1978, and produced 568 kilolitres (150,000 gall.) the following year, selling his brands Koshu Masamune for restaurants and Numano's Sake for home consumers.[14] Like all sake brewers in

North America to this day, Numano made an 'all rice' (junmaishu) sake because adding alcohol requires a more expensive distillers' licence. Some Japanese sake experts had a chance to sample some of Numano's sake exported to Japan, and they praised its quality, 'exclaiming, "I had no idea that seishu could taste so good"', a statement testifying to the rarity of junmaishu in Japan at the time.[15]

Numano sold his brewing company to Takara Shuzō in 1982, which revamped Numano's brewery to sell Sho Chiku Bai sake under the Takara USA label, making sake for the domestic market but also for export, moves that established Takara USA as America's largest sake producer. In 1988, Numano opened a new brewery in Vernon, California, called American Pacific Rim, where by 1993 he produced some 1,135 kilolitres (299,835 gall.) annually. American Pacific Rim offered the brands California Ki-Ippon Dry Sake and California Ki-Ippon Premium Dry, selling these mostly to the West Coast and parts of the Midwest and East Coast cities.[16] Pacific Rim is now Yaegaki Corporation USA, the American branch of a brewery in Himeji. In May 2023, Takara made a strategic investment in Izumi, a craft brewery that opened in 2011 in Toronto, Canada, to help grow that local sake business.

California once again became the epicentre for sake brewing in the United States, with major Japanese brands establishing breweries, beginning with Ozeki in Hollister in 1979, joining Takara Shuzō (Takara Sake USA) in Berkeley, Gekkeikan in Folsom in 1989 and Kohnan Incorporated, which opened (the now closed) Hakusan Brewery in Napa Valley in 1990. All of these California breweries benefited from access to Calrose rice grown in the Sacramento and San Joaquin Valleys and from the lower prices of making sake in the United States. In 1989, a bottle of sake that cost U.S.$7.50 to create in Japan cost only $2.50 to produce in California.[17]

OZEKI SAKE USA

The venerable Nada brewer Ozeki (Ōzeki in Japanese), established in 1711, opened its facilities an hour's drive south of San Jose in Hollister, California, in 1979, allowing it to cut costs since American rice was one-third less expensive than using the rice grown in Japan, and the taxes American breweries paid were also lower.[18] Kozue Miyagi, director of sales and marketing for Ozeki USA, offered another reason for establishing a brewery in California:

> Forty-five years ago, we could only export our sake, and it took a couple of months sometimes to get into the warehouse. During that time, I don't believe we could use refrigerated containers for shipping, so the flavour of sake was not as good as the original. Our goal was to deliver fresh sake and good sake for everyone in the States.

Opening a brewery in Hollister made providing fresh sake to the United States markets much easier.

Besides economic and logistical reasons, Ozeki's decision to locate overseas was also in light of the soy sauce company Kikkoman opening new facilities in Walworth, Wisconsin, in 1973, another signal of the growing popular demand for Japanese food products in the United States. 'At that time, we had a great relationship with Kikkoman,' explained Miyagi, 'and it was a time that they were expanding their market and their production facilities to the States as well. Japanese food and Japanese sake go hand in hand, so we decided to expand our production facility at the same time that they did, and the reason we picked Hollister is because that's where grapes are grown.'[19] Hollister lies north of

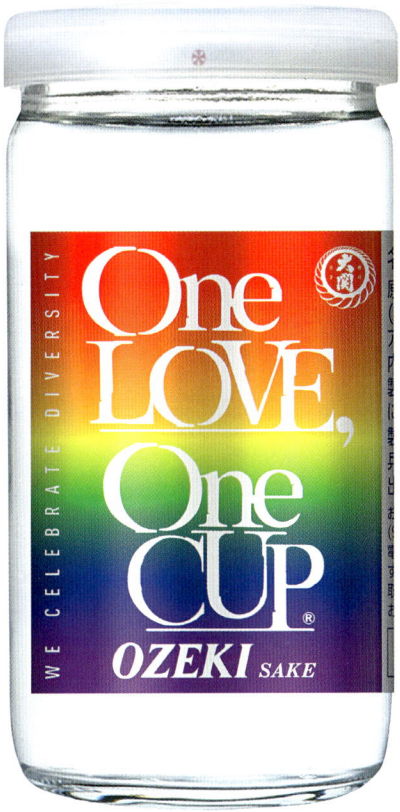

Meant to celebrate diversity,
Ozeki Sake released a version of
their famous One Cup sake in 2021
in the United States.

California's Cienega Valley wine region, and Ozeki opened its plant in a former winery.

Restaurants remain more than half of Ozeki USA's sales, according to Kozue Miyagi, with the remainder in retail liquor stores, which Ozeki hopes to expand:

Our next focus will be retail stores and local liquor stores. Because sake can be paired with a lot of food – cheese, fried chicken or pizza – and we offer a lot of types of sake. So we want consumers to find their favorites and the best pairings.

Ozeki produces more than forty products, including its famous One Cup, introduced in Japan in 1964, which allowed for sake drinking on the go.[20] Ozeki also produced strawberry, pineapple and yuzu nigori as well as a sparkling style and the sake named Ikezo, a 'sake jelly shot' in three flavours, peach, berry mix and yuzu – 'each flavor has its own unique deliciousness along with supplements good for your skin,' according to the company's promotions. Ozeki also makes soap and skincare products using sake and sake kasu.[21]

GEKKEIKAN USA

A decade after Ozeki began production in Hollister, Gekkeikan opened its facility a thirty-minute drive from Sacramento in Folsom. At the time that Gekkeikan chose to expand its operations to California the company was 'at the height of its power, at the height of its performance, influence, and sales in the 1970s', stated Mark Zheng-Garratt, Sales and Logistics Manager for Gekkeikan USA.

During that time there was certainly a recognition that sake exports were going to be a thing in the future. The U.S. was the first natural choice for an overseas location because of the history between Japan and the U.S., and because Americans will be the predominant consumers

of sake exports, and it would just be that more cost effective
to produce that locally for that market.

Besides the ability to source California rice, 'the water was the
more important factor to consider when selecting a location in
the U.S.,' according to Zheng-Garratt.

> We chose Folsom because of the rice that is grown in the
> Sacramento Valley. It's very close. That also helps reduce costs
> and there is plenty of it. Also the water here in Folsom . . .
> It is quite a soft water, and it is also very close in mineral
> content to the water that we use at our headquarters in
> Fushimi in Kyoto. Part of the attraction of Folsom was the
> similarity of the mineral content of the water because at
> least you have some kind of a constant that the brewers who
> come over from Japan to brew sake here, they know how the
> water behaves and you can achieve a similar style as part of
> that brand identity.

Recent droughts have caused challenges in sourcing rice locally
in California, admits Zheng-Garratt. 'We have nearly a four hundred year history, and we plan to emphasize sustainability' in the
future, explained Gekkeikan USA president Kengo Matsumura.

Zheng-Garratt defined Gekkeikan as a 'gateway brand' for
U.S. sake consumers:

> If the only sake that someone can find in their supermarket
> in the middle of nowhere is Gekkeikan and they grow to love
> sake, they buy our sake, they learn more about it, and then
> the go off to other brands, then honestly that's fine. We have
> generated a new consumer for the sake market.[22]

Modesty aside, Gekkeikan's 750-millilitre (1½ pint) bottle remains the leading sake sold at retail in the United States.

SAKÉONE

Outside of California, SakéOne began brewing in Forest Grove, Oregon, in 1998. 'It was started by a chance meeting between an Oregon entrepreneur named Grif Frost and Toru Murai who at the time was the CEO of Momokawa Brewing of Japan in Aomori prefecture,' recounts Steve Vuylsteke, current president and CEO of SakéOne.

> At the time, they [Momokawa] were the thirty-third largest brewery in Japan, and Toru had this idea . . . that we should build a sake brewery that focuses on ginjō grade and higher quality level sake meant to be served chilled, and that's what really started it . . . and they ended up building it in Forest Grove, primarily because they found that the quality of the water was very similar to that in Aomori.

Establishing a sake brewery brought many challenges, explained Vuylsteke:

> The company should have gone bankrupt a few times, but it managed to survive, and slowly by the time I took over the company was actually making some money and developing a foothold in the market primarily for the brands that we produced in Oregon.[23]

Vuylsteke came to the sake business after a long career in the Oregon wine industry through his parents, who 'caught the amateur wine bug in the mid-1960s, and that translated into a partnership with a neighbor and ended up being one of the pioneering wineries in Oregon'. The winery Vuylsteke's parents founded in 1970 was Oak Knoll Winery, one of only five wineries in Oregon at the time with a combined total of less than a hundred acres of vines. Today, there are over a thousand Oregon wineries and 31,000 acres of vines, according to Vuylsteke. After university, where he studied for a business degree, he went to work for his family's winery.

> I spent twenty-eight years professionally in the Oregon wine industry, mostly with the family winery although I did leave in 2002, and became the general manager of Erath Vineyards, which was another Oregon pioneer winery, and I ran that for six years.

After Vuylsteke left Erath he received a call from a headhunter:

> At the time, it was kind of funny, because he said, 'I am calling you because of your expertise in the Oregon wine business and managing wineries, and I got this operation.' And I said, 'well, what is it?' He said, 'well, it's an adult beverage company.'

Vuylsteke laughs,

> I had never really heard that term before. Well, I kind of put two and two together, and figured out it was SakéOne that was looking for a president to run the company. I didn't know a lot about sake having spent all my career in the wine business, but there's a lot of parallels once you get the product

in the bottle that poised me to be successful in making a sort of sideways shift.

Vuylsteke's background in raising the profile of Oregon wine made him appealing to SakéOne's attempt to grow its market share.

I took my experience growing up in a fledgling industry in Oregon that really there was no reputation even in Oregon for premium Oregon wine per se, particularly Pinot Noir as a variety back in the 1980s. Americans were just starting to come to grips with varietal wines like Cabernet Sauvignon, Pinot Grigio and Chardonnay. It was basically a jug wine market or port and sherry. So having worked with the pioneers to help establish a reputation for Oregon when there was really none, not only for Oregon, but also for Pinot Noir in this country, even California wasn't successful for the most part with Pinot Noir. So, it was interesting when this opportunity came along, and I started understanding the position of sake in the American market it was like déjà vu all over again because most Americans had no idea what sake was, only that it was a Japanese drink that you drank in little cups when you went to a Japanese restaurant.

In 2011 Momokawa Japan, the majority stakeholder in SakéOne, sold some of its shares to Hakutsuru Brewing Company of Kobe, which opened the doorway to import Hakutsuru's products, but that development brought new challenges:

It presented some challenges for me because it became apparent that they, like most Japanese sake companies,

knew very little about the American marketplace and how
to engage in a strategy that would be successful in the short
term and long term. It really took three years before they
understood SakéOne's position in the marketplace as really
one of the only companies in the United States that was
sake specific, and we . . . were dealing with mostly the larger
distributors who had ample footprint in the marketplace.
So, once they saw that, then finally in 2014 we reached an
agreement where SakéOne would take over as their exclusive
U.S. importer for the American market, so that alone changed
our dynamic.

Today 60 per cent of SakéOne's sales come from imports. 'Not
that our Oregon craft sake sales have gone down: they have
actually gone up,' indicates Vuylsteke.

In terms of its own products, Vuylsteke explains how his
company honours Japanese brewing traditions while at the same
time adapting their beverages to American taste preferences:

We honor the traditions that come from Japan in terms of the
sake making, but we think we have a little better idea of what
Americans are actually looking for, how the American palate
works with sake, and when I say that it has to do more with
the intensity of the sake, and generally that's a little higher
acidity level than what comes out of Japan. Products that
really can stand up better to the stronger flavored cuisines
in the United States. Americans like big bold flavors. A lot
of times the traditional sakes that can be lighter and ethereal
with a lighter aroma, they get stampeded by barbecue or
strong flavors.

Despite its growth into a major brand, Vuylsteke affirms the company's focus as a craft brewer:

> We are very proud of the fact we are the original craft brewery on the mainland. We were really the first to take the dynamic that worked in wine, that worked in beer, and apply it to sake. We are also proud that we really uphold the traditions of Japanese sake brewing.

DASSAI BLUE

SakéOne's status as America's pre-eminent craft brewer faced a significant challenge in 2023 when Asahi Shuzō invested $80 million in a production facility in Hyde Park, New York, a two-hour car ride from New York City. The 60,851-square-metre (655,000 sq. ft) brewery complex includes its own facility for rice polishing and a state-of-the-art water-filtration system that alone cost $6.7 million.[24] Asahi Shuzō in Yamaguchi prefecture, which in the mid-1980s switched from making table sake for the local market to premium junmai daiginjō sake, launched its Dassai brand in 1992 with styles differentiated by polishing rate (seimai-buai). The brewery's 'Dassai 23' is a sake where the rice is milled down to just 23 per cent remaining of its original size. Asahi Shuzō enjoyed tremendous growth in the early 2000s at 30 per cent annually, which provided both the capital and confidence to begin brewing premium sake in the United States.[25]

Half of Asahi Shuzō's recent growth in sales is due to the international market, and if the New York plant is successful that will certainly grow even further, explains Dassai Blue president Kenzo Shimotori. His company's decision to locate in New York's Hudson River Valley came after an invitation from the nearby

Culinary Institute of America, which had sought to collaborate with a Japanese brewery to advance its education programmes in Japanese food culture. Another reason, according to Shimotori, is that New York City is an important cultural centre, key to the popularization of Japanese culinary culture globally. Dassai's American brand, Dassai Blue, conforms to the company's focus on producing only junmai ginjō sake and is advertised as 'an idea born in Japan, but now brewed in New York'.[26] Rather than rely on rice from California, which Shimotori explains has seen short-falls due to recent droughts, Dassai Blue initially used rice from Japan but now contracts with Isbell Farms in Arkansas to grow the variety Yamada Nishiki, cherished by sake makers, and the only rice Dassai Blue uses. Arkansas is not only America's top rice-producing state, it shares practically the same latitude as Japan's Hyōgo prefecture, home of some of the country's best sake rice,

Dassai Blue, Type 23, brewed in the United States.

particularly Yamada Nishiki.[27] Viewing Dassai Blue's investment from afar, SakéOne's president, Steve Vuylsteke, observes:

> One thing that the Japanese do very well is look at investment with a very long-term perspective. They are not at the mercy of venture capitalists and private equity, where you got to get that return right away. They are looking at this as a way to combat some of that decline of consumption in Japan by having these locations where they can preach what premium sake is all about. The success of Japanese sake is going to be increasing its viability as a global alternative to the other beverage alcohols.

Eyes will be on Dassai Blue in the coming years to see what dividends they reap on their investment, whether premium sake will have a larger market in the United States and globally, and how these developments will affect the brewing scene in North America and back in Japan.

SMALLER CRAFT BREWERS AND THE ROLE OF MOTO'I

For their focus on premium beverages, SakéOne and Dassai could be called craft brewers, but they are giant producers compared to the wave of smaller craft breweries that have opened in North America since around 2020. Anyone who wants to build their own sake brewery from the ground up faces tremendous challenges beginning with the cost of equipment, as Weston Konishi, president of the Sake Brewers Association of North America (SBANA) explains:

> Rice mills are super-expensive. Most Japanese producers have their own, but most of our people don't. In Japan

things like that are often subsidized by the government because a lot of sake equipment, even things like alcohol meters, can be prohibitively expensive, but they tend to be subsidized in Japan whereas here there is no such system. A lot of our brewers are not only busy brewing things, they're actually making their own equipment. Most of our people wind up making their equipment, repurposing beer equipment or wine equipment or what have you to make sake brewing equipment. So that's another dimension that makes it complicated.

Besides making sake, 'If you are a brewer owner you have to do it all yourself, all of the business development, all the contracts, working with sourcing the ingredients, marketing, social media marketing, all of that essentially has to be done by yourself. So it's really tough to do all that,' Konishi observes.

I really have respect for our brewers because they pour their guts out for what they do because they love what they do, they love sake. Excuse my language, but it's kind of like an asshole filter, because you can't half-ass brew sake. You are in it to win it or nothing. So, it tends to weed out people who are phony and half-assed about what they do, and it tends to be something for people who are really driven by passion genuinely.[28]

Establishing a sake brewery was even more difficult in 2008 when Blake Richardson opened Moto'i in Minneapolis, the first sake brewpub in the United States or anywhere else outside of Japan.[29] Looking back at the time he started the brewery, Richardson recalled:

I didn't have a blueprint. Finding the equipment was hard, and the only thing that we got from Japan was the Yabuta [sake] press. Everything else came from different parts of the world. We got tanks from Italy and Germany. We just pieced it together. Luckily I had the basics of the brewing background, but a lot of it was 'I hope this works.'

Richardson is Moto'i's head brewer (tōji), but he started in the beer making business, becoming a brewer at a brewpub at the age of 23. He went on to earn a degree in brewing and opened his own beer pub, The Herkimer, before catching the sake bug in 2002.

Another early challenge for Richardson was obtaining rice milled to the specifications for sake brewing. Initially, he purchased milled rice from SakéOne, but when that company reached brewing capacity, he needed a new source. A phone call led him to travel to Chico, California, to purchase a rice mill the day after he learned it was for sale.

I had no idea what I am doing but let's see if we can make this work. We got the mill, and we brought it here, but we didn't even take into account where to put it. [Mills] are so tall and it's hard to explain how rare a building with that high ceilings is, at least in Minneapolis, Minnesota. It took forever to find the space and that was quite an ordeal.

With the mill set up and working in 2012, Richardson could now polish rice for his use and for other craft brewers.

We were happy to bring something in for you and mill it to whatever percentage that you wanted and ship it back to you. We were the only people doing that at the time. We had a handful of customers, but it was a slow start, and Moto'i the brewpub was the biggest customer for a very long time.

In 2023, Richardson sold the mill to a partnership in Arkansas that includes Isbell Farms, mentioned earlier for its production of Yamada Nishiki rice. At one time, Richardson considered growing his own rice in Minnesota, observing that the weather was similar to Japan's Niigata region. But, 'it didn't go well, and there is so much to rice. That's another career.' Besides Yamada Nishiki, Moto'i uses Jupiter and Titan strains of rice from Arkansas, which have their heritage based in Africa, according to Richardson who regularly rotates the sake available on his brewpub menu.[30]

What set Moto'i apart from earlier sake breweries in North America or Japan was the setting of the brewpub, which has become a model for the taprooms of smaller brewers in the United States. Taprooms are a main way that North American sake brewers can put their products in front of customers, when they are unable to produce the volume of sake needed to distribute their products nationally, explained SBANA president Weston Konishi. 'Most of our brewers have taprooms,' Konishi observed, 'and it's really on-premises sales that's a big part of their business. What that means for some people is that for a lot of states, if you have a taproom, then you have to have a food service of some sort, which makes your overall operation a whole lot more involved and complicated.' In other words, to be able to serve sake, brewers also need to offer food, which means managing a restaurant. A restaurant also offers another source of income to augment sake sales, as Motoi's Richardson describes:

> I chose a brewpub only because that was the model I knew
> well. It was also a safer bet, because if the brewery didn't

work out, I still had a full functioning entity that could pivot
and focus just on bottled sake or something. It was also what
I wanted. I didn't want to do anything but a brewpub.

Currently, all of Moto'i's sales are on premises or to go, according
to Richardson. The main advantage of a brewpub is that sake
makers can take time to introduce their products to a receptive
audience, as Richardson explains:

> We get to get in front of the person in real time at the time of
> purchase and they don't leave. So we have every opportunity
> available to us. We can educate them. We can suggest a pairing.
> If they don't like it we can replace it. We take advantage of
> every type of interaction that we can.

The model works for Moto'i where sake sales as a percentage of
bar sales keep increasing year to year, according to Richardson.

PROPER SAKE

Proper Sake of Nashville, Tennessee, follows a similar brewpub
model to Moto'i, and initially Proper's owner and chief fermentation officer Byron Stithem processed his rice in Motoi's mill.
Stithem's love of sake began in New York City when he was working in the culinary field after graduating from university in 2007.
He recalls, 'There is a sake bar called Decibel up there, and that
was the first time that I tasted premium sake and also yamahai
sake in particular. That's what set things in motion.' Yamahai
became a trademark brewing style for Stithem at Proper Sake, but
it is one thing to appreciate drinking a sake and another to try to
brew it oneself.

My background up to that point had been in hospitality and culinary specifically so I was deep in on fermentation already . . . Having that kind of foundation allowed me to mess around [brewing] even at a small scale early on. After the first two batches I made, several were actually reasonably good in my mind. It just kind of occurred to me that this might be a unique way to make a living, for one because I really enjoyed Japanese culture. I really enjoy the beverage, and the process I think is uniquely romantic as well. That's when I started traveling to Japan and trying to learn enough to open a brewery, and I still feel like I am trying to learn enough to operate a brewery, but you are never done.

Stithem describes his sake as following 'premodern styles', eschewing even lactic acid used by most brewers in Japan since the 1920s. Stithem instead builds up lactic acid naturally using the techniques brewers developed in premodern Japan such as the bodaimoto method. Proper Sake's focus on yamahai and kimoto styles made with rice from Arkansas help to distinguish its products from other breweries in the United States and Japan for their bolder flavours of sake. 'There is going to be a bit more umami, maybe a little more depth of flavor,' notes Stithem, who also contends that this sort of flavour-forward sake translates well for American foods and can help introduce newcomers to sake.

The key to introducing any sake in a way that makes new consumers comfortable is what Weston Konishi describes as de-mystifying sake. 'It helps when you have a bearded guy with tats who is pouring sake for you as opposed to like a really coquettish, charming kimono-clad young woman,' contrasting American sake servers with the typical brand ambassadors of Japanese brewer-ies. 'It's much more approachable when it's somebody who speaks the same language and kind of looks like you and maybe comes from your hometown.'

Stithem's brewpub Rice Vice is not exclusively sake. It also offers sake craft beers.

Our biggest beer product is called Koji Gold, and it's a Japanese-style lager, but it is brewed with kōji as well.

Byron Stithem working the tap at Rice Vice by Proper Sake Co., Nashville.

A certain portion of the mash is kōji – and there are certainly many kōji-related flavor profiles that come through, but it also helps dry out the beer a little more with its high enzyme content. We also do a kōji pale ale that's dry-hopped with kōji as well, so it's got kōji in the main mash and then it has kōji in the dry-hopping as well.

The customer-facing approach for introducing sake at Rice Vice is succeeding. Stithem has plans to open two more locations, in Huntsville, Alabama, and New Orleans.[31]

THE VOID

Another brewery that once purchased milled rice from Moto'i and sought to open a taproom is Kentucky's first sake maker, The Void, which opened in Lexington in 2021. Like Richardson of Moto'i and Stithem of Proper Sake, The Void's three founders started as home brewers. Justin LeVaughn, co-owner and head brewer of The Void, recounts how he began experimental brewing and met his future co-owners after obtaining a job in the beer brewing industry.

We always did fun, different, unique fermentations with wild yeasts, some different wines, different beer-infusions, and we did a mini festival with Japanese cuisine and some beers, and that's where we discovered kōji. From there the rest is history. We fell in love with the organism and the process of sake making because it is so different from beer brewing. It's pretty intimate because you have your hands on it throughout the whole process. It's more laborious and a labor of love.[32]

In 2018, LeVaughn and his collaborators began their sake 'research and development' in earnest, learning as they brewed. According to LeVaughn, 'at that point there was hardly any translated material [about sake brewing] available. There was a Facebook group of home brewers and a handful of commercial brewers, and that's how we connected with them.' After three years of refining their process and products, the sake 'got to the point where we decided it was good enough that I thought that we could sell it'. The Void produced its first batch for distribution in February 2021.

The pandemic forced the decision to put the planned brewpub on hold and focus on distribution first. 'Initially we were going to do a taproom restaurant and then the shutdown happened, and we had to pivot away from that,' recounted LeVaughn. The taproom was intended to have an interior reminiscent of an izakaya. But, as soon as they could, The Void owners tried to realize their goals for their taproom. 'We quickly realized that the money is not in distribution: it's in the taproom sales or self-distribution.' So in June 2021, The Void opened a taproom in part of their 158-square-metre (1,700 sq. ft) warehouse space that also houses their brewery. Initially local food trucks provided meals. A year later, The Void began serving Japanese street food and other Asian-inspired izakaya fare. 'People can only have so many 15 and 13 per cent [ABV] drinks without any food,' observed LeVaughn, who also debuted several lower-alcohol carbonated sake for customers who wanted something lighter. In March 2024, The Void moved its taproom to a space three times the size of its original drinking area, allowing it also to expand its brewing operations in its first facility.

The name 'The Void' speaks to the owners' ambitions to fill the sake void for Kentucky and the South, and it also reflects their love of science fiction and mystery and that many consumers might view sake as an unknown entity. The Void decided to play up the mysterious aspects of sake to dispel the idea that the unknown is something to fear and to draw in drinkers already coming to Kentucky, a region famous for bourbon, local wines and craft beers. 'There's already a huge segment of craft beer drinkers or craft alcohol consumers in general that want something different besides beer or they are beer drinkers that are accustomed to a lot of those very bold flavors,' LeVaughn explains. Many of The Void's signature brands are flavoured nigori, as described below, crafted to entice new customers to the brewery's taproom. 'It's a vehicle to bring them in and once they are here then we can educate them on more traditional methods or styles.' Customers also enjoy seeing The Void's bartenders pour sake into cups placed inside wooden *masu* boxes, premodern measuring containers for sake that are served with a plate underneath. Watching that traditional pouring method introduces newcomers to sake culture and has been a selling point for The Void, as have its 'sake socials', which invite members of its 'sake club' to the taproom to try new releases with food.

BROOKLYN KURA

Brooklyn, New York, is rapidly becoming a sake capital in the United States with SakeBrooklyn Brewing Company slated to open soon and become Brooklyn's third brewery behind Kato Sake Works, which opened in 2016, and Brooklyn Kura, which has gained national fame. Brooklyn Kura is the creation of Brian Polen, company president, and Brandon Doughan, its master brewer. Polen, who studied applied maths and finance and worked as a data scientist, met Doughan in 2013 on a trip to Japan for a wedding of a mutual friend. Doughan's own background was in research science, and he had been an avid home brewer of wine, beer and soy sauce since the age of sixteen, a passion he shared with Polen. Three years of conversations about sake, home brewing and sake's commercial potential led the pair to quit their jobs and to Doughan moving from Portland, Oregon, to join Polen in Brooklyn. Polen remembers,

> We wanted to make something that was special, compelling, challenging, and different. Create something that was connected to our experience in Japan, but also had the potential to be something unique. We got a small, little laboratory space in Bushwick, Brooklyn, and started making our batches there.[33]

Fourteen experimental batches later, the pair felt they had a winning recipe, one that is enshrined in their brand Number Fourteen, a junmai ginjō.

In March 2017 Polen and Doughan signed a lease for a 22-square-metre (3,100 sq. ft) brewing space in Brooklyn and entered into commercial production in December of that year, selling their first bottle in January 2018. Brooklyn Kura continues production at their first brewery, but it has since moved in 2023 to a 1,860-square-metre (20,000 sq. ft) space in Industry City, an entertainment and workspace in the Sunset Park neighbourhood where Polen and Doughan began brewing in March 2024. Polen recalls the enthusiasm he received from New York and the larger sake world when he and Doughan were starting out:

> From September 2016 to the launch of the brewery in Industry City the amount of support that we received from the industry up and down the supply chain, from

farmers to laboratories that grow kōji and yeast all the way up through the people who are hustling to sell sake across the u.s., we have had them with us and supportive of us. That support also resulted in interest from a range of different potential investors.

Besides attracting the interest of investors to Brooklyn, master brewer Doughan was excited to speak with the tōji from Japan, dozens of whom have visited Brooklyn Kura so far, allowing him to ask questions and seek their opinions. 'If I had gone to study in Japan, that would have taken me years to travel around and have those conversations with those tōjis.' Brooklyn Kura's location helped make these visits possible. 'That's a benefit from being in New York. If a brewer is going to come to the United States, they are probably going to come to New York because it's the largest market. And if they are going to come here they are going to come and visit us,' Doughan explained.

Even before they started commercial sales, one of the first visitors to Brooklyn Kura was the Japanese brewery Hakkaisan. Conversations with the Niigata-based brewery led to partnership talks in 2020 that were finalized in 2021 when Hakkaisan became a strategic investor in Brooklyn Kura. Hakkaisan is also lending technical expertise and personnel to Brooklyn Kura as it plans to scale up production. Doughan clarifies:

I have been self-taught in all of my sake making, and this jump to our new scale is significant and they have a lot of experience in that, and they have hundreds of years of sake brewing knowledge. They want us to keep doing what we are doing, but at the same time they are a tremendous brewing resource.

Brooklyn Kura also plans to market sake imported from Hakkai-san alongside their own, taking advantage of the Japanese brewer's wider sales network in the United States. And Brooklyn Kura has plans to export their sake to Japan.

When Brooklyn Kura began to think about a wider distribution for its products, it opted to shift to bottle-pasteurized sake to ensure quality, but unpasteurized sake remains a feature of its taproom, and Polen promised that he would pour that for me or another first-time visitor.

> The first thing I would pour for you is *shiboritate* (freshly pressed sake). It is this special thing that is essentially unadulterated, undiluted, un-fined and unfiltered beyond the initial pressing sake that comes at the end of fermentation. It's essentially when the tax authority in Japan would deem it to be sake. It's got this brightness, richness, texture and weight that you can't really find outside of stuff like shiboritate. We do shiboritate flights in the taproom. We produce between two and four cases of shiboritate with every batch that we make. This is what sake from a brewery anywhere in Japan tastes like the day it is pressed.

Brooklyn Kura's sake flights, a selection of small servings of sake to allow customers to taste different types, are based on different rice, kōji or yeast blends, and their sake are on the dry end of the spectrum. 'We pour people samples and treat them like they were walking into a beer brewery or winery,' explains Polen.

Doughan and Polen wanted their taproom to emulate a hip wine or beer bar so that Brooklyn Kura would be familiar to customers, and having a taproom was fundamental to the brewery's business model. 'If you are going to do something like this in New York City and you don't have a taproom, you might as well not do this here,' Polen observed. 'So much of the consumption culture around breweries in New York state and around the country is about meeting the makers and enjoying it in the place it is made.' Having a taproom, Polen continued, is also the 'fastest way to revenue', and a way of reaching consumers directly given the challenges of wholesale distribution.

Brooklyn Kura's taproom is also a classroom for their Sake Studies Center, which began in 2023, in partnership with Japan's National Tax Agency and the Japanese Consulate General of New York, with Timothy Sullivan serving as education director. Sullivan is one of a handful of 'sake samurai', a title granted by the Japan Sake Brewers Association for work popularizing sake and educating people about the beverage. The studies centre offers learning experiences for the general public, such as on how to pair food with sake, but its main audience is professionals in the beverage industry including buyers, beverage managers, restaurant owners and retail owners, whom Polen calls 'gatekeepers' for consumers exploring sake.

Brooklyn Kura's taproom, evoking beer and wine bars, exemplifies its attempt to acculturate new customers to sake by presenting sake, still a novel beverage for most Americans, in a familiar context. But Polen and Doughan are not trying also to reinvent sake. Their aim is to produce Japanese sake (Nihonshu) in the USA, as Doughan relates:

> We are trying to make very traditional Japanese-style sake. We want to give something to people the first time that accurately represents what Nihonshu is. [But] we are not presenting it as Japanese. There's no kanji [Japanese writing]

[on the bottle]. We are not Japanese. We use domestically grown rice. We use Brooklyn water, and we push those things.

Providing a new context for a traditional beverage gives new opportunities not just for Brooklyn Kura and its partner Hakkai-san but potentially for other Japanese breweries wanting to market their products globally and domestically. 'The cool kids in Japan are drinking IPAs and Japanese whiskey,' observed Doughan, but brewers might say 'look what they are doing in Brooklyn' as a way to move younger Japanese consumers back to sake. Polen affirms that while they are striving for the success of their own brewery, they also feel connected to a community of brewers in Japan and recognize sake's potential to become a global beverage.

SAWTELLE SAKE

On the other coast is Sawtelle Sake, named after a Los Angeles neighbourhood with a historic Japanese community. Sawtelle's brewing once occurred at a distillery 105 kilometres (65 mi.) north of Los Angeles, but they moved their operation back to the city in 2024. Business partners Troy Nakamatsu and Maxwell Leer have the ambition to sell their sake well beyond Los Angeles. Nakamatsu is the head brewer and Leer runs operations for the company, although both take on many roles. Nakamatsu observes, 'I am the CEO, but I also am the janitor. My job spans everything in between.'[34]

Nakamatsu began as a home brewer. 'I had been home brewing sake since 2012, just out of curiosity and out of an appreciation for sake and just being a bit of an experimenter and just wanting to do something fun.' Nakamatsu left a career in finance to open

Sawtelle Sake in 2019. 'Had I known how difficult this would be, starting from nothing and growing a brewery, I'm not sure I would have embarked on this journey.' But he persevered. 'As I was home brewing it became more and more clear to me that this is a good opportunity. If somebody in the U.S. could make sake more approachable, more understandable, and brew a good product here, the market is massive.'

Maxwell Leer joined Sawtelle in 2021. Leer, who describes his job title as head of strategy, came to Sawtelle from the world of food and beverage promotion, which he described as 'working in trying to communicate the value to the end user of really well made stuff, typically wine for almost two decades'.

One of the main venues for Sawtelle to promote its products and receive feedback from consumers is at Sake Day, an annual event held in late September in San Francisco since 2005 to coincide with 'sake day' (*Nihonshu no hi*) celebrated in Japan on 1 October. Sake Day's organizers advertise it as 'the largest day of sake celebration in the world'.[35] Leer explains, 'every year at Sake Day in San Francisco, we put what we think the consumer is going to like in front of the consumer and we let the consumer tell us what they like and what they don't like.'

As much as both Nakamatsu and Leer support this celebration of sake, they also warn that making high-quality sake is not enough. Nakamatsu stated:

> We can't be thinking like a lot of the other craft sake breweries in the U.S. It's a small community and all of the guys and gals are wonderful, and we know most of them. But I think a lot of those breweries are in large part just trying to replicate the Japanese models, and maybe the labels look a little different, and maybe they are a little more Americanized

in terms of their branding, but what they are trying to do
is make Nihonshu (Japanese sake) in the United States. As
much as we love Nihonshu, and as much as we could drink it
every single day, what we are trying to do is make something
completely new that's our own creation. We have taken the
methods and the processes, and the tradition and everything,
and we have absorbed as much of it as we can from Japan; we
are implementing that on a daily basis, but we are trying to
create something new. We almost hesitate to use the term
'sake' when we are describing our products, because we found
that it really doesn't mean much to people.

Leer concurs:

At the end of the day, sake tastes like sake to most people
because it tastes like sake. But the reality is that no one
is ready for that yet. We are not at a historical moment
where Americans are ready for that. Outside of the izakaya
no one is ready for that. So, we have to position ourselves
as any first-generation idea in this space, in this country,
with that knowledge of the consumer base to be listening
to them, letting them tell us what they like, and guiding
our business through that purview, and there is no other
way to do it.

For Leer and Nakamatsu, the types of sake available at izakaya are
all brands that are sold at five to six times their retail price to the
consumer. Their goal, in contrast, is to make an affordable beverage alcohol available to the supermarket shopper. Referring to
rival brands, Leer opines,

We are taking a radical approach. We want them [other
makers] to hold the izakayas. We want them to hold the sake
stores. We want them to take all of the Michelin-rated sushi
restaurants in America. We don't want them. We want to be
in the grocery store.

Leer admits that as a small producer they are facing a leviathan's
task to compete in the North American sake market for entry-
level customers in supermarkets:

What you are up against is Goliath. You are up against
companies that have the scale of Anheuser-Busch and
Dassai. These companies can afford to blip an $80 million
marketing project into Hyde Park without ever feeling any
weirdness about the future profitability of that investment.
Who can do that?

For Sawtelle, making excellent sake is the starting point for
that future beverage. Nakamatsu shares,

Being a home brewer, I guess I was really ambitious when
we started, and the one goal I had in mind was if I can't make
a good nama junmai ginjō with California-grown Yamada
Nishiki [rice], 901 yeast, and a pretty standard kōji from
Akita Konno [a noted kōji producer in Japan], then I don't
think we have any business being a sake brewery. For the first
three years, I was basically fanatically just brewing that, and
making tweaks to the recipe along the way. Clear Skies was the
first product that we came out with. All the other derivative
products have Clear Skies at their base.

Clear Skies is Sawtelle's focal brand. The question Leer then poses is:

> How are we going to take this water-like, crystalline, nama junmai ginjō muroka genshu [unfiltered and unpasteurized] sake and spin it in favor of the consumers' preference? That is exactly what we do, and that is something very different from what our competitors do, because they reach the line of junmai ginjō genshu muroka nama sake, and that's Nihonshu, and think that's good enough. But, it's not.

The answer for Sawtelle is to produce a variety of flavoured sake, which combine ingredients like yuzu and perilla leaves, as introduced in more detail below.

Leer and Nakamatsu admit the challenges they have in reaching their goals. Nakamatsu comments:

> We have been struggling to get this to break even, and profitability has made us a little rough around the edges, but I think it's important. No one really talks about this. There are a lot of passion projects. There are a lot of really wonderful sake breweries in North America that are funded by massive millionaire families that don't really help you think about the economics of sake brewing. It's a very interesting parallel in what's going on in this nascent, early days industry, versus what's going on in Japan where you have these multigenerational breweries that really never made a profit, but it was part of upholding the family name, or the family company, or whatever, and they funded it that way. It's difficult in both countries for different reasons, but here we are trying to be very

pragmatic about the fact that this is a business at the end
of the day . . . This is not just a passion project because there
are a lot less frustrating passion projects we could embark
on if we really wanted to.

Sawtelle's may not be a passion project, but both Nakamatsu and
Leer bring passion to their work to define a new place for sake
in North America.

BREWING AMERICAN SAKE

Sawtelle shares with all other North American brewers the
challenge of making a sake for Americans, most of whom have
yet to try sake, and those who have drunk it have not always had
a positive experience. 'They had it in a mediocre way,' complains
Maxwell Leer, such as having sake warmed in a microwave at a
restaurant. Leer explains, 'the word "sake" to most people in
America is not a net positive. Because if your point of engage-
ment is a lackluster beginning, what's the point of coming back
for more?' Steve Vuylsteke, president of SakéOne, concurs:

One of the real challenges is if you put a clear liquid in a
little cup in front of an American, they are going to look
at it and they are going to think it's a shot. They are going
to think it's distilled. Americans think all sake comes from
Japan and a lot of them think it's distilled because it's clear.
And if they drink hot sake in a restaurant and they say the
next day that they felt like crap, well, they didn't understand
that it's the lowest quality grade out there and maybe it had
15–16 percent alcohol.

And just because a sake is well received in Japan does not mean it will be in the American market, explained Vuylsteke:

> The Japanese struggle with what I call a market-driven approach to your product. They have been historically more production-driven, where they make the sake like they make and sell it in Japan, and say 'OK, here, drink this product. We like it in Japan, and you should like it in America.' No, because Americans didn't grow up drinking sake. In fact, they probably drank beer or wine or spirits. So, you have a different reference point. To just simply stick a Japanese-style sake out there and to expect it to be just as successful, or Americans are going to love it . . . well, no.

Mark Zheng-Garratt, Sales and Logistics Manager for Gekkeikan, said something similar:

> Over time, we have come to realize that the taste of consumers, the expectations of consumers, the preconceptions of consumers are very different in Japan and here in the U.S. What would be considered a good, real sake, those preconceptions and expectations are much weaker here in the U.S. where people have less knowledge and expectations of sake. Yes, there is less appreciation of it, but you have a wider definition of what sake is and what sake could be. So the sakes that we import from Japan and sell in the U.S., you could call more conservative than the sake that we make here in the U.S.

The million-dollar question is how to determine what Americans are looking for in a sake and then how to create it.

Zheng-Garratt explains Gekkeikan's approach to answering this question:

> We didn't know really, so we needed to do some better market research, so for example, our first project was a case study in sweetness. Do Americans prefer something that is very sweet, or less sweet? . . . We took it to restaurants and got data. We found that the 'sweet spot' – pun not intended – was somewhere in the middle between those, and then we used that data to relaunch one of our products . . . That's the kind of thing we need to focus on to make sure that what we are making is appealing to consumers.

The resulting sake that Gekkeikan 'produces in the U.S. are a little more bold in all directions than the ones you get in Japan', noted Mark Zheng-Garratt.

Sake Brewers Association of North America (SBANA) president Weston Konishi stated that the craft brewers in his organization are all trying to adjust the formula for sake to suit American taste preferences:

> If you really want to insult an American sake brewer, tell them that their sake is just as good as Japanese sake. That's really insulting to them. They are just trying to make the best sake they can given the material that they have to work with. No one is trying to make 'Japanese sake' here. They are trying to make their own sake with their own personalities reflected in their products. That doesn't necessarily mean that they are always doing wacky things. They could be doing things that are more what you might call Japanese-style, but I would say even then the intention is not to make

a Japanese-style daiginjō or Japanese-style kimoto. The intention is to make the best kimoto they can make. If that is evocative of Japanese kimoto then so be it, but that's not their ultimate objective.

This sentiment resonates well with Justin LeVaughn, who describes The Void's brewing as 'where Japanese tradition meets American craft'. He explains, 'We want to make American sake its own unique thing because we are not Nihonshu. We're not making it in Japan.'

Bold flavours may better suit the American palate, but they are also the result of the fact that many craft sake brewers have a background in beer making and are accustomed to big tastes from hops and malt, explains Brandon Doughan of Brooklyn Kura. And there are technical reasons why some American craft sake is more acidic, according to Doughan, because smaller brewers have a more difficult time controlling brewing temperatures and their beverages are more exposed to other organisms that can raise acidity. Plus, many craft brewers have relied on Calrose, which is a table rice and has more protein and fat and less of a starchy core than sake rice. Access to better sake rice varieties, a wider variety of yeasts, and years and years of skill-building will be needed to take American craft sake to the next level. An American style of sake will be years in the making according to Doughan, and his co-owner at Brooklyn Kura, Brian Polen, agrees.

SAKE AND AMERICAN FOOD

Any discussion of efforts to create sake that suits the American palate invariably moves into the pairing of sake with food, a reflection of the long interest and rules for pairing wines with food in the West, notwithstanding the complete absence of any similar traditions of food pairing in sake's long history in Japan. Pairing sake with food may be a very recent notion, but it is one that has taken hold, especially in the United States. Drawing from his experience in the adult beverage industry, SakéOne's Vuylsteke contends that sake is a much more versatile beverage for food pairing than wine.

> Unlike wine where there are these distinct pillars that you have to be careful that you don't cross otherwise it's going to completely destroy the gastronomic experience, sake is so much easier to pair and to talk about pairing sake with cuisines other than Japanese. We tell people, if you have Italian food, do you only drink Italian wine? Probably not. Maybe in an Italian restaurant you might. So, sake doesn't work only with Japanese food. It works with anything . . . You can have sake with fried chicken, with pizza, pasta. Japanese [food] is obvious but in some cases, the sake actually pairs better than wine and I have a long history in wine. I have tried sake with all types of cuisine, and I have yet to find something where it doesn't work.

Blake Richardson of Moto'i agrees about sake's versatility with food although he admits that it can be a challenge to pair sake with spicy Southeast Asian curries. 'Sake is so expansive,' Richardson indicates. 'The flavor components are more than four hundred or double what's in wine. You just have to find the right one to pair with food. I have a certain sake that I go to every time that I am eating pizza . . . There is a hamburger sake out there. There is a hotdog sake out there. You just got to find it.'

One of the reasons why Byron Stithem of Proper Sake focuses on yamahai and kimoto is precisely because those types of bold sake pair well with American cooking, he explains:

> I think a lot of times Japanese sake can be lost with
> American cuisine or even some of your spicier cuisines
> from Southeast Asia for that matter. But yamahais on the
> aggregate are going to be a little bit more flavor forward
> than a clean contemporary ginjō or daiginjō, especially

SakéOne's Moonstone brand in three flavours and serving suggestions.

where a lot of the notes of the sake are coming on the nose
and less on the palate.

FLAVOURED SAKE

Making bolder sake is one approach, but many North American
brewers are taking a further step by also adding flavouring.
SakéOne's website advertises its Moonstone brand as 'the first
of its kind', and it could well be the first flavoured sake ever
produced.[36] Company president Steve Vuylsteke explained the
inspiration:

> The idea came from the founders and there is no question
> that they were looking for a way to present sake to Americans
> who had no experience drinking sake, or very limited
> experience, only drinking hot sake out of ochokos [small
> sake cups]. This would be a way to show them the platform
> of sake . . . By adding these flavors, it gave them something
> to identify with, and definitely was sort of an entry point.

Flavourings might be new to sake, but they are familiar in other
beverage alcohols, as Vuylsteke continues,

> It's like in the wine business where depending on what
> era you grew up in, whether wine coolers were around,
> or whether it was White Zinfandel, those products were
> gateways for wine as . . . very fruity Chardonnays for example
> became the gateways. Recently, you have got sweet reds. So
> anytime you look at an industry, you have got to find a way
> to make products that can appeal to people that haven't
> developed a sophistication level of their palate yet.

While flavoured sake might be a gateway to unflavoured sake, it does not necessarily have to be, observes Vuylsteke:

> We saw people who started off drinking our Moonstone Asian Pear or Plum, eventually start gravitating towards a Momokawa Diamond, which is a junmai ginjō. But we have people who start drinking Moonstone and still drink Moonstone. It's not like you can only move away from Moonstone.

Other major U.S. brewers have also tried flavoured sake, with varying success. Gekkeikan once produced a flavoured sake, according to Mark Zheng-Garratt, but not currently. He explains:

> It's not that we are entirely against the concept. The past few years have been a period of re-evaluation of what we want to do. For the flavored sakes it's a step away from adding lots of flavors and sugar and things like that, and instead trying to go back to the basics and create really interesting sake that almost feel like they are flavored, because of the yeast, and create some very aromatic and bold flavors.

This view resonates with veteran craft brewer Blake Richardson of Moto'i:

> As far as flavoring sake, you can look at it from two angles. There's an economic point of view. Making sake is not cheap. It requires a ton of labor. Your raw ingredients are expensive, and I just think there are other avenues to drinking something that tastes like lychee that's just more economical. I would never tell someone that they shouldn't

do it. That's not my place. But I think that this company
should stick to trying to get the most flavorful sake that
we can with the four ingredients that we have. You can get
lychee flavor in sake. You just have to brew it that way, and
that's a skill.

Although he remains open to the idea of creating a flavoured
sake for the U.S. market, Dassai Blue's president Shimotori feels
that the future is likewise in premium rather than flavoured sake.
'America is a cocktail society, but people drink beer straight,'
Shimotori said.

Outside of Japan, Ozeki sells flavoured nigori sake in strawberry, pineapple and yuzu. In describing how flavoured sake can
appeal to newcomers to sake, Ozeki's Kozue Miyagi drew upon
her personal experience:

I personally could not drink red wine, but as a sangria, wine
cocktail, that's how I started drinking wine, and I became
more of a fan of red wine. So, as a gate[way], we thought nigori,
cloudy sake, especially with a fruit flavour, could attract new
consumers. We don't use flavorings, we use fresh ingredients,
for example, strawberry puree, and those strawberries are
picked in California and Oregon, and the pineapple puree is
from Costa Rica. Yuzu juice is freshly squeezed and shipped
frozen from Japan. We use only natural ingredients to make
a gate product for beginners. We do brew traditional sake in
the States, but at the same time, we started offering something
more approachable for consumers in the States.

Although these products, innovated in Ozeki's California brewery, were meant to introduce drinkers outside of Japan to sake,

Strawberry nigori sake
from Ozeki Sake.

Miyagi explains that they have since been introduced back in Japan:

A brewmaster was sent from Japan to Hollister. That person developed strawberry- and pineapple-flavored nigori, and when he returned to Japan he talked about how successful

these products were in the United States and Europe. Now
Japan has started to make the same nigori, although the
ingredients are not from California.

Miyagi imagines that flavoured sake could help to reinvigorate
Japan's sake market at home:

> Japanese sake brewing companies are very traditional.
> Sometimes we think that this should only be this way,
> or in this shape, but changes like nigori-flavored sake or
> sparkling sake will, I think, create a new market in Japan as
> well, especially if [it's] proven in the States or other countries
> that these beverages can be popular.

In fact, Brian Polen of Brooklyn Kura observes that licensed makers of doburoku in Japan are increasingly turning to flavours to
appeal to new customers. However, his colleague, Brooklyn
Kura's master brewer Brandon Doughan, views those sorts of
additives as antithetical to making sake in the United States equal
to the Nihonshu produced in Japan. Doughan concedes that in
some North American markets it is a necessary step to draw new
drinkers into sake's orbit:

> There are people who are making things that wouldn't be
> considered Nihonshu in Japan, like doing a lot of fruit- and
> herb-infused things. But it's what works in their area. There
> are some people in more rural areas, and they are doing
> whatever it takes to get people in the door and get them
> introduced to something that maybe in those towns they
> would never get introduced to.

Brooklyn Kura offers one sake called the Occidental that Doughan describes as 'non-traditional', a junmai sake that is dry-hopped after pressing. The fruity hops are meant to be reminiscent of beer, while the blush colour is supposed to appeal to wine drinkers. It is a popular choice at Brooklyn Kura, according to Doughan.

Ozeki also produces the brand Ikezo, a sake made with Jello, and currently the only Jello-sake in the United States according to Ozeki's Noe Arakawa. 'There is Jello in the can, and you shake it before you open the can to break the Jello. There is also a small amount of carbonation with a Jello texture. That's a very fun drink, and the alcohol is only 5.5% ABV.' Miyagi explains the inspiration for the name of this beverage. 'When you flip Ozeki, the spelling is Ikezo.' The inversion signifies that Ikezo is 'not a traditional sake', explains Miyagi.

Sake purists might turn their noses up at flavoured sake in the same way that some hardcore sushi mavens spurn the California Roll, but flavoured sake play an important role in introducing the beverage to consumers, contends SBANA president Konishi:

> I think flavored sake plays an important role in spreading the joy of sake. If you have never had sake before, then having really fresh flavors that are recognizable and approachable can be exciting for people. The other advantage that you have with flavored sake is that when you are doing those little pouring samples, like one or two ouncers, flavored sake tends to show very well because you are not really delving into nuanced aromas and flavors in the sake itself. Flavored sakes can also be a lot of fun if enjoyed as aperitifs, dessert drinks, and paired with bolder cuisines like Indian and Thai food.

An example of a flavoured sake proving itself at a tasting festival is Sawtelle's Pink Can, released at Sake Day in San Francisco on 30 September 2022. Sawtelle's Maxwell Leer recalled, 'I am pretty sure it was the most talked-about sake in a room of thousands of sakes.' The inspiration for the beverage came from a sun tea Leer was making when he started working at Sawtelle:

> 'I would show up to work every day with a sun tea that
> I had made, that was at base hibiscus flower but it has
> raspberry leaves, blackberry leaves, orange peel, ginger,
> sassafras, roasted chicory. It's a deeply pink sun tea that
> I would be drinking out of a bottle, and Troy [Nakamatsu]
> in a few days mustered up, 'what the fuck are you drinking?'

The pair added the tea to Sawtelle's Clear Skies sake, which is the base for all of its sake blends, along with some yuzu juice imported from Yamaguchi prefecture and Japanese rock sugar (*korizato*) from Okinawa, added carbonization, and had a hit. Another Sawtelle product, Northern Lights, uses locally grown Japanese perilla leaves. Leer explains:

> We contract-farmed one hundred pounds of red shiso
> from a local organic farm in Santa Barbara called Coleman
> Farms, and Romeo grew this for us and harvested it in
> the summer. We took it. We juiced it. We blended it
> with our sake and some korizato, and we call it Northern
> Lights because the plant itself at harvest literally looks
> like that harlequined green to red hued ephemera in
> the sky. It's this electrically colored seasonally available
> herb sake.

Sawtelle Sake's Pink Can and its contents.

Although innovative, Sawtelle's blend consciously evokes and pays tribute to the traditional Japanese culinary repertoire, explained Leer:

> We could just as easily have blended it with orange juice. But the intention here is not to be terribly dismissive of Japanese ingredients. When we prepare these flavorized sakes, we are intensely aware of what flavors are recognizably Japanese and doing our best through local agriculture to assimilate those traditions and then make them our own. This isn't about cultural appropriation. It's more about taking the idea at its purest form and then showing everybody what they can do with these flavors with their sake so as to increase the bandwidth of their consumer excitement.

At Sake Day, Nakamatsu and Leer poured their Clear Skies brand and followed that with a sample of Northern Lights. They concluded that customers greatly preferred their flavoured sake.

Justin LeVaughn, who has a graduate degree in STEM (Science, Technology, Engineering and Maths) Education, sounds a bit like a mad scientist in the way he and his co-owners of The Void come up with their flavoured sake. 'We usually just sit down and have a bunch of different stuff and just play and mix like the little science kits that you would do as a kid. Sometimes they are duds and sometimes there is something there.' And sometimes there are sake that are 'way out there', in LeVaughn's words, in terms of their flavouring. The Void's taproom offers one sake that blends lemon nigori with squid ink garnished with gold leaf. One popular flavoured nigori is The Shining One, a tangerine-flavoured sake meant to evoke a creamsicle, a frozen dessert that combines vanilla ice cream with fruit juice. That sake is one of The Void's top sellers since it offers a nostalgic taste for southern drinkers, especially millennials and Gen-Xers. Nigori and horchata, blended in The Void's brand called Echoes, seemed another natural pairing for LeVaughn. 'You already have the nutty kind of creamy character with it and some vanilla and some cinnamon. Playing with those ratios and once you hit it, it tastes just like it.'

SAKE COCKTAILS

Before the debut of flavoured sake, using sake in cocktails has been a longstanding way of trying to broaden the sake consumer base in the United States. In the early 1960s, sake producers in Japan hoped to grow the North American market by popularizing Sake Manhattans, Sake (Tom) Collins and Sake Martinis, suggesting sake as a substitute for the spirits typically used in these drinks.[37] Sake brewers in Hawaii in the immediate post-war period experimented with sake cocktails to introduce their beverage, and they also pioneered carbonated sake before the Second World War and sold a style of bubbly sake called Polo Champion post-war.[38] In 1974, Johnrae Earl (1928–1978), restaurant critic for the *Chicago Tribune*, described a cocktail called the Geisha as 'lovely to look at but dangerous to flirt with' due to its 'lethal combination of rum, vodka, and sake' served at the Tanizake Japanese Steak-house in Chicago, which also sold a mixed drink called the Black Belt, made of sake and Kahlua on the rocks.[39] The North American establishment with the highest volume of sake sales nationally in 1979 was not a Japanese restaurant but the Cheshire Cat 'student bar' in Berkeley, where sake featured in a cocktail as a replacement for tequila.[40] Restaurant critic Michelle Huneven describes a similar 'hip scene' a decade later in Los Angeles's Tokyo Delve Sushi Bar, where 'smartly dressed secretaries downing Bailey's-flavored Shogun sake cocktails' share the space with 'kids with purple hair drinking Kirin' beer.[41] Popular sake cocktails of the late 1980s included 'sake margaritas, sake with orange juice and grenadine ("Rising Sun"), and sake 'n' cider (hot) on ski slopes'.[42]

Some breweries have cocktail recipes on their websites. SakéOne suggests making a Sake Sunrise with sake, pineapple juice and a dash of Grenadine, or a Bloody Mariko consisting of tomato juice, dashi and soy sauce to be combined with their junmai daiginjō garnished with wasabi and fuki, a Japanese vegetable similar to celery.[43] Blake Richardson of Moto'i and Byron Stithem of Proper Sake do not make flavoured sake but both have sake cocktails on the menus in their taprooms. 'The ultimate goal', explains Stithem, 'is to trick people into drinking sake. If they drink the cocktail and they like it, maybe that convinces them to go over to the sake menu.'

Sake's versatility as potential for mixed drinks is not lost on Ozeki's Miyagi, and she forecasts sake becoming a new ingredient in canned ready-to-drink cocktails:

> The hard seltzer market has grown so much in the past five years, and they usually use distilled alcohol like tequila or vodka or sugar cane base. But the hard seltzer market with the ingredients coming from those vodka and tequila is saturated, so a lot of companies are trying some new ingredients and some co-packers and blending houses have come to us. We would like consumers to try our sake as is, but this also could be a good start to know what sake is like.

In 2022, Hiro Sake, a beverage packaging company, launched the 'ready-to-drink' Saketini cocktail packed in a 12-ounce (0.35 litre) can in watermelon and black cherry flavours.

Cocktails have also inspired sake flavours. Justin LeVaughn of The Void claimed inspiration for his brewery's Reanimator coffee nigori by watching a bartender in Tokyo describe a house drink:

> We had a trip planned to Japan and then everything got shut down [due to the pandemic] so we did a sake tasting virtual tour and the person doing it was a bartender in some izakaya in downtown Tokyo. He talked about doing a nigori with a coffee ice cube like a sake cocktail, and that's when it kind of clicked that we could do something like that.

Coffee had long been a favourite of craft beer brewers, indicated LeVaughn, but nigori sake has a complexity and flavour that is especially well suited for different flavours, especially for

Americans who tend to like bolder, sweeter tastes. Nigori also stands well without any food, which is especially appropriate for The Void's flavoured sake reminiscent of other foods and drinks like ice cream, coffee and horchata.

THE AMERICAN SAKE BOTTLE

Americans who encounter sake outside of a restaurant or a brewpub often need to decipher a bottle with unique technical terms and Japanese writing. Japanese bottles are notoriously difficult to read because of their calligraphic text. One of the most frequently asked questions on r/Sake on Reddit is a photo of a bottle captioned, 'what is this sake?'

Gekkeikan USA has long had the most traditional-looking sake bottle that emulated labelling once used in Japan, according to Zheng-Garratt, who admits it can be tricky balancing the need for authentic-looking labelling while at the same time making it readily understood by consumers outside of Japan.

> You want to have some kind of Japanese elements to evoke that sense that it is a Japanese product, despite being made in the U.S. But you also want it to be easily understood with terms that are easily understood by consumers. That's the million-dollar question: how do you strike that perfect balance?

Answering that question depends on the target market for that sake, explains Zheng-Garratt:

> Our role as one of the pioneers of the sake industry in the U.S. is not to focus on that top tiny sliver of the market,

Gekkeikan's 'traditional' bottle label.

Gekkeikan's bottle label updated in 2024,
indicating that it is a junmai sake.

but it's really to appeal to the masses and democratize sake and make it more approachable and more accessible to everyone, and deliver that quality at a reasonable, affordable price. For example, this new Haiku product, on the front we mention that it is a tokubetsu junmai, and we try to briefly explain how we bottle it in a namazume fashion [pasteurized only once before cellaring] on the back of the label, adding just a little bit of information to make it stand out. But we really don't want to delve too much into that technical information, because I personally feel that it can scare people off.

Gekkeikan's traditional bottle never mentioned that the sake was a junmai because that term would not have resonated with consumers in North America or Japan when the brand debuted in 1989, according to Zheng-Garratt. Now, however, Gekkeikan's bottle has evolved along with the North American sake market.

Steve Vuylsteke of SakéOne thinks it is only a matter of time before consumers in the United States become conversant with the terms on sake labels. 'Americans learned how to say Merlot and they can say Pinot Noir.' SakéOne's bottles display terms like junmai ginjō or tokubetsu, albeit it in a smaller font than the brand name. Vuylsteke explains the reasoning: 'We think that there's significance to [Japanese] terms. The wine terms that have come out of Europe, like cuvée, or some of the sparkling wine terms, once you understand those terms you understand that they are very relevant.' Justin LeVaughn of The Void agrees about the utility of these terms, reflecting on his time teaching science in graduate school. 'In my mind, the more you learn and know about a thing, you begin to appreciate it a little bit more.' The Void educates its consumers about the meaning of Japanese terms by using translations on its taproom menu, where it lists nigori as 'cloudy' and calls *genshu*, undiluted sake, 'uncut'.

Sawtelle's Leer and Nakamatsu disagree about the utility of Japanese technical terms, although they have used Japanese technical terms on their labels in the past. Leer remarks, 'Think about junmai ginjō. That term gets in the way of advancement because . . . those two words . . . mean nothing to most people.'

Thus, among craft sake brewers in North America there is a lot of debate about the utility of Japanese technical terms on bottles, as Weston Konishi observes:

> There are people here who very vehemently believe we should not stick to that model because it is meaningless, and you tend to lose customers when you have to go to the lengths of explaining mill rates and things like that. It doesn't make for very effective elevator pitch. So there are people who think we should just really not do that at all. Then there are others who stick to it because there's a certain cachet to calling your sake daiginjō. But my sense is that compared to the Japanese producers with their seimaibuai mill rates, there is less of a religious following of that model than there is in Japan.

One point that brewers would agree on is that a daiginjō sake is not necessarily superior to a table sake. Ozeki's Miyagi says,

> people tend to think that junmai daiginjō is good sake and futsūshu [table sake] is not, but that is not true. Each sake has unique character and I hope everyone enjoys the diversity of sake. I can't pick my favorite sake, just like you can't pick your favorite child. They are all good.

It is also important to point out that junmai and ginjō are des-
ignations coined by the Japanese Tax Agency, not styles of sake,
as Justin LeVaughn of The Void is quick to point out. However,
their utility is that they can suggest different flavour experiences,
explains LeVaughn.

At the heart of the debate over technical terms is whether
or not brewers give sake brand names. Blake Richardson recalls:

> In the beginning we didn't brand anything. We just said this
> is junmai ginjō or this is junmai. If it was kimoto or yamahai
> we would note that but otherwise we wouldn't say what type
> of yeast it was. Over the years, we found recipes that we liked
> and wanted to repeat, and then we brand them, but we really
> only have maybe six brands.

Among Moto'i's brands is Another Dalliance, which is the brewery's flagship brew. 'Coming up with the names is very hard,'
admits Justin LeVaughn of The Void. LeVaughn and his co-owners
have found inspiration in science fiction and the horror stories
of H. P. Lovecraft. The Void's sake, The Reanimator, is named after
a 1922 Lovecraft story, which became a 1985 film about a scientist
who invents a serum to raise the dead, fitting for coffee-flavoured
nigori. 'Opalescent' was the name chosen to describe the pearl
colour of The Void's junmai nigori while also preserving an air
of mystery about the beverage. Another sake called 'Harbinger'
signals to the drinker that it is an undiluted (genshu) sake higher
in alcohol.

Byron Stithem of Proper Sake observes that a style of labelling found on beer bottles, where brand names are typically in a
larger font than the names of styles like lager, are trending among
sake bottles, even those from Japan.

It is no secret that Japanese sake, especially the premium stuff, has been relatively hard to decipher, even for people who are pretty familiar, if they don't read and write in the native language there. A lot of Japanese brands have over the years consulted with us in an informal manner about how we think their beverage could be best interpreted by the general public in the States and what advice we might have to offer there. To that end you are definitely starting to see more fanciful names of sakes and in English as well.

Proper Sake's trademark sake,
The Diplomat.

Stithem's own inspiration for his sake brand names comes from an attempt to clarify the style for the consumer. Proper Sake's trademark brand is The Diplomat, named to express that the sake is a flavour-forward but clean yamahai ginjō created to be the most versatile beverage in Proper Sake's lineup and the one Stithem pours first for new customers.

Instead of beer bottles, Steve Vuylsteke of SakéOne traces the origins of this style of labelling to the wine trade.

> American [sake] producers and certainly importers have gone more in the direction with what we call the screen names, where you come up with something like Wandering Poet or Bride of the Fox . . . Those work in certain ways because for Americans who don't understand the nomenclature then they understand, 'oh yeah it has the fox,' or whatever the image is on the label. In the wine business we call those 'critter labels'. You put a duck or you put a beaver [on the label]. It gives the consumer something to identify the wine without having to know all the knowledge of whatever it was about the wine.

Sawtelle Sake's Maxwell Leer explained they could have called their perilla-flavoured sake 'shiso sake',

> but 99% of the people who come in contact with Northern Lights have never tasted shiso before. They have certainly never tasted red shiso before. However, they like the taste, and that has more of an impact than me explaining to them any of the technical shit.

Rather than look to wine or beer packaging, Sawtelle found inspiration for its labels in an iconic American soft drink. 'The single most successful beverage brand in the history of the world is Coca-Cola,' states Leer. 'From that we gleaned you should put your font sideways on a label and make it bold. So we did that.'

A BRIEF LOOK AT SAKE IN ENGLAND

Looking briefly at the craft sake scene in England reveals some similarities with the United States, but also suggests some alternative routes for the beverage to develop along. Britain's first sake brewery is Kanpai, which opened in Peckham in southeast London in 2016. Kanpai is the creation of owners Tom and Lucy Wilson, who were inspired by a trip they took to Japan to try their hand at brewing. Kanpai has since moved to a location in south London, claiming a spot on the Bermondsey Beer Mile, a stretch of more than a dozen beer breweries and a few gin distilleries in south London, many of which, like Kanpai, are tucked beneath Victorian railway arches. American craft brewers would quickly recognize the brewpub setting of Kanpai as a way to appeal to consumers familiar with beer pubs, and Kanpai produces sake in a way to make it friendly to newcomers. Its brands feature easy-to-remember two-syllable Japanese names like Kaze, Kumo, Tori and Sora, with minimal Japanese technical terms on the boldly designed front labels. Kanpai's entry-level sake is affordably priced at £17 ($22) a bottle, but it also offers some premium selections.

Dojima Brewery, which began producing sake in 2018, represents an entirely different approach to sake. Located on Fordham Abbey Estate in Cambridgeshire, an eighteenth-century manor on a 200-acre property, Dojima is owned by the Hashimoto family, who invested £9,000,000 ($11.8 million) in purchasing and renovating the setting, building a sake brewery as well as a Japanese

Kanpai London Sake Brewery & Taproom.

garden and Shinto shrine honouring the deity of sake. The Hashimoto family are the hereditary owners of Kotobuki Shuzō Brewery, makers of sake in Osaka since 1822 and more recently the craft beer line Kuninocho. Dojima frequently hosts Japanese culture festivals, and from this aristocratic setting produces two premium brands, Dojima Junmai and Vintage Sake Cambridge, stored for three to five years. Both sell for £1,000 ($1,320) per bottle.

England's third sake brewery, the Sparkling Sake Company, is also located in Cambridgeshire. Beginning production in 2021, the same year as Dojima, Sparkling Sake focuses on its namesake variety, producing effervescent sake, the only brewery with that speciality globally. Naoki Toyota, who trained in Japan, guides the brewing process, and he founded the company in collaboration with the American sake educator Tracey Delaney. Sparkling Sake's main brand is its nigori Awa (sparkling) sake (£30, $40 a bottle) and it also offers a different seasonal flavoured sake each year in limited batches, a homage to the importance of nature and impermanence in Japanese culture.

These three British sake brewers, which opened within a few years of each other, share the fact that they import their rice, but each stakes its future on a different vision for sake. Kanpai, like most American craft sake brewers, would like sake to share the table with beer in a familiar pub setting. To the extent that Kanpai fits well among other brewpubs, Dojima begs comparison with a French wine château, one that can command high prices for its bottles due to its prestige. Sparkling Sake has turned a novelty sake style into a business model. All three position sake as a drink adjacent to the experiences of consumers more familiar with beer and wine, and such steps are needed to familiarize newcomers to the ancient beverage.

WHAT THE FUTURE MIGHT BRING

Blake Richardson, who has set the course for many North American craft sake brewers, predicts that within a decade there will be as many sake brewpubs as there are cities with National Football League teams. 'That's an easy prediction to make,' claims Richardson, 'but it does mean that there will be 32 sake breweries in this country for certain if that comes true.' Beyond that, expansion of the sake industry in North America will be much more difficult:

> When you look at other markets that have emerged, call it craft, whatever, coffee, wine, beer, all those movements were started with the lesser of two. You had Starbucks, but before Starbucks there was Maxwell House. Before Jordan Vineyards there was Ernest and Julio Gallo; and before Sierra Nevada there was Anheuser-Busch. Everyone had the early years of the previously not as good version, but that isn't the case in America for sake. It is the complete adoption of a new alcohol, a new drink that ultimately will have to replace what you are currently consuming that is not sake. Therefore, the runway is longer. It's not going to happen like the beer movement or the wine movement or the coffee movement. I do think it will happen though because people are inquisitive and they like new things, and you have early adopters who want to show their friends something incredibly good. It's just going to take a while.

Key to the future of sake brewing in North America, according to Richardson, is the brewpub experience, which allows sake makers to guide new consumers' appreciation of sake. Those brewpubs might also form the basis for distinct local flavours and styles of sake, imagines The Void's LeVaughn, with regions like Kentucky drawing tourists not just for bourbon and craft beer but to sample the local sake.

With its $80-million investment in New York to produce exclusively junmai daiginjō sake, Dassai USA is betting on the future premiumization of the sake market, a vision that SakéOne's Steve Vuylsteke shares and defines in this way:

> If you follow what's happened in wine and beer and spirits, you probably heard an industry term 'premiumization'. It relates to the concept to consumers that if you give them the right amount of information and knowledge, they will be curious and want to trade up. If you buy a $10 bottle of Riesling, you wonder what the $15 or $20 bottle tastes like. From a sustainability standpoint and a financial standpoint, it makes sense to pursue those types of consumers, because once they are engaged in the category, they are going to trade up. That's where craft beer has succeeded, craft spirits, boutique wine or high-quality wine as well. So that's the niche we focus on and say that our goal is to become the leading premium sake company in America.

While some North American brewers are betting that consumers will desire premium sake, Japanese brewers are also taking note of the popularity of flavoured brands in the USA, Vuylsteke indicates, referencing his time as SakéOne's president.

> When I came on board fourteen years ago, you would never see any Japanese sake company release a product that had any flavors added to it. That was just unheard of. And now, they will do anything to get new customers . . . low alcohol, sparkling, anything to try and present it in a different way.

Legally, a sake cannot be sold with flavourings in Japan, so these beverages are usually relabelled as liqueurs.

Besides possibly drawing inspiration from the innovative techniques of American craft brewers, an increase in sake's popularity in North America could also help revitalize the brewing industry in Japan, a point that many American brewers I spoke with articulated. Weston Konishi, president of SBANA, put it this way:

> If we can make sake more popular here, I do think there is
> a better chance of it becoming popular again with young
> Japanese consumers because there is nothing more cool than
> Brooklyn, New York. It's the cool capital of the world. We are
> now going to have three sake breweries in Brooklyn alone.
> That cachet I am hoping will rub off on sake's broader image
> in Japan.

Beyond the desire of young Japanese to emulate the cool sake scenes of America's East or West coasts, or even in the heartland of Nashville, Minneapolis or Lexington, Kentucky, sake also offers what younger drinkers are looking for in an alcoholic beverage, according to Konishi:

> If you look at the checklist of what millennials and
> Gen-Z'ers want out of beverages, sake hits all of those
> marks. For instance, young people like natural products.
> They like to know where the ingredients come from. They
> like gluten-free products. They like things that are new yet
> grounded in some sort of craft tradition. All of these things
> play to sake's strengths. So that's where I see us having real
> potential for growth here, and I am hoping that younger
> generations of Japanese share those values. The key word
> here is values. For previous generations I am not so sure

that their values were part of their consumerism. It was more like they just liked the damn stuff, or it got them drunk, or whatever. Whereas for these younger generations, values matter. I think that's a global trend; and if that's the case, then sake has a chance to appeal to young consumers again too.

Sake has long historic roots in Japan, but the globalization of sake is what might save breweries in Japan, where sake's market share fell to 5.3 per cent in 2020, alcohol drinkers consume four times more beer than sake, and more people, especially younger consumers, are swearing off alcohol altogether.[44]

GLOSSARY

Amazake – A beverage that is non-alcoholic when made just with kōji but can contain some alcohol if produced from the lees (kasu) left over from brewing.

Doburoku – 'Unfiltered sake', which historically was an inexpensive recipe for sake that was made illegal to produce in 1899. Today, makers in a government-sanctioned 'doburoku district' can legally produce the alcoholic beverage for sale.

Jizake – 'Local sake'; a term that developed in the 1970s and 1980s meant to highlight the quality of regional brands that were officially 'second rank' but often tasted better than the first- and special-rank sake that dominated the market – thanks to the fact that these producers simply paid higher tax rates. This distinction ended in 1992 with the establishment of a new method of differentiating and taxing sake.

Kasu – Also called sake kasu. The mashed rice (lees) left over after sake is pressed and often finding culinary uses such as to make pickles or soups.

Koji – The term encompasses a variety of moulds, but *Aspergillus oryzae* is the one used in sake making to break down the starches in rice into sugars needed for fermentation.

Koku – A traditional way of measuring volume still used by Japanese sake makers. One koku is 180 litres or 47½ gallons.

Morohaku – An 'all white' sake made entirely from polished rice.

Moto – 'The fermentation starter' also known as shubo; a small batch of ingredients meant to facilitate the growth of yeast.

Nigorizake – A 'cloudy sake' distinguished from doburoku in that it is filtered but it still retains some of the lees, giving the beverage an opaque appearance.

Nihonshu – 'Japanese sake'; used in this text to refer to the artificial sake (sanzōshu) made in the post-war period, but conventionally Nihonshu refers to sake made in Japan.

Sake kasu – See **kasu**

Sandan jikomi/shikomi – A way of 'preparing ingredients' (shikomi) that developed by the late sixteenth century where rice, kōji and water are introduced in 'three stages' (sandan) so as to make more sake without overwhelming the yeast.

Sanzōshu – Also called sanbaijōshu; a method making 'three times more sake' by adding brewers' alcohol, flavourings and sugars. Developed late in the Second World War, this was the dominant recipe for sake until 1992.

Seishu – The legal term for sake in Japan.

Shubo – See **moto**

Tōji – A term popularized in the early modern era for a brewery's 'master brewer', but in ancient times once referred to a female village leader who also made sake.

REFERENCES

INTRODUCTION

1 Nihon Jōzō Kyōkai, Nihonshu Sābisu Kenkyūkai and Sakashō Kenkyūkai Rengōkai, eds, *Nihonshugaku: Sake ga motto umaku naru!* (Tokyo, 2016), p. 12.

2 Yoshida Hajime, *Sake* (Tokyo, 2015), p. 16.

3 Ibid., p. 19; Yoshida Hajime, *Kindai Nihon no sakezukuri: Bishu tankyū no gijutsushi* (Tokyo, 2013), p. 6.

4 Mori Motoko, *Nihon no shokuseikatsu zenshū*, vol. XXI: *Kikigaki Gifu no shokuji* (Tokyo, 1990), p. 89; Eric C. Rath, *Japan's Cuisines: Food, Place and Identity* (London, 2016), p. 214.

5 Yoshida, *Sake*, p. 9.

6 Kurahashi Atsushi, 'Kōji amazake no seibu, kinōsei, anzensei', *Seibutsu kagaku*, XCVII/4 (2019), p. 190.

7 Aoki Takahiro, *Kindai shuzōgyō no chiikiteki tenkai* (Tokyo, 2002), p. 162.

8 *Shogakukan Unabridged Dictionary of the Japanese Language*, cited at https://japanknowledge.com, accessed 30 November 2023.

9 Yunoki Manabu, *Sakezukuri no rekishi, shinsōpan* (Tokyo, 2005), p. 1.

10 For a profile of Miho Imada and several more prominent women brewers in Japan today, see Ayuko Yamaguchi, 'Women Leading the Way', *Sake Today: Celebrating the World of Sake Culture*, 17 (2018), pp. 29–39.

11 Suzuki Yoshiyuki, *Nihonshu no kin-gendaishi: Shuzōchi no tanjō* (Tokyo, 2015), pp. 16–17.

12 Furukawa Yoshimi, *Sobayazake: Ā 'Edomae' no shiawase* (Tokyo, 2011), p. 18.

13 Kobayashi Tsuneo, *Kyūshū no shuzōgyō to tōji shūdan* (Tokyo, 2023), p. 24.
14 Kanzaki Noritake, 'Naze ima "kanpai no bunkashi" kenkyū ka', in *Kanpai no bunkashi*, ed. Kanzaki Noritake (Tokyo, 2007), p. 15.

ONE CLOUDY BEGINNINGS, 1000 BCE TO 1000 CE

1 Yoshida Hajime, *Sake* (Tokyo, 2015), p. 9.
2 Saeki Arikiyo, *Treatise on the People of Wa in the Chronicle of the Kingdom of Wei: The World's Earliest Written Text on Japan*, trans. Joshua A. Fogel (Portland, ME, 2018), p. 371.
3 Yokota Hiroyuki, *Horoyoibanashi: Sake no Nihon bunkashi* (Tokyo, 2019), pp. 12–15.
4 Satō Nobuo, *Sake to utsuwa no hanashi* (Fukuoka, 2005), pp. 19–20.
5 Werner Steinhaus et al., eds, *An Illustrated Companion to Japanese Archaeology*, 2nd edn (Oxford, 2020), p. 41.
6 Yoshida Hajime, *Edo no sake: Tsukuru, uru, ajiwau* (Tokyo, 2016), pp. 81–2; Yoshida, *Sake*, p. 10.
7 Yoshida, *Sake*, pp. 10, 12–14, 19.
8 Ōshima Akeo, 'Shōwa shoki ni okeru kome no suihanhō to yōgu: Jikyoku no kakawari kara', in *Shoku no Shōwa bunkashi*, ed. Tanaka Nobutada and Kenzō Matsuzaki (Tokyo, 1995), p. 145.
9 Suzuki Shigeo, 'Mochi no hanashi are kore', *Koko chishin*, 15 (1978), p. 27.
10 Yoshida, *Sake*, pp. 48–9.
11 *Ōsumi no kuni fudoki*, in *Shinpen Nihon koten bungaku zenshū*, vol. V: *Fudokī*, ed. Uegaki Setsuya (Tokyo, 1997), p. 564.
12 Sakaguchi Kin'ichirō, 'Kamosukō', *Nihon jōzō kyōkai zasshi*, LXXIII/1 (1978), pp. 1–2. In terms of classical Japanese grammar, the word for brewing – *kamu*, or simply *kam* in old Japanese – falls in the *yodan* verb class, while chewing (*kamu*) is in a verb class called *kami nidan*, meaning the two verbs are conjugated differently, providing further evidence that they are different words. Alexander Vovin, personal correspondence, 13 October 2021.
13 Yunoki Manabu, *Sakezukuri no rekishi, shinsōpan* (Tokyo, 2005), p. 1.
14 Li Liu et al., 'The Origins of Specialized Pottery and Diverse Alcohol Fermentation Techniques in Early Neolithic China',

Proceedings of the National Academy of Sciences of the United States of America, CXVI/26 (2019), p. 12773.

15 Ueda Seinosuke, *Nihonshu no kigen: Kabi, kōji, sake no keifu* (Tokyo, 1999), p. 19; Hsing-Tsung Huang, *Science and Civilization in China*, vol. VI: *Biology and Biological Technology*, part V: *Fermentation and Food Science* (Cambridge, 2000), p. 154.

16 Yamashita Masaru, 'Kuchikami sake to wa (1)', *Nihon jōzōkyō-kaishi*, XCIV/1 (1999), pp. 39–40; Jeffrey M. Pilcher, *Hopped Up: How Travel, Trade, and Taste Made Beer a Global Commodity* (New York, 2024), p. 25.

17 For an overview of the historical and ethnographic evidence of kuchikami sake in the Ryukyu Islands, see Hagio Toshiaki, *Awamori o meguru Okinawa no sake bunkashi* (Naha, Okinawa, 2022), pp. 26–30, 106–11.

18 Yoshida, *Sake*, pp. 5–6.

19 Eric C. Rath, *Japan's Cuisines: Food, Place and Identity* (London, 2016), p. 72.

20 Ishige Naomichi, 'Japan', in *The Cambridge World History of Food*, vol. II, ed. Kenneth F. Kiple and Kriemhild Coneè Ornelas (New York, 2000), p. 1180.

21 Rath, *Japan's Cuisines*, pp. 138, 150–51; Alan Christy, *A Discipline on Foot: Inventing Japanese Native Ethnography, 1910–1945* (Lanham, MD, 2012).

22 Ueda, *Nihonshu no kigen*, p. 20.

23 Eric C. Rath, *Oishii: The History of Sushi* (London, 2021), p. 37.

24 Harada Nobuo, *Washoku to Nihon bunka: Nihon ryōri no shakaishi* (Tokyo, 2005), pp. 218–22; Kumakura Isao, 'Nihon no dentōteki shoku bunka to shite no washoku no inkikata', in *Nihon no shoku no kinmirai*, ed. Kumakura Isao (Kyoto, 2013), p. 8.

25 Gautier Roussille, *Nihonshu: Japanese Sake* (n.p., 2017), p. 16.

26 Koizumi Takeo, *Kōji kabi to kōji no hanashi* (Tokyo, 1984), p. 64.

27 Yamashita, 'Kuchikami sake to wa (1)', pp. 39–40, 41–3.

28 Matsumoto Buichiro, '"Fudoki" in arawareta sake', *Nihon jōzō kyōkai zasshi*, LXVIII/7 (1973), p. 494.

29 Antonis Rokas, 'Aspergillus', *Current Biology*, XXIII/5 (2013), p. R188.

30 Ogura Hiraku, 'Song of Kōji', www.youtube.com, accessed 21 February 2022.

31 Perng-Kuang Chang and Kenneth C. Ehrlich, 'What Does Genetic Diversity of *Aspergillus flavus* Tell Us about *Aspergillus oryzae?*', *International Journal of Food Microbiology*, CXXXVIII/3 (2010), p. 189.

32 Masayuki Machida, Osamu Yamada and Katsuya Gomi, 'Genomics of *Aspergillus oryzae*: Learning from the History of Koji Mold and Exploration of Its Future', *DNA Research*, XV/4 (2008), pp. 173–4.

33 Victoria Lee, *The Arts of the Microbial World: Fermentation Science in Twentieth-Century Japan* (Chicago, IL, 2021), p. 15.

34 Nihon Jōzō Gakkai, 'Declaration', www.jozo.or.jp, accessed 11 July 2022.

35 Lee, *The Arts of the Microbial World*.

36 Ichishima Eiji, *Kōji* (Tokyo, 2007).

37 *Shogakukan Unabridged Dictionary of the Japanese Language*, cited at https://japanknowledge.com, accessed 15 February 2023.

38 Kurahashi Atsushi, 'Kōji amazake no seibu, kinōsei, anzensei', *Seibutsu kagaku*, XCVII/4 (2019), p. 191.

39 Rich Shih and Jeremy Umansky, *Koji Alchemy: Rediscovering the Magic of Mold-Based Fermentation* (White River Junction, VT, 2020), p. 16.

40 Chang and Ehrlich, 'What Does Genetic Diversity of *Aspergillus flavus* Tell Us?', p. 190; Machida, Yamada and Gomi, 'Genomics of *Aspergillus oryzae*', p. 175.

41 Melinda A. Zeder, 'The Domestication of Animals', *Journal of Anthropological Research*, LXVIII/2 (2012), pp. 163–4.

42 John G. Gibbons et al., 'The Evolutionary Imprint of Domestication on Genome Variation and Function of the Filamentous Fungus *Aspergillus oryzae*', *Current Biology*, XXII/15 (2012), p. 1403.

43 C. P. Kurtzman et al., 'DNA Relatedness among Wild and Domesticated Species in the *Aspergillus flavus* Group', *Mycologia*, LXXVIII/6 (1986), p. 955; Gibbons et al., 'The Evolutionary Imprint', p. 1403.

44 John G. Gibbons and Antonis Rokas, 'The Function and Evolution of the *Aspergillus* Genome', *Trends in Microbiology*, XXI/1 (2012), p. 15.

45 Masayuki Machida et al., 'Genome Sequencing and Analysis of *Aspergillus oryzae*', *Nature*, CDXXXVIII/22 (2005), p. 1160.

46 Chang and Ehrlich, 'What Does Genetic Diversity of *Aspergillus flavus* Tell Us?', p. 196.

47 *Dōmō shuzōki*, in *Nihon nōgyō zenshū*, vol. LI: *Dōmō shuzōki, Kanmoto zōyō gokuiden*, ed. Yoshida Hajime (Tokyo, 1996), pp. 3–178, p. 45.

48 Ishige Naomichi, 'Shuzō to inshu no bunka', in *Ronshū sake to inshu no bunka*, ed. Ishige Naomichi (Tokyo, 1998), pp. 45–6.

49 Ibid., p. 46.

50 Liu et al., 'The Origins of Specialized Pottery and Diverse Alcohol Fermentation Techniques in Early Neolithic China', pp. 12767, 12773; Huang, *Science and Civilization in China*, vol. VI, pp. 157–9.

51 Ishige, 'Shuzō to inshu no bunka', p. 52.

52 Hanai Shirō, 'Nihonshu no kita michi', in *Ronshū sake to inshu no bunka*, ed. Ishige Naomichi (Tokyo, 1998), pp. 233–4.

53 Machida, Yamada and Gomi, 'Genomics of *Aspergillus oryzae*', p. 175.

54 Koizumi Takeo, 'Kome kōji no hassei to Nihon no sakezukuri: Inakōji no shūhen kara no ikōsai', in *Ronshū sake to inshu no bunka*, ed. Ishige Naomichi (Tokyo, 1998), pp. 168, 177.

55 Suminoe Kinshi, 'Sakeshi ni kan suru ni san no chiken', *Nihon jōzō kyōkai zasshi*, LXV/9 (1970), p. 772.

56 *Harima fudoki*, in *Shinpen Nihon koten bungaku zenshū*, vol. V: *Fudoki*, ed. *Uegaki Setsuya* (Tokyo, 1997), p. 85.

57 Huang, *Science and Civilization in China*, vol. VI, pp. 161–2.

58 Suminoe, 'Sakeshi ni kan suru ni san no chiken', p. 772.

59 Koizumi Takeo, 'Kome kōji no hassei to Nihon no sakezukuri', pp. 170–71.

60 Ibid., p. 175.

61 *Kokushi taikei*, vol. XL: *Engishiki*, pp. 883–95, cited at https://japanknowledge.com, accessed 3 August 2023.

62 Itō Nobihiro and Itō Akitoshi, 'Kome to sake soshite no sono shūhen: Kankyō no shiza kara', in *Yoi no bunkashi: Girei kara yamai made*, ed. Itō Nobuhiro (Tokyo, 2020), p. 149.

63 Yoshida, *Sake*, p. 56; Yunoki, *Sakezukuri no rekishi, shinsōpan*, p. 18.

64 Huang, *Science and Civilization in China*, vol. VI, p. 157.

65 Yoshida, *Sake*, pp. 62–4.

66 Yunoki, *Sakezukuri no rekishi, shinsōpan*, p. 19.

67 Nakayama Keiko, *Jiten wagashi no sekai* (Tokyo, 2006), p. 7.

68 The table is based on Yoshida, *Sake*, pp. 57–8.

69 Basil Hall Chamberlain, *The Kojiki: Records of Ancient Matters* (Rutland, VT, 1981), p. 72.

70 Yoshida Hajime, *Nihon no shoku to sake: Chūsei no hakkō gijutsu o chūshin ni* (Tokyo, 1991), p. 154.

71 Yoshida Hajime, *Kyō no sakegaku* (Kyoto, 2016), p. 50.

72 The following descriptions of these sake are based on the analysis of Yoshida, *Sake*, pp. 56–61; Matsumoto Buichirō, '"Engishiki" no sake: "Un" no kōshō', *Nihon jōzō kyōkai zasshi*, LXXVI/7 (1981), pp. 46–65.

73 Yoshida Hajime, *Kindai Nihon no sakezukuri: Bishu tankyū no gijutsushi* (Tokyo, 2013), p. 10.

74 Yoshida, *Kyō no sakegaku*, p. 47.

75 Ibid., p. 30.

76 Yunoki, *Sakezukuri no rekishi, shinsōpan*, pp. 15–16.

77 Yoshida, *Sake*, pp. 53–6.

78 Joan R. Piggott, 'Mokkan: Wooden Documents from the Nara Period', *Monumenta Nipponica*, XLV/4 (1990), pp. 452–3.

79 Yoshida, *Kyō no sakegaku*, pp. 34–5.

80 Segawa Kiyoko, *Shoku seikatsu no rekishi* (Tokyo, 2001), p. 237.

81 Ningen Bunka Kenkyū Kikō Kokuritsu Rekishi Minzoku Hakubutsukan, *Jendā no Nihon shi* (Chiba-ken Sakura-shi, 2020), pp. 53–4.

82 Yoshiko Kurata Dykstra, *The Konjaku Tales: Japanese Section (i)* (Hirakata City, Osaka, 1998), p. 391.

83 Yoshino Shuji, *Kodai no shoku seikatsu: Taberu, hataraku, kurasu* (Tokyo, 2020), p. 44.

TWO ENLIGHTENED BREWS: MEDIEVAL TOWN AND TEMPLE SAKE
BREWERIES, 1400-1600

1 Yoshida Hajime, *Sake* (Tokyo, 2015), p. 87.

2 The data point is not only important for sake history: it is one that demographers use to deduce Kamakura's population. With the assumption that a household was five people, and each household had three or four jars for brewing, that places Kamakura's population around 50,000 commoners with an additional 10,000–20,000 samurai and clerics. Ishii Susumu,

'Bunken kara saguru jinkō', in *Yomigaeru chūsei*, vol. III: *Bushi no miyako Kamakura* (Tokyo, 1989), pp. 59–61.

3 William Wayne Farris, *Japan to 1600: A Social and Economic History* (Honolulu, HI, 2009), pp. 115–17.

4 Yoshida, *Sake*, p. 88.

5 Katō Hyakuichi, *Sake wa morohaku: Nihonshu to unda gijutsu no bunka* (Tokyo, 1989), pp. 18–19.

6 Eric C. Rath, 'Hell's Kitchen and the Joy of Cooking: Culinary Themes in Kumano Mandala', *Impressions*, 37 (March 2016), p. 116.

7 Yoshida, *Sake*, p. 102.

8 Suzuki Yoshiyuki, *Nihonshu no kin-gendaishi: Shuzōchi no tanjō* (Tokyo, 2015), p. 25.

9 Yoshida Hajime, *Kyō no sakegaku* (Kyoto, 2016), p. 89.

10 Suzanne Gay, *The Moneylenders of Late Medieval Kyoto* (Honolulu, HI, 2001), p. 39.

11 Yunoki Manabu, *Sakezukuri no rekishi, shinsōpan* (Tokyo, 2005), pp. 20–21; Imatani Akira, 'Shuen no hajimari', in *Shuen no katachi*, ed. Tamura Toyō (Tokyo, 1997), p. 56.

12 Yunoki, *Sakezukuri no rekishi, shinsōpan*, pp. 21–2.

13 Yoshida, *Kyō no sakegaku*, pp. 113–16.

14 Ibid., pp. 90–91.

15 Yoshida Hajime, *Edo no sake: Tsukuru, uru, ajiwau* (Tokyo, 2016), p. 61.

16 Yoshida, *Sake*, pp. 94–5.

17 Yoshida, *Kyō no sakegaku*, p. 92.

18 Yoshida, *Sake*, pp. 95, 99.

19 Gay, *The Moneylenders of Late Medieval Kyoto*, pp. 40, 225–8.

20 Ibid., p. 120.

21 Yoshida, *Kyō no sakegaku*, pp. 92–3.

22 Gay, *The Moneylenders of Late Medieval Kyoto*, pp. 120–23; Yoshida, *Kyō no sakegaku*, pp. 93 4.

23 Koizumi Takeo, *Kōji kabi to kōji no hanashi* (Tokyo, 1984), pp. 89–91.

24 Yunoki, *Sakezukuri no rekishi, shinsōpan*, pp. 29–30.

25 Yoshida, *Sake*, pp. 102–3.

26 Yoshida Hajime, *Kindai Nihon no sakezukuri: Bishu tankyū no gijutsushi* (Tokyo, 2013), p. 222.

27 Jeffrey M. Pilcher, *Hopped Up: How Travel, Trade, and Taste Made Beer a Global Commodity* (New York, 2024), p. 4.

28 Gautier Roussille, *Nihonshu: Japanese Sake* (n.p., 2017), p. 143.

29 Hsing-Tsung Huang, *Science and Civilization in China*, vol. VI: *Biology and Biological Technology*, part V: *Fermentation and Food Science* (Cambridge, 2000), p. 282.

30 Yoshida, *Sake*, p. 56.

31 As a manuscript that depended on secret professional expertise, oral tradition and physical/sensory learning to make it understandable, the *Sake Journal* presents some challenges for readers today, and for the translator. I referenced three modern commentaries on the text, and often found variations in how the original was interpreted, even on such basic matters as to whether recipes required brown or polished rice. *Goshu no nikki*, in *Shiryō tsūshin sōshi*, ed. Kondō Heijō (Tokyo, 1893–7), pp. 33–6. In translating, I referred to the commentaries from Katō, *Sake wa morohaku*, pp. 39–51; Matsumoto Buichirō, '"Goshu no nikki" to sono kaigi – Satake monjo yori', *Nihon jōzō kyōkai zasshi*, LXXIV/11 (1979), pp. 748–51; and Yoshida, *Kyō no sakegaku*, pp. 102–7.

32 Soaking the kōji also facilitates the release and melting of diastatic enzymes, which breaks starch down into maltose: Yoshida, *Kyō no sakegaku*, p. 103.

33 Katō (*Sake wa morohaku*, p. 46) interprets this as white rice, but Matsumoto and Yoshida contend it is brown rice: Matsumoto, '"Goshu no nikki" to sono Kaigi', p. 748; Yoshida, *Kyō no sakegaku*, p. 103. To me, the original 'good rice with the chaff removed' ([w]*are mo naki no umai*) suggests brown rice. The direction to 'steam it thoroughly' is also consistent with other passages that indicate brown rice.

34 The text indicates that 'one should make rice' (*odai ni subeshi*). The commentators equate the rice here with cooked rice (*gohan*): Yoshida, *Kyō no sakegaku*, p. 104; Matsumoto, '"Goshu no nikki" to sono Kaigi', p. 749. Steaming was one of the ways of cooking rice for eating in the medieval period and the preferred method for preparing rice for sake brewing, so it is likely that the cooking method here is steaming. One of the advantages of steaming is that the grain remains much firmer and therefore less likely to dissolve compared to boiling. For more on premodern rice

cooking methods, see Eric C. Rath, *Japan's Cuisines: Food, Place and Identity* (London, 2016), pp. 76–83.

35 Presumably, the covering was removed later, and the container sat for two additional days.

36 This section comes after the recipe for Amano sake, but I follow Yoshida and move it to the end since pasteurization occurs after brewing the sake. Yoshida, *Kyō no sakegaku*, pp. 106–7.

37 Yoshida, *Sake*, p. 58; Yoshida, *Kyō no sakegaku*, p. 44.

38 Yoshida, *Sake*, pp. 102–3.

39 Katō, *Sake wa morohaku*, p. 26.

40 Ibid., pp. 28–9.

41 Hiroshi Kondō, *Sake: A Drinker's Guide* (New York, 1984), p. 44.

42 Katō Hyakuichi, 'Nara Shōrakuji no shubo seizō menkyo kōfu', *Nihon jōzō kyōkai zasshi*, XCIV/7 (1990), p. 537.

43 Ibid., pp. 50–51.

44 Yoshida, *Kyō no sakegaku*, p. 55.

45 Unfortunately, Roussille does not provide a citation for this fourteenth-century reference. Roussille, *Nihonshu*, p. 18. The use of ash to clarify sake is discussed in Chapter Four.

46 Matsumoto, '"Goshu no nikki" to sono kaigi', p. 150.

47 *Shogakukan Unabridged Dictionary of the Japanese Language*, https://japanknowledge.com, accessed 24 January 2025.

48 Hioki Shōichi, *Monoshiri jiten, inshokuhen* (Tokyo, 2005), vol. V, p. 236.

49 *Ryōri monogatari*, in *Nihon ryōri hiden shūsei: Genten gendaigoyaku*, vol. I (Kyoto, 1985), p. 72.

50 Rath, *Japan's Cuisines*, pp. 72, 74.

51 Yoshida, *Kyō no sakegaku*, p. 103.

52 Matsumoto, '"Goshu no nikki" to sono kaigi', p. 749.

53 *Shogakukan Unabridged Dictionary of the Japanese Language*, https://japanknowledge.com, accessed 24 January 2025.

54 Yoshida, *Sake*, p. 109.

55 Katō, *Sake wa morohaku*, pp. 53, 56, 58.

56 Yoshida, *Kyō no sakegaku*, p. 111.

57 Yoshida, *Sake*, pp. 109–10.

58 Yoshida, *Kyō no sakegaku*, p. 110.

59 Suzuki, *Nihonshu no kin-gendaishi*, p. 25.

60 Katō, *Sake wa morohaku*, p. 64.

61 Suzuki, *Nihonshu no kin-gendaishi*, p. 25.

62 Ningen Bunka Kenkyū Kikō Kokuritsu Rekishi Minzoku Haku-butsukan, *Jendā no Nihon shi* (Chiba-ken Sakura-shi, 2020), p. 130.

THREE DRINKING IN ANCIENT AND MEDIEVAL JAPAN, 700–1600

1 Wakamori Tarō, *Sake ga kataru Nihonshi* (Tokyo, 1971), pp. 61–2.

2 *Man'yōshū*, book 5, poem 892, cited in Wakamori, *Sake ga kataru Nihonshi*, p. 27

3 Abe Takeshi, *Doburoku to onna: Nihon josei inshukō* (Tokyo, 2009), p. 36.

4 *Hitachi no kuni fudoki*, in *Shinpen Nihon koten bungaku zenshū*, vol. v: *Fudokī*, ed. Uegaki Setsuya (Tokyo, 1997), pp. 361–2.

5 Nippon Gakujutsu Shinkōkai, trans., *The Manyōshū, One Thousand Poems with the Texts in Romaji* (New York, 1965), p. 222.

6 Abe, *Doburoku to onna*, pp. 60–61.

7 Yoshida Hajime, *Sake* (Tokyo, 2015), pp. 216, 218.

8 Hirabayashi Akihito, *Kamigami no nikushoku to kodaishi* (Tokyo, 2007), pp. 173, 178, 181.

9 Yokota Hiroyuki, *Horoyoibanashi: Sake no Nihon bunkashi* (Tokyo, 2019), pp. 111–12.

10 Jeremy Robinson, trans., 'Thirteen Poems in Praise of Saké', in *Traditional Japanese Literature, an Anthology, Beginnings to 1600*, ed. Haruo Shirane (New York, 2007), pp. 101–2.

11 Sato Hideki, *Senju sake gassen to gosuichōki* (Tokyo, 2021), pp. 42–3.

12 Yoshida Hajime, *Kyō no sakegaku* (Kyoto, 2016), p. 68.

13 Takeshi Watanabe, 'Gifting Melons to the Shining Prince: Representations of Food in the Late Heian Period', in *Devouring Japan: Global Perspectives on Japanese Culinary Identity*, ed. Nancy Stalker (New York, 2018), p. 48.

14 Ivan Morris, trans., *The Pillow Book of Sei Shōnagon* (New York, 1991), p. 254.

15 Ibid., p. 45.

16 Ibid., p. 117.

17 Takahashi Tōru, 'Heian kizoku on "yoi" to "matsurigoto"', in *Yoi no bunkashi: Girei kara yamai made*, ed. Itō Nobuhiro (Tokyo, 2020), p. 74.

18 Ziro Uraki, trans., *The Tale of the Cavern* (*Utsuho monogatari*) (Tokyo, 1984), pp. 100, 112, 114.

19 Imazeki Toshiko, 'Ōchō jidai no shurei to shuen', in *Kanpai no bunkashi*, ed. Kanzaki Noritake (Tokyo, 2007), pp. 41–2.

20 G. Cameron Hurst III, 'Michinaga's Maladies: A Medical Report on Fujiwara no Michinaga', *Monumenta Nipponica*, XXXIV/1 (1979), p. 104.

21 Murasaki Shikibu, *The Tale of Genji*, trans. Royal Tyler (New York, 2001), pp. 563–4.

22 Imazeki, 'Ōchō jidai no shurei to shuen', p. 41.

23 Katō Hyakuichi, 'Genji monogatari ni mieru sake' (3), *Nihon jōzō kyōkaishi*, CV/3 (2011), pp. 287–8.

24 Murasaki Shikibu, *The Tale of Genji*, pp. 155–7.

25 Ibid., p. 565.

26 Yoshida Kenkō, *Essays in Idleness: The Tsurezuregusa of Kenkō*, trans. Donald Keene (New York, 1998), p. 4.

27 Ibid., p. 150.

28 Ibid., p. 151.

29 Ibid., p. 152.

30 Sakurai Eiji, *Nihon no rekishi kōza*, vol. XII: *Muromachibito no seishin* (Tokyo, 2011), p. 238.

31 Satō Toyozō, 'Shōgun no onari to cha no yu', in *Buke chadō no keifu*, ed. Bukeshi Danka (Tokyo, 1983), pp. 156–7.

32 Kaneko Hiraku, 'Utage no kiroku to shite no "onariki" to "chakaiki"', in *Utage no chūsei: Ba, kawarake, kenryoku*, ed. Ono Masatoshi, Gomi Fumihiko and Hagihara Mitsuo (Tokyo, 2008), p. 206.

33 Kurushima Noriko, 'Matsurigoto to matsuri no shuenshi', in *Utage no chūsei*, pp. 17–18.

34 Mori Yukio, *Chūsei no buke kanryō to bugyōnin* (Tokyo, 2016), p. 185.

35 Futaki Ken'ichi, *Chūsei buke no sahō* (Tokyo, 1999), pp. 125–6.

36 Michael Cooper, trans. and ed., *This Island of Japon: João Rodrigues' Account of 16th-Century Japan* (Tokyo, 1973), p. 213.

37 Nakai Atsushi, 'Kyōen bunka to hajiki: Girei no juyō no kachi', in *Utage no chūsei*, p. 133.

38 For further discussion of the shikisankon, see Eric C. Rath, *Food and Fantasy in Early Modern Japan* (Berkeley, CA, 2010), pp. 66–71.

39 The unglazed ceramics used in the medieval period were plain and drab. It was not until the end of the sixteenth century that more vibrant, colourful glazed ceramic plates were used for banquet meals among the ruling elite. Kanzaki Noritake, 'Shokki no hayari sutari', in *Rakugo ni miru Edo no shokubunka*, ed. Tabi no Bunka Kenkyūkaijo (Tokyo, 2000), pp. 7–76.

40 Charlotte von Verschuer, 'Illustrated Debate over Wine and Rice (*Shuhanron emaki*): Dining and Socializing in Late Muromachi Japan', *Monumenta Nipponica*, LXXII/2 (2017), p. 189.

41 Kitajima Daisuke, 'Ōuchishi wa nani o tabeta ka: Shokuzai to shite dōbutsu riyō', in *Nihonshi kōza*, vol. IV: *Chūsei shakai no kōzō*, ed. Rekishigaku Kenkyūkai and Nihonshi Kenkyūkai (Tokyo, 2004), pp. 130–32.

42 Matthew Stravos, *Kyoto: An Urban History of Japan's Premodern Capital* (Honolulu, HI, 2014), p. 123.

43 Morimoto Masahiro, *Zōtō to enkai no chūsei* (Tokyo, 2008), p. 45.

44 Matsuoka Shinpei, *Utage no shintai: Basara kara Zeami e* (Tokyo, 1991), pp. 70–75.

45 *Sakamori* is a medieval term dating from the late twelfth century. See Nagaike Kenji, 'Sakamorikō, En no chūseiteki keitai to Muromachi ko'uta', in *Chūsei denshō bungaku to sono shūhen*, *Tomohisa Takefumi sensei koki kinen ronbunshū*, ed. Tomohisa Takefumi Sensei Koki Kinen Ronbunshū Kankōkai (Hiroshima, Keisuisha, 1997), p. 118.

46 Von Verschuer, 'Illustrated Debate over Wine and Rice (*Shuhanron emaki*)', p. 196. There are thirty extant copies of the work in Japan and others outside of the country such as in the New York Public Library Spencer Collection and France's Bibliothèque Nationale. Itō Nobuhiro, '"Shuhanron emaki" ni egakareru shokumotsu ni tsuite', in *'Shuhanron emaki' no sekai: Nichifutsu kyōdo kenkyū*, ed. Abe Yasurō and Itō Nobuhiro (Tokyo, 2014), p. 70.

47 *'Shuhanron emaki' no sekai*, pp. 5–6.

48 Von Verschuer, 'Illustrated Debate over Wine and Rice (*Shuhanron emaki*)', p. 192.

49 Chadō Shiryōkan, ed., *Shuhanron emaki: Yōkoso chūsei Nihon no utage no seki e heisei sanjūnen shūki tokubetsuten* (Kyoto, 2018), pp. 118, 122.

50 Nagayama Hisao, *Nihon no sake unchiku hyakka* (Tokyo, 2008), pp. 124, 131.

51 Chadō, ed., *Shuhanron emaki*, pp. 118–19, 122–3.

52 Takeshi Watanabe, 'Wine, Rice, or Both? Overwriting Sectarian Strife in the Tendai *Shuhanron* Debate', *Japanese Journal of Religious Studies*, XXXVI/2 (2009), p. 270.

53 Sakurai Eiji, 'Enkai to kenryoku', in *Utage no chūsei*, p. 232.

54 Sakurai, *Muromachibito no seishin*, p. 240.

55 Watanabe, 'Wine, Rice, or Both?', p. 270.

56 Sakurai elaborates that it was not until the late sixteenth century that elite samurai showed more discretion and avoided vomiting in public. Sakurai, 'Enkai to kenryoku', p. 232.

57 Katō Hyakuichi, 'Muromachiki ni okeru kuge, bukeshū no shuen (3): Sono sahō to yūgika', *Nihon jōzō kyōkaishi*, XCVIII/12 (2003), pp. 841–2.

58 Yoshida, *Sake*, p. 111.

59 Katō, 'Muromachiki ni okeru kuge, bukeshū no shuen (3): Sono sahō to yūgika', pp. 841–2.

60 Futaki, *Chūsei buke no sahō*, p. 136.

61 Katō, 'Muromachiki ni okeru kuge, bukeshū no shuen (3)', pp. 843–4.

62 Yoshida, *Kyō no sakegaku*, p. 96.

63 Sakurai, 'Enkai to kenryoku', p. 237; Sakurai, *Muromachibito no seishin*, pp. 238–9.

64 Yoshida, *Essays in Idleness*, p. 150.

65 Sakurai, 'Enkai to kenryoku', pp. 236–7; Sakurai, *Muromachibito no seishin*, pp. 238–9.

66 Sakurai, 'Enkai to kenryoku', pp. 220–21.

67 Yoshizawa Hajime, 'Sōbō shuen tsuikō', in *Yoi no bunkashi: Girei kara yamai made*, ed. Itō Nobuhiro (Tokyo, 2020), p. 41.

68 Yoshida, *Essays in Idleness*, pp. 46–7.

FOUR THE EARLY MODERN SAKE INDUSTRY, 1600–1868

1 Mark Teeuwen et al., eds and trans., *Lust, Commerce, and Corruption: An Account of What I Have Seen and Heard, by an Edo Samurai* (New York, 2014), p. 372.

2 Yoshida Hajime, *Edo no sake: Tsukuru, uru, ajiwau* (Tokyo, 2016), p. 100; Yoshida Hajime, 'Kaidai', in *Nihon nōgyō zenshū*, vol. LI: *Dōmō shuzōki, Kanmoto zōyō gokuiden* (Tokyo, 1996), p. 217.

3 Suzuki Yoshiyuki, *Nihonshu no kin-gendaishi: Shuzōchi no tanjō* (Tokyo, 2015), pp. 50–51.

4 Harada Nobuo, '"Kome shikō" saikō', in *Shokubunka kara shakai ga wakaru!*, ed. Yano Keiichi (Tokyo, 2009), p. 20.

5 Food scholar Arizono Shōichirō estimates that 15 per cent of the rice went to sake making in the early modern period, based upon his study of domanial ordinances and Meiji-period records. See Arizono Shōichirō, *Kinsei shomin no nichijōshoku: Hyakushō wa kome o taberarenakatta ka?* (Ōtsu, 2007), p. 48. Koyama Shūzō's study of the *Latter Gazetteer of Hida* (*Hida gofudoki*), compiled in 1873, finds that 20 per cent of the rice grown in the eighteen villages that comprised the mountainous Hida region of modern Gifu prefecture went to sake making. A remarkable total for a place where growing any rice at all was difficult due to the mountainous terrain and high altitude. Likely the rice was grown to pay rents and taxes and then was directed to breweries as in nearby Takayama. See Koyama Shūzō, '"Hida gofudoki" ni miru Edo jidai no shokuseikatsu', in *Zenshū Nihon no shokubunka*, vol. II: *Shoku seikatsu to shokumotsushi*, ed. Haga Noboru and Ishikawa Hiroko (Tokyo, 1999), p. 219.

6 Yoshida, 'Kaidai', p. 215.

7 Katō Hyakuichi, *Sake wa morohaku: Nihonshu to unda gijutsu no bunka* (Tokyo, 1989), p. 109.

8 Sugama Seinosuke, *Saketsukuri no takumi tachi: Rō-tōji no kataru Nihon no sake* (Tokyo, 1987), p. 232.

9 Yoshida Hajime, *Kyō no sakegaku* (Kyoto, 2016), p. 142.

10 Gautier Roussille, *Nihonshu: Japanese Sake* (n.p., 2017), p. 74.

11 Katō, *Sake wa morohaku*, pp. 67–8, 70.

12 Ibid., p. 79.

13 Yamaguchi Shōzō, *Nihon no sakagura* (Fukuoka-shi, 2009), p. 5.

14 Yoshida, *Edo no sake*, p. 61.

15 Yoshida, 'Kaidai', p. 216.

16 Katō, *Sake wa morohaku*, pp. 83–4.

17 Yoshida, 'Kaidai', p. 217; Sugama, *Saketsukuri no takumi tachi*, p. 227.

18 Katō, *Sake wa morohaku*, pp. 133, 189–90.

19 Ibid., pp. 193–4.

20 Ibid., pp. 236–7.

21 Ibid., p. 147.

22 Translated from the original included in Yoshida Hajime, *Sake* (Tokyo, 2015), pp. 205–6.

23 *Nihon ryōri hiden shūsei: Genten gendaigoyaku*, vol. XIV: *Tsukemono hidenshū*, ed. Issunsha (Kyoto, 1985), p. 239.

24 Yoshida Hajime, 'Edo, Tōkyō no doburokuya', *Sakeshi kenkyū*, 36 (2021), p. 2.

25 Andō Yūichirō, 'Nihonshu bunka ni okeru doburoku jōzō no rekishi: Seishu to hikaku kara', *Shoku seikatsu kagaku bunka oyobi chikyū kankyō kagaku ni kan suru kenkyū josei kenkyū kiyo*, 13 (2003), pp. 65, 67, 69.

26 Yoshida Hajime, *Kyō no sakegaku*, p. 142.

27 *Dōmō shuzōki*, in *Nihon nōgyō zenshū*, vol. LI: *Dōmō shuzōki, Kanmoto zōyō gokuiden* (Tokyo, 1996), pp. 96, 152.

28 Gerald Groemer, *The Land We Saw, The Times We Knew: An Anthology of 'Zuihitsu' Writing from Early Modern Japan* (Honolulu, HI, 2019), p. 307.

29 Sugama, *Saketsukuri no takumi tachi*, p. 225.

30 Katō, *Sake wa morohaku*, pp. 220–21.

31 Yunoki Manabu, *Sakezukuri no rekishi*, shinsōpan (Tokyo, 2005), p. 30; Katō, *Sake wa morohaku*, pp. 219, 220.

32 Kamatani Chikatoshi and Katō Hyakuichi, 'Dōmō shuzōki: Sono honkoku to kaisetsu', *Shushi kenkyū*, 8 (1990), p. i.

33 For a translation and discussion of the instructions to make kōji in *The Idiot's Guide to Sake Brewing*, see Eric C. Rath, 'It Gives the Rice a Kick: Sweetness and Kōji in Early Modern Sake Brewing', *Gastronomica: The Journal for Food Studies*, XXIII/4 (2023), pp. 36–40.

34 Yoshida, *Sake*, pp. 144–5.

35 Eric C. Rath, *Japan's Cuisines: Food, Place and Identity* (London, 2016), pp. 72–3.

36 Katō, *Sake wa morohaku*, p. 160.

37 Ibid., p. 163.

38 Yunoki, *Sakezukuri no rekishi*, shinsōpan, pp. 34–5.

39 *Dōmō shuzōki*, pp. 79, 80.

40 Ibid., pp. 96–7.

41 Yoshida Hajime, *Kindai Nihon no sakezukuri: Bishu tankyū no gijutsushi* (Tokyo, 2013), p. 44.
42 *Dōmō shuzōki*, pp. 86–7.
43 Sugama, *Saketsukuri no takumi tachi*, p. 228.
44 Yoshida, *Edo no sake*, pp. 30–31; Yoshida, *Sake*, p. 135.
45 Yoshida, *Sake*, p. 136.
46 Yunoki, *Sakezukuri no rekishi, shinsōpan*, p. 34.
47 Katō, *Sake wa morohaku*, p. 102.
48 Sugama, *Saketsukuri no takumi tachi*, pp. 225–6.
49 Yunoki, *Sakezukuri no rekishi, shinsōpan*, p. 86.
50 Yoshida, *Edo no sake*, p. 100.
51 Yoshida, *Sake*, p. 155.
52 Katō, *Sake wa morohaku*, p. 156.
53 Yunoki, *Sakezukuri no rekishi, shinsōpan*, p. 30.
54 Yoshida, *Sake*, p. 139.
55 Yoshida Hajime, *Nihon no shoku to sake: Chūsei no hakkōgijutsu o chūshin ni* (Tokyo, 1991), p. 157.
56 Suzuki, *Nihonshu no kin-gendaishi*, p. 29.
57 Yoshida, *Edo no sake*, p. 52.
58 For this section, I found very helpful Yoshida Hajime's brief discussion of the sake-brewing images from *Nihon sankai meisan zue*, in *Nihon nōgyō zenshū*, vol. LI: *Dōmō shuzōki, Kanmoto zōyō gokuiden*, ed. Yoshida Hajime (Tokyo, 1996), pp. ii–iv.
59 Yunoki, *Sakezukuri no rekishi, shinsōpan*, pp. 38–40.
60 Katō, *Sake wa morohaku*, p. 159.
61 Yunoki, *Sakezukuri no rekishi, shinsōpan*, p. 38.
62 Rath, 'It Gives the Rice a Kick', p. 38.
63 Suzuki, *Nihonshu no kin-gendaishi*, p. 33.
64 Yoshida, *Sake*, p. 139.
65 Sugama, *Saketsukuri no takumi tachi*, p. 235.
66 Yoshida, *Kindai Nihon no sakezukuri*, p. 35.
67 Yunoki, *Sakezukuri no rekishi, shinsōpan*, pp. 40–41.
68 Yoshida, *Kindai Nihon no sakezukuri*, pp. 36–7.
69 Yunoki, *Sakezukuri no rekishi, shinsōpan*, p. 42.
70 Yamaguchi, *Nihon no sakagura*, pp. 13, 15, 17, 20; Yunoki, *Sakezukuri no rekishi, shinsōpan*, p. 173.
71 Katō, *Sake wa morohaku*, pp. 126, 127.

72 Suzuki, *Nihonshu no kin-gendaishi*, pp. 190–91.

73 Ibid., p. 72.

74 Yamaguchi, *Nihon no sakagura*, pp. 5–6.

75 Yunoki, *Sakezukuri no rekishi, shinsōpan*, p. 191.

76 Katō, *Sake wa morohaku*, pp. 270, 272.

77 Suzuki, *Nihonshu no kin-gendaishi*, p. 36.

78 Ibid., pp. 58–9.

79 Yoshida, *Edo no sake*, pp. 52–4.

80 Suzuki, *Nihonshu no kin-gendaishi*, p. 58.

81 Katō, *Sake wa morohaku*, pp. 131, 143.

82 Yunoki, *Sakezukuri no rekishi, shinsōpan*, p. 79.

83 Katō, *Sake wa morohaku*, p. 144.

84 Sugama, *Saketsukuri no takumi tachi*, p. 16.

85 Katō, *Sake wa morohaku*, pp. 61–2, 132–3, 263.

86 Suzuki, *Nihonshu no kin-gendaishi*, pp. 29, 31.

87 Yoshida, *Kindai Nihon no sakezukuri*, p. 47.

88 Yoshida, *Edo no sake*, pp. 149–50.

89 Conrad Totman, *Early Modern Japan* (Berkeley, CA, 1993), pp. 240, 241; Yoshida, *Edo no sake*, pp. 150–51.

90 Yoshida, *Edo no sake*, p. 89.

91 Ibid., pp. 90–91.

92 Katō, *Sake wa morohaku*, p. 117.

93 Yoshida, *Edo no sake*, p. 92.

94 Yoshida, *Sake*, pp. 132–3; Suzuki, *Nihonshu no kin-gendaishi*, pp. 39–41.

95 Yoshida, *Edo no sake*, p. 95.

96 Suzuki, *Nihonshu no kin-gendaishi*, p. 50.

97 Yoshida, *Sake*, p. 137; Sugama, *Saketsukuri no takumi tachi*, p. 229.

98 Yunoki, *Sakezukuri no rekishi, shinsōpan*, pp. 112–13.

99 Suzuki, *Nihonshu no kin-gendaishi*, p. 59.

100 Katō, *Sake wa morohaku*, pp. 240, 244, 246.

101 Sugama, *Saketsukuri no takumi tachi*, p. 231.

102 Yunoki, *Sakezukuri no rekishi, shinsōpan*, p. 38.

103 Katō, *Sake wa morohaku*, pp. 259–62.

104 Yoshida, *Sake*, p. 145; Suzuki, *Nihonshu no kin-gendaishi*, p. 52.

105 Katō, *Sake wa morohaku*, p. 252.

106 Yunoki, *Sakezukuri no rekishi, shinsōpan*, p. 93.

107 Ibid., pp. 112–13.
108 Suzuki, Nihonshu no kin-gendaishi, pp. 50–51.
109 Katō, Sake wa morohaku, p. 255.
110 Suzuki, Nihonshu no kin-gendaishi, p. 55; Yoshida, Kindai Nihon no sakezukuri, p. 178.
111 Suzuki, Nihonshu no kin-gendaishi, pp. 60–61.
112 Yoshida, Kyō no sakegaku, p. 164.
113 Ibid., p. 198.
114 Katō, Sake wa morohaku, p. 104; Yoshida, Edo no sake, pp. 2, 14.
115 Yoshida, Edo no sake, pp. 15, 28–9; Yunoki, Sakezukuri no rekishi, shinsōpan, p. 32.
116 Suzuki, Nihonshu no kin-gendaishi, p. 70.

FIVE THE RISE OF NIHONSHU, 1868-1989

1 The word Nihonshu was not widely used until after the 1964 Tokyo Olympics. Suzuki Yoshiyuki, Nihonshu no kin-gendaishi: Shuzōchi no tanjō (Tokyo, 2015), pp. 1, 3.
2 Gautier Roussille, Nihonshu: Japanese Sake (n.p., 2017), p. 194.
3 The Mayo Clinic warns of possible serious side effects of ingesting salicylic acid, including 'swelling of the face, fingers, feet, and/or lower legs; severe stomach pain, black, tarry stools, and/or vomiting of blood or material that looks like coffee grounds; unusual weight gain; and/or skin rash. Also, signs of serious heart problems could occur such as chest pain, tightness in chest, fast or irregular heartbeat, or unusual flushing or warmth of skin.' Mayo Clinic, 'Salicylate (Oral Route, Rectal Route)', www.mayoclinic.org, accessed 25 July 2023.
4 Nishimura Takaharu, Nada no kuramoto sanbyakunen: Kokushu, Nihonshu no nazo ni semaru (Tokyo, 2014), p. 213.
5 This calculation assumes the nineteenth-century exchange rate of 1 ryō to 6,500 mon of copper, Bank of Japan Currency Museum, www.imes.boj.or.jp, accessed 19 October 2023; Miyoshi Ikkō, ed., Edo seigyō bukka jiten (Tokyo, 2002), p. 101.
6 Yoshida Hajime, Kindai Nihon no sakezukuri: Bishu tankyū no gijutsushi (Tokyo, 2013), p. 100.
7 Ibid.

8 Yoshida Hajime, *Kyō no sakegaku* (Kyoto, 2016), pp. 179–80; Andō Yūichirō, 'Nihonshu bunka ni okeru doburoku jōzō no rekishi: Seishu to hikaku kara', *Shoku seikatsu kagaku bunka oyobi chikyū kankyō kagaku ni kan suru kenkyū josei kenkyū kiyo*, 13 (2003), p. 70.

9 Abe Takeshi, *Doburoku to onna: Nihon josei inshukō* (Tokyo, 2009), p. 280.

10 Yoshida Hajime, 'Edo, Tokyo no doburokuya', *Sakeshi kenkyū*, 36 (2021), p. 5.

11 Yoshida, *Kindai Nihon no sakezukuri*, pp. 100–101.

12 Andō, 'Nihonshu bunka ni okeru doburoku jōzō no rekishi', p. 70.

13 Abe, *Doburoku to onna*, p. 280.

14 Yamaguchi Shōzō, *Nihon no sakagura* (Fukuoka-shi, 2009), p. 6.

15 Andō, 'Nihonshu bunka ni okeru doburoku jōzō no rekishi', p. 71.

16 Yoshida, 'Edo, Tokyo no doburokuya', p. 5.

17 Abe, *Doburoku to onna*, p. 271.

18 Miyoshi, *Edo seigyō bukka jiten*, p. 101.

19 Abe, *Doburoku to onna*, p. 272.

20 Yoshida, 'Edo, Tokyo no doburokuya', pp. 5, 7.

21 Saitsu Yumiko, 'Kinjirareta sakezukuri to yurusareta sakezukuri no aida', in *Sake yomi: Bungaku to rekishi de yomu osake*, ed. Horoyoi Bukkusu Henshūbu (Tokyo, 2012), p. 82.

22 Abe, *Doburoku to onna*, pp. 281–2.

23 Yoshida, *Kindai Nihon no sakezukuri*, p. 101.

24 Yamaguchi, *Nihon no sakagura*, p. 7.

25 Yoshida, *Kindai Nihon no sakezukuri*, p. 103.

26 Suzuki, *Nihonshu no kin-gendaishi*, p. 94.

27 Abe, *Doburoku to onna*, pp. 283, 285, 306.

28 Saitsu, 'Kinjirareta sakezukuri to yurusareta sakezukuri no aida', p. 82.

29 Kanzaki Noritake, *Sake no Nihon bunka* (Tokyo, 1991), p. 34.

30 Suzuki, *Nihonshu no kin-gendaishi*, p. 95.

31 Yoshida, 'Edo, Tokyo no doburokuya', pp. 5, 7.

32 Andrew Gordon, *A Modern History of Japan: From Tokugawa Times to the Present* (New York, 2014), pp. 94–5.

33 Suzuki, *Nihonshu no kin-gendaishi*, p. 97.

34 Yoshida, *Kindai Nihon no sakezukuri*, p. 104.

35 Abe, *Doburoku to onna*, p. 305.

36 Yoshida, *Kindai Nihon no sakezukuri*, pp. 109–10.

37 Ibid., pp. 103–4.

38 Ibid., p. 110.

39 Ibid., p. 104.

40 Andō, 'Nihonshu bunka ni okeru doburoku jōzō no rekishi', p. 71.

41 Suzuki, *Nihonshu no kin-gendaishi*, pp. 95, 103–4.

42 Aoki Takahiro, *Kindai shuzōgyō no chiikiteki tenkai* (Tokyo, 2002), p. 172.

43 Suzuki, *Nihonshu no kin-gendaishi*, p. 73.

44 Yamaguchi, *Nihon no sakagura*, p. 7.

45 Yoshida, *Kindai Nihon no sakezukuri*, pp. 65–6.

46 Yoshida, *Kyō no sakegaku*, p. 214.

47 Yamaguchi, *Nihon no sakagura*, p. 21.

48 Saitō Tokio, ed., *Nihon shokubunka jinbutsu jiten: Jinbutsu de yomu Nihon shokubunkashi* (Tokyo, 2005), p. 72.

49 Yamaguchi, *Nihon no sakagura*, pp. 9–10; Suzuki, *Nihonshu no kin-gendaishi*, p. 83.

50 Yoshida, *Kyō no sakegaku*, pp. 209–10.

51 Suzuki, *Nihonshu no kin-gendaishi*, p. 130.

52 Yoshida, *Kindai Nihon no sakezukuri*, p. 79; Suzuki, *Nihonshu no kin-gendaishi*, pp. 130–31; Yoshida, *Kyō no sakegaku*, pp. 209–10, 213.

53 Suzuki, *Nihonshu no kin-gendaishi*, p. 191.

54 Yoshida, *Kindai Nihon no sakezukuri*, pp. 54–6; Yamaguchi, *Nihon no sakagura*, p. 20.

55 Yoshida, *Kyō no sakegaku*, p. 198; Suzuki, *Nihonshu no kin-gendaishi*, pp. 132–3.

56 Yoshida, *Kindai Nihon no sakezukuri*, p. 173.

57 Yamaguchi, *Nihon no sakagura*, pp. 21, 217–18.

58 Yoshida, *Kindai Nihon no sakezukuri*, pp. 101–2, 104, 106.

59 Ibid., pp. 78–83, 106; Suzuki, *Nihonshu no kin-gendaishi*, p. 106.

60 Suzuki, *Nihonshu no kin-gendaishi*, pp. 108–10, 222.

61 Yoshida, *Kindai Nihon no sakezukuri*, p. 113.

62 Ibid., p. 132.

63 Roussille, *Nihonshu*, pp. 144–5.

64 Yoshida, *Kindai Nihon no sakezukuri*, p. 70.

65 Suzuki, *Nihonshu no kin-gendaishi*, pp. 11–14; Roussille, *Nihonshu*, pp. 133–4.

66 Yoshida, *Kindai Nihon no sakezukuri*, pp. 73, 77.

67 Suzuki, *Nihonshu no kin-gendaishi*, p. 161.

68 Ibid., pp. 85, 87–9; Yoshida, *Kindai Nihon no sakezukuri*, pp. 86–7; Nancy Matsumoto and Michael Tremblay, *Exploring the World of Japanese Craft Sake: Rice, Water, Earth* (North Clarendon, VT, 2022), p. 61.

69 Yoshida, *Kindai Nihon no sakezukuri*, pp. 94–6.

70 Ibid., p. 171.

71 Jeffrey W. Alexander, *Brewed in Japan: The Evolution of the Japanese Beer Industry* (Vancouver, 2013), pp. 86, 93.

72 Oana Fujio, 'Shuzō gyō no suii', *Nihon jōzō kyōkai zasshi*, LXV/4 (1970), p. 310.

73 Yoshida, *Kyō no sakegaku*, p. 219; Eric C. Rath, *Japan's Cuisines: Food, Place and Identity* (London, 2016), p. 129.

74 Hashimoto Kenji, *Izakaya no sengoshi* (Tokyo, 2015), p. 123.

75 Alexander, *Brewed in Japan*, pp. 108, 126, 143.

76 Yoshida, *Kindai Nihon no sakezukuri*, p. 220; Yoshida, *Kyō no sakegaku*, p. 210.

77 Hashimoto, *Izakaya no sengoshi*, p. 124.

78 Nihon Shōhisha Renmei, *Honmono no sake o!* (Tokyo, 1982), pp. 35–9.

79 Suzuki, *Nihonshu no kin-gendaishi*, pp. 156–8; Nishimura, *Nada no kuramoto sanbyakunen*, p. 223; Hashimoto, *Izakaya no sengoshi*, p. 187.

80 Yoshida, *Kindai Nihon no sakezukuri*, pp. 211–13; Funase Shunsuke, *Honmono no nihonshu o!* (Tokyo, 2005), p. 6.

81 Yoshida, *Kindai Nihon no sakezukuri*, pp. 214–17.

82 Ibid.; Suzuki, *Nihonshu no kin-gendaishi*, p. 168.

83 Nihon Jōzō Kyōkai, Nihonshu Sābisu Kenkyūkai and Sakashō Kenkyūkai Rengōkai, eds, *Nihonshugaku: Sake ga motto umaku naru!* (Tokyo, 2016), p. 149.

84 Funase, *Honmono no nihonshu o!*, p. 8.

85 Yoshida, *Kindai Nihon no sakezukuri*, p. 211; Nishimura, *Nada no kuramoto sanbyakunen*, p. 222.

86 Hashimoto, *Izakaya no sengoshi*, p. 124.

87 Alexander, *Brewed in Japan*, pp. 156, 171, 180.

88 Hashimoto, *Izakaya no sengoshi*, p. 127.

89 Yoshida, *Kindai Nihon no sakezukuri*, pp. 217, 219.

90 Roussille, *Nihonshu*, p. 177.

91 Yoshida, *Kindai Nihon no sakezukuri*, pp. 216–17.

92 Suzuki, *Nihonshu no kin-gendaishi*, pp. 191–2.

93 Robert M. Marsh and Hiroshi Mannari, *Modernization and the Japanese Factory* (Princeton, NJ, 1976), p. 19.

94 Nihon Jōzō Kyōkai Zasshi, ed., 'Okeuri ni tsuite no ankēto', *Nihon jōzō kyōkai zasshi*, LXIII/6 (1968), p. 630.

95 John Gauntner, *Sake Professional Course* (Chicago, IL, 2012), pp. 96–7.

96 Funase, *Honmono no nihonshu o!*, p. 3.

97 'Seishu "okegai" jitai akarumi', *Asahi Shimbun*, 3 January 1981, p. 23.

98 Nishimura, *Nada no kuramoto sanbyakunen*, pp. 214–15.

99 'Survey Reveals the Realities of Kurabito Life', *Sake Industry News*, 68 (July 2022).

100 Suzuki, *Nihonshu no kin-gendaishi*, pp. 195–6.

101 Hitoshi Utsunomiya, 'About the Production Status of Sake', Japan Sake and Shochu Makers Association (2021), https://japansake.or.jp, accessed 19 October 2023.

102 The authors keep the name of the plant they studied anonymous. Marsh and Mannari, *Modernization and the Japanese Factory*, pp. 23, 34, 59, 61, 63, 64.

103 Oana, 'Shuzō gyō no suii', pp. 308, 310.

104 Tomita Tadao, 'Ankēto chōsa kara mireru seishu gyōkai no kongo no hōkō to mondaiten (1)', *Nihon jōzō kyōkai zasshi*, LXVI/6 (1971), p. 537.

105 Suzuki, *Nihonshu no kin-gendaishi*, pp. 1, 3.

106 Hashimoto, *Izakaya no sengoshi*, p. 190.

SIX A BRIEF HISTORY OF IZAKAYA

1 Yoshida Hajime, *Kindai Nihon no sakezukuri: Bishu tankyū no gijutsushi* (Tokyo, 2013), p. 19; Kanzaki Noritake, '*Utsuwa' o kurau: Nihonjin to shokuji no bunka* (Tokyo, 2017), pp. 196, 200.

2 Hashimoto Kenji, *Izakaya horoyoi kōgengaku* (Tokyo, 2014), p. 33.

3 Yoshida Hajime, *Edo no sake: Tsukuru, uru, ajiwau* (Tokyo, 2016), pp. 100–101.

4 Iino Ryōichi, *Izakaya no tanjō: Edo no nomiore bunka* (Tokyo, 2001), pp. 22, 34.

5 Iino, *Izakaya no tanjō*, pp. 40–41.
6 Ibid., p. 37.
7 Unno Hiroshi, 'Edo no sakaba hanjōki', in *Sakaba no tanjō*, ed. Tamura Toyō (Tokyo, 1998), pp. 23–4.
8 Yoshida, *Edo no sake*, p. 102.
9 Iino, *Izakaya no tanjō*, p. 35.
10 Ibid., pp. 50–54; Itō Yoshisuke, *Edo no izakaya* (Tokyo, 2017), p. 102.
11 Unno, 'Edo no sakaba hanjōki', pp. 45–6.
12 Itō, *Edo no izakaya*, p. 57.
13 Unno, 'Edo no sakaba hanjōki', p. 45.
14 Iino, *Izakaya no tanjō*, pp. 132–3.
15 Itō, *Edo no izakaya*, p. 93.
16 Kanzaki Noritake, 'Edo kara Meiji e: Izakaya, ryōriya no hensen', in *Sakaba no tanjō*, ed. Tamura Toyō (Tokyo, 1998), p. 73.
17 Yoshida, *Edo no sake*, pp. 104–5.
18 Conrad Totman, *Early Modern Japan* (Berkeley, CA, 1993), p. 153.
19 Itō, *Edo no izakaya*, p. 93.
20 Abe Takeshi, *Doburoku to onna: Nihon josei inshukō* (Tokyo, 2009), p. 2; Imazeki Toshiko, 'Ōchō jidai no shurei to shuen', in *Kanpai no bunkashi*, ed. Kanzaki Noritake (Tokyo, 2007), p. 51.
21 Itō, *Edo no izakaya*, p. 112.
22 Kanzaki, 'Edo kara Meiji e', pp. 72, 74; Iino, *Izakaya no tanjō*, pp. 143–4.
23 Nagayama Hisao, *Nihon no sake unchiku hyakka* (Tokyo, 2008), pp. 255–6; Inflation Tool, www.inflationtool.com, accessed 31 October 2023.
24 Iino, *Izakaya no tanjō*, p. 23.
25 Itō, *Edo no izakaya*, pp. 96–7, 101–2.
26 Iino, *Izakaya no tanjō*, pp. 119, 121, 123.
27 Ehara Ayako, Ishikawa Naoko and Higashiyotsuyanagi Shōko, *Nihon shokumotsushi* (Tokyo, 2009), p. 151.
28 The 2006 number also includes beer halls, yakitori restaurants and oden shops. Iino, *Izakaya no tanjō*, pp. 16–17.
29 Iino, *Izakaya no tanjō*, pp. 125, 128–9, 135, 138.
30 Hirade Kōjirō, *Tōkyō fūzokushi* (Tokyo, 1968), pp. 153–4, 159.
31 Eric C. Rath, 'For Gluttons, Not Housewives: Japan's First Gourmet Magazine, *Kuidōraku*', in *Feeding Japan: The Cultural and*

Political Issues of Dependency and Risk, ed. Tine Walravens and
Andreas Niehaus (Cham, Switzerland, 2017), pp. 83–111.

32 Jiji Shinposha, ed., *Tōkyō meibutsu tabearuki* (Tokyo, 1929),
pp. iv–vi.

33 Eric C. Rath, 'Technologies of Taste: Restaurant Guides, Diners,
and Dining Halls in Interwar Tokyo', *Gastronomica: The Journal for
Food Studies*, xx/4 (2020), pp. 75–85, p. 81.

34 Matsuzaki Tenmin, *Tōkyō tabearuki*, republished in *Gurume annaiki*,
ed. Kondō Hiroko (Tokyo, 2005), pp. 33–4, 83–5.

35 Iino, *Izakaya no tanjō*, p. 211.

36 Tanaka Hiroko, *Shokusābisu sangyō no kōgyōka: Gaishoku, chūshoku
sangyō o chūshin ni* (Kyoto, 2022), p. 102.

37 Jeffrey W. Alexander, *Drinking Bomb and Shooting Meth: Alcohol and
Drug Use in Japan* (Ann Arbor, mi, 2018), p. 53.

38 Jeffrey W. Alexander, *Brewed in Japan: The Evolution of the Japanese
Beer Industry* (Vancouver, 2013), p. 182.

39 Hashimoto Kenji, *Izakaya no sengoshi* (Tokyo, 2015), pp. 17, 26, 54.

40 Hashimoto Kenji, *Izakaya horoyoi kōgengaku*, pp. 107–8, 131, 137.

41 Kon Tōji, *Famirī resutoran: Gaishoku no kin-gendaishi* (Tokyo, 2003),
pp. 92–3; Nakamura Yoshihei, *Izakaya chēn sengokushi* (Tokyo,
2018), pp. 34–6.

42 Nakamura, *Izakaya chēn sengokushi*, pp. 46–58, 61.

43 Tanaka, *Shokusābisu sangyō no kōgyōka*, p. 101.

44 Tsuji Shigeaki, *Kane no nai hito koso shōbai o yare: Shōshihon 'yakitori
izakaya' seikō kaigyōhō* (Tokyo, 1996), pp. 101, 116, 215.

45 Kokkudoa, www.cookdoor.jp/izakaya, accessed 3 November 2023.

46 Taro Futamura and Kazuaki Sugiyama, 'The Dark Side of the
Nightscape: The Growth of *Izakaya* Chains and the Changing
Landscape of Evening Eateries in Japanese Cities', *Food, Culture
and Society*, xxi/1 (2018), pp. 102, 106.

47 Tanaka, *Shokusābisu sangyō no kōgyōka*, p. 102.

48 Alexander, *Brewed in Japan*, p. 185.

49 Hashimoto, *Izakaya no sengoshi*, pp. 226–7.

50 Hatanaka Mioko, *Fashon fūdo, arimasu: Hayari no tabemono
kuronikuru 1970–2010* (Tokyo, 2013), pp. 60, 77–8, 81.

51 Hashimoto, *Izakaya no sengoshi*, pp. 158–60, 223–4; Hashimoto,
Izakaya no sengoshi, pp. 80–81.

52 Hatanaka, *Fashon fūdo, arimasu*, p. 131; Ako Mari, *Shōwa no yōshoku, Heisei no kafe meshi: Katei ryōri hachijūnen* (Tokyo, 2013), p. 114.
53 James Farrer et al., 'The Izakaya as Global Imaginary', in *The Global Japanese Restaurant: Mobilities, Imaginaries, and Politics*, ed. James Farrer and David L. Wank (Honolulu, HI, 2023), pp. 255–88, p. 280.
54 Ibid., p. 277.
55 Hashimoto, *Izakaya no sengoshi*, pp. 189, 199.
56 Farrer et al., 'The Izakaya as Global Imaginary', p. 255.

SEVEN THE QUEST FOR 'REAL SAKE', 1970–2020

1 Nihon Shōhisha Renmei, *Honmono no sake o!* (Tokyo, 1982); Funase Shunsuke, *Honmono no nihonshu o!* (Tokyo, 2005), pp. ii, 3–4. Nishimura Takaharu, *Nada no kuramoto sanbyakunen: Kokushu, Nihonshu no nazo ni semaru* (Tokyo, 2014), pp. 213–14.
2 Abe Takeshi, *Doburoku to onna: Nihon josei inshukō* (Tokyo, 2009), pp. 288–9, 291, 297.
3 'Campaign Scheduled against Bootlegging', *Nippon Times*, 29 September 1955, p. 3.
4 'Tipsy Japanese Horses Give Tip on Bootleg Sake', *Los Angeles Times*, 10 December 1959, p. 22.
5 'Brewing of Illicit "Doburoku" Is Nat'l Pastime: Tax Agency', *Japan Times*, 12 December 1962, p. 4.
6 Hongō Akemi, *Do wa doburoku no do: Ushinawareta sake o tazunete* (Tokyo, 2011), pp. 146–8.
7 Quoted in Abe, *Doburoku to onna*, pp. 355–6.
8 Eric C. Rath, *Japan's Cuisines: Food, Place and Identity* (London, 2016), pp. 150–57.
9 Abe, *Doburoku to onna*, p. 356.
10 Hongō, *Do wa doburoku no do*, p. 8.
11 These prior texts have been reissued as Kaihara Hiroshi, Araya Rakuzan and Sasano Kōtarō, *Shokoku doburoku hōten: Tsukuru, nomu, mawaru* (Tokyo, 2020).
12 Rath, *Japan's Cuisines*, pp. 157–9.
13 Tomiko Shirakigawa, 'Talking Shop', *Japan Times*, 8 January 1982, p. 8.

14 Nihon Shōhisha Renmei, *Honmono no sake o!*, pp. 62–3.

15 Okumura Ayao, ed., *Kikigaki furusato no katei ryōri*, vol. VIII: *Tsukemono* (Tokyo, 2003), p. 127.

16 Kaihara, Araya and Sasano, *Shokoku doburoku hōten*, p. 88.

17 Nōbunkyō Henshūbu, 'Seishubanare no bōshi wa doburoku no kaikin de', in *Doburoku o tsukurō*, ed. Maeda Toshihiko (Tokyo, 2020), pp. 58–9, 60–63.

18 David E. Apter and Nagayo Sawa, *Against the State: Politics and Social Protest in Japan* (Cambridge, MA, 1984), pp. 145–7.

19 *Doburoku o tsukurō*, ed. Maeda, p. i.

20 Maeda Toshihiko, 'Jo: Ima, "Doburoku o tsukurō" to naniyue iu ka', in *Doburoku o tsukurō*, ed. Maeda Toshihiko (Tokyo, 2020), p. 21.

21 *Doburoku o tsukurō*, ed. Maeda, pp. 1–2, 196–220.

22 Ibid., pp. 190–91.

23 Ibid., p. 191.

24 Ibid., pp. 191–2, 204–7.

25 Apter and Sawa, *Against the State*, p. 147.

26 'Home Brewed Sake Party Given in Defiance of Gov't', *Japan Times*, 21 December 1981, p. 2.

27 'Tax Officials Search Home of Defiant Sake Brewer', *Japan Times*, 22 December 1981, p. 2.

28 'Home Brewer Loses Sake Tax Case', *Japan Times*, 26 March 1986, p. 2.

29 'Supreme Court Backs Guilty Verdict of 80-Year-Old Home Sake Brewer', *Japan Times*, 15 December 1989, p. 4.

30 Saitsu Yumiko, 'Kinjirareta sakezukuri to yurusareta sakezukuri no aida', in *Sake yomi: Bungaku to rekishi de yomu osake*, ed. Horoyoi Bukkusu Henshūbu (Tokyo, 2012), pp. 93–4; Abe, *Doburoku to onna*, p. 374.

31 Ayako Yamaguchi, 'Nihonshu Tokku: Special Sake Brewing Zones', *Sake Today: Travel in Japan, Food and Sake Culture*, 34 (2022), pp. 36–43.

32 Rath, *Japan's Cuisines*, pp. 19, 160–61, 177–8.

33 Hashimoto Kenji, *Izakaya no sengoshi* (Tokyo, 2015), p. 187.

34 'Ichi, ni kyū mo honrai kara haishi: Jizake gyōkai, aji de shōbu', *Asahi Shimbun*, 18 December 1991, p. 5.

KANPAI

35 Nihon Shōhisha Renmei, *Honmono no sake o!*, pp. 36–9.
36 Ibid., p. 40.
37 Ibid., pp. 230–31, 676–7.
38 Hashimoto, *Izakaya no sengoshi*, pp. 192–3, 195.
39 Ibid., pp. 192–3, 195.
40 Ibid., p. 188.
41 Nihon Shōhisha Renmei, *Honmono no sake o!*, pp. 51–2.
42 Oota Hiroshi, 'Jizake: Nihonshu ninki "fukken" no tachiyakusha', *Asahi Shimbun*, 5 December 1982, p. 11.
43 Ibid.
44 Tomiko, 'Talking Shop', p. 8.
45 'Jizake būmu ni kōmei motomei', *Asahi Shimbun*, 10 March 1981, p. 8.
46 'Chikagoro jizake, conbiini ni: Nedan mo tegoro wakamono ni mo ninki', *Asahi Shimbun*, 20 February 1996, p. 18; Nihon Jōzō Kyōkai, Nihonshu Sābisu Kenkyūkai and Sakashō Kenkyūkai Rengōkai, eds, *Nihonshugaku: Sake ga motto umaku naru!* (Tokyo, 2016), p. 154.
47 'Ichi, ni kyū mo honrai kara haishi: Jizake gyōkai, aji de shōbu', *Asahi Shimbun*, 18 December 1991, p. 5.
48 John Gauntner, *Sake Confidential: A Beyond-the-Basics Guide to Understanding, Tasting, Selection and Enjoyment* (Berkeley, CA, 2014), pp. 68–70.
49 Okamoto Susumu, *Sekai de ichiban atsui Nihonshu* (Tokyo, 2023), pp. 123–4; Nihon Jōzō Kyōkai, Nihonshu Sābisu Kenkyūkai and Sakashō Kenkyūkai Rengōkai, eds, *Nihonshugaku*, p. 13.
50 Okamoto, *Sekai de ichiban atsui Nihonshu*, p. 126.
51 Hashimoto, *Izakaya no sengoshi*, p. 198.
52 Sakagura Kankyō Kenkyūkai, ed., *Chosen suru sakagura: Honmono no Nihonshu o motomete* (Tokyo, 2007), p. 41.
53 Seko Kazuho, Tsuchida Osamu, *Nihonshu, komezukuri kara hajimeru: Sakagura saizensen* (Tokyo, 2018), p. 58.
54 Sakagura Kankyō Kenkyūkai, ed., *Chosen suru sakagura*, pp. 37, 40.
55 Nihon Jōzō Kyōkai, Nihonshu Sābisu Kenkyūkai and Sakashō Kenkyūkai Rengōkai, eds, *Nihonshugaku*, pp. 13, 16.
56 Ibid., p. 154.

57 Kobayashi Tsuneo, *Kyūshū no shuzōgyō to tōji shūdan* (Tokyo, 2023), p. 21; Nishimura, *Nada no kuramoto sanbyakunen*, pp. 217, 219, 223.

58 Richard Grant, 'Sake in the USA', *Smithsonian Magazine*, October 2021, pp. 40–49.

59 Okamoto, *Sekai de ichiban atsui Nihonshu*, pp. 313–14.

EIGHT SAKE IN NORTH AMERICA, 1908-TODAY

1 Sake Brewers Association of North America, https://sakeassociation.org/sake-map, accessed 30 November 2023.

2 Akiko Katayama, 'Making Japanese Sake a Local Beverage: Leading Brand Dassai Opens Its First Brewery Abroad in New York', *Forbes*, 30 September 2023, accessed at www.forbes.com; Eric Asimov, 'Sake Moves into the American Mainstream', *New York Times*, 1 March 2023, p. d2.

3 Conversation with Brandon Doughan, master brewer and co-owner of Brooklyn Kura, 4 February 2024.

4 Yoshida Hajime, *Kindai Nihon no sakezukuri: Bishu tankyū no gijutsushi* (Tokyo, 2013), pp. 148–53.

5 Ibid., pp. 142–7; Fred Eckhardt, *Sake (USA): The Complete Guide to American Sake, Sake Breweries and Homebrewed Sake* (Portland, OR, 1992), p. 63.

6 Eckhardt, *Sake (USA)*, p. 63. Eckhardt provides a list of historical breweries from 1902 to 1992 and their locations, ibid., pp. 70–73.

7 Sam Jameson, 'Sake Makers Worry about U.S. Market', *Los Angeles Times*, 4 September 1984, p. e3.

8 Charles Hillinger, 'Sake: As American as California Wine', *Los Angeles Times*, 14 April 1990, p. ocd4.

9 Cited in Nihon Shōhisha Renmei, *Zoku honmono no sake o!: Kitare! bishu, meishu no jidai* (Tokyo, 1984) pp. 74–6.

10 Dena Kleiman, 'On Sake Bottles, More Labels Say "Made in USA"', *New York Times*, 13 September 1989, p. c1.

11 William Chapman, 'Beer, Whiskey Sales Soaring: Sake Use Falls with Japan's Traditions', *Los Angeles Times*, 29 October 1978, p. h4.

12 Martin Rossman, 'Japanese Forsaking Sake but Westerners Think Wine Fine', *Los Angeles Times*, 3 April 1972, p. D10.

13 Eckhardt, *Sake (USA)*, p. 21.

14 Mark Blackburn, 'Japan Comes to California to Brew a Cheaper – and Maybe Better – Sake', *Chicago Tribune*, 30 June 1980, p. C1.

15 Nihon Shōhisha Renmei, *Zoku honmono no sake o!*, p. 78.

16 Iris Yokoi, 'Wine That Found Its Time', *Los Angeles Times*, 16 September 1993, p. sgj8.

17 David Smollar, 'Sake with Twist: It's Made in U.S.', *Los Angeles Times*, 9 December 1979, p. E1.

18 Shōhisha Renmei, *Zoku honmono no sake o!*, p. 78.

19 Conversation with Kozue Miyagi, director of sales and marketing Ozeki USA, 8 December 2023. Subsequent quotes from this speaker come from this interview.

20 Ry Beville, 'Ozeki usa: An Industrial Pioneer', *Sake Today: Travel in Japan, Food and Sake Culture*, 35 (2023), p. 43.

21 Ozeki, www.ozeki.co.jp, accessed 8 December 2023.

22 Conversation with Mark Zheng-Garratt, Marketing and Control Manager for Gekkeikan U.S., and Kengo Matsumura, president of Gekkeikan USA, 6 December 2023. Subsequent quotes from these speakers come from this interview.

23 Conversation with Steve Vuylsteke, president and CEO of SakéOne, 13 December 2023. Subsequent quotes from this speaker come from this interview.

24 Katayama, 'Making Japanese Sake a Local Beverage', accessed at www.forbes.com.

25 John Gauntner, 'Dassai: Sake Revolutionaries', *Sake Today: Travel in Japan, Food and Sake Culture*, 16 (2018), pp. 42–3.

26 'Dassai Blue', https://dassai.com, accessed 8 December 2023.

27 Conversation with Kenzo Shimotori, president of Dassai USA, 5 December 2023. Subsequent quotes from this speaker come from this interview.

28 Conversation with Weston Konishi, president of the Sake Brewers of North America, 6 December 2023. Subsequent quotes from this speaker come from this interview.

29 John Gauntner, 'Blake Richardson: A Case of Sake Insanity', *Sake Today: Travel in Japan, Food and Sake Culture*, 3 (2014), p. 44.

30 Conversation with Blake Richardson, tōji of Moto'i, 10 February 2024. Subsequent quotes from this speaker come from this interview.

31 Interview with Byron Stithem, owner of Proper Sake, 6 February 2024. Subsequent quotes from this speaker come from this interview.

32 Conversation with Justin LeVaughn, head brewer and co-owner of The Void, 22 February 2024. Subsequent quotes from this speaker come from this interview.

33 Conversation with Brian Polen, president of Brooklyn Kura, and Brandon Doughan, master brewer and co-owner, 4 February 2024. Subsequent quotes from these speakers come from this interview.

34 Conversation with Maxwell Leer and Troy Nakamatsu of Sawtelle Sake, 19 January 2024. Subsequent quotes from these speakers come from this interview.

35 'Sake Day', sakeday.com, accessed 19 February 2024.

36 'Moonstone', www.sakeone.com/oregon-craft/moonstone, accessed 22 February 2024.

37 Emerson Chaplin, 'Japanese Push U.S. Sake Sales: Brewers Start Campaign to Mix It in Cocktails', *New York Times*, 2 October 1965, p. 6.

38 Yoshida, *Kindai Nihon no sakezukuri*, p. 147; Eckhardt, *Sake* (USA), p. 65.

39 Johnrae Earl, 'Food and Fun, Orient Style', *Chicago Tribune*, 15 December 1974, p. e26.

40 Smollar, 'Sake with Twist', p. e1.

41 Michelle Huneven, 'Sushi Bar Fulfills Dream of Owner, Offers Hip Haven with a Jazz Beat', *Los Angeles Times*, 20 May 1988, p. CV20.

42 Eckhardt, *Sake* (USA), p. 59.

43 SakéOne, https://sakeone.com, accessed 16 December 2023.

44 Kobayashi Tsuneo, *Kyūshū no shuzōgyō to tōji shūdan* (Tokyo, 2023), p. 20.

SELECT BIBLIOGRAPHY

Abe Takeshi, *Doburoku to onna: Nihon josei inshukō* (Tokyo, 2009)

Dōmō shuzōki, in *Nihon nōgyō zenshū*, vol. LI: *Dōmō shuzōki, Kanmoto zōyō gokuiden*, ed. Yoshida Hajime (Tokyo, 1996), pp. 3–178

Eckhardt, Fred, *Sake (USA): The Complete Guide to American Sake, Sake Breweries and Homebrewed Sake* (Portland, OR, 1992)

Gay, Suzanne, *The Moneylenders of Late Medieval Kyoto* (Honolulu, HI, 2010)

Goshu no nikki, in *Shiryō tsūshin sōshi*, ed. Kondō Heijō (Tokyo, 1893–7), pp. 33–6

Hanai Shirō, 'Nihonshu no kita michi', in *Ronshū sake to inshu no bunka*, ed. Ishige Naomichi (Tokyo, 1998), pp. 233–65

Harima Fudoki, Japanese Historical Text Initiative, https://jhti. studentorg.berkeley.edu, accessed 15 February 2022

Harima fudoki, in *Fudoki*, vol. V: *Shinpen Nihon koten, bungaku zenshū*, ed. Uegaki Setsuya (Tokyo, 1997), pp. 17–123

Hitomi Hitsudai, *Honchō shokkan*, ed. Shimada Isao, 5 vols (Tokyo, 1976)

Huang, Hsing-Tsung, *Science and Civilization in China*, vol. VI: *Biology and Biological Technology*, Part V: *Fermentation and Food Science* (Cambridge, 2000)

Ichishima Eiji, *Kōji* (Tokyo, 2007)

Ishige Naomichi, 'Shuzō to inshu no bunka', in *Ronshū sake to inshu no bunka*, ed. Ishige Naomichi (Tokyo, 1998), pp. 25–85

Itō Nobihiro and Itō Akitoshi, 'Kome to sake soshite no sono
    shūhen: Kankyō no shiza kara', in *Yoi no bunkashi: Girei kara yamai
    made*, ed. Itō Nobuhiro (Tokyo, 2020), pp. 148–70
Iwasaki Kae et al., *Shin Nihon koten bungaku taikei*, vol. LXI: *Shichijū
    ichiban shokunin uta'awase*, ed. Iwasaki Kae (Tokyo, 1993),
    pp. 1–146
Kaihara Hiroshi, *Shokoku doburoku hōten: Tsukuru, nomu, mawaru*
    (Tokyo, 2020)
Kamatani Chikatoshi and Katō Hyakuichi, 'Dōmō shuzōki: Sono
    honkoku to kaisetsu', *Shushi kenkyū*, 8 (1990) pp. i–xxvi
Katō Hyakuichi, *Sake wa morohaku: Nihonshu to unda gijutsu no bunka*
    (Tokyo, 1989)
Kidder, J. Edward Jr, *Himiko and Japan's Elusive Chiefdom of Yamatai:
    Archaeology, History, and Mythology* (Honolulu, HI, 2007)
Kitamoto, Katsuhiko, 'Molecular Biology of Koji Molds', *Advances
    in Applied Microbiology*, 51 (2002), pp. 129–53
Koizumi Takeo, *Kōji kabi to kōji no hanashi* (Tokyo, 1984)
—, 'Kome kōji no hassei to Nihon no sakezukuri: Inakōji
    no shūhen kara no ikōsai', in *Ronshū sake to inshu no bunka*,
    ed. Ishige Naomichi (Tokyo, 1998), pp. 167–80
Kurahashi Atsushi, 'Kōji amazake no seibu, kinōsei, anzensei',
    Seibutsu kagaku, XCVII/4 (1990), pp. 190–94
Kurtzman, C.P., et al., 'DNA Relatedness among Wild and
    Domesticated Species in the *Aspergillus flavus* Group', *Mycologia*,
    LXXVIII/6 (1986), pp. 955–9
Lee, Victoria, *The Arts of the Microbial World: Fermentation Science in
    Twentieth-Century Japan* (Chicago, IL, 2021)
Liu, Li, et al., 'The Origins of Specialized Pottery and Diverse
    Alcohol Fermentation Techniques in Early Neolithic China',
    *Proceedings of the National Academy of Sciences of the United States
    of America*, CXVI/26 (2019), pp. 12767–74
Machida, Masayuki, et al., 'Genome Sequencing and Analysis of
    Aspergillus oryzae', *Nature*, CDXXXVIII/22 (2005), pp. 1157–61
Machida, Masayuki, Osamu Yamada and Katsuya Gomi, 'Genomics
    of *Aspergillus oryzae*: Learning from the History of Koji Mold
    and Exploration of Its Future', *DNA Research*, 15 (2008), pp. 173–83
Maeda Toshihiko, ed., *Doburoku o tsukurō* (Tokyo, 2020)

Matsumoto Buichirō, '"Goshu no nikki" to sono kaigi – Satake monjo yori', *Nihon jōzōkyōkai zasshi*, LXXIV/11 (1979), pp. 748–51

Nakayama Keiko, *Jiten wagashi no sekai* (Tokyo, 2006)

Nihon Jōzō Gakkai, 'Declaration', www.jozo.or.jp, 2013, accessed 11 July 2022

Nihon Shōhisha Renmei, *Honmono no sake o!* (Tokyo, 1982)

Nishimura Takaharu, *Nada no kuramoto sanbyakunen: Kokushi, Nihonshu no nazo ni semaru* (Tokyo, 2014)

Rath, Eric C., *Food and Fantasy in Early Modern Japan* (Berkeley, CA, 2010)

—, *Japan's Cuisines: Food, Place and Identity* (London, 2016)

—, *Oishii: The History of Sushi* (London, 2021)

Rokas, Antonis, 'Aspergillus', Current Biology, XXIII/5 (2013), r187–8

Roussille, Gautier, *Nihonshu: Japanese Sake* (n.p., 2017)

Shih, Rich, and Jeremy Umansky, *Koji Alchemy: Rediscovering the Magic of Mold-Based Fermentation* (White River Junction, VT, 2020)

Shogakukan Unabridged Dictionary of the Japanese Language, cited at https://japanknowledge.com, accessed 15 February 2023

Steinhaus, Werner, et al., eds, *An Illustrated Companion to Japanese Archaeology*, 2nd edn (Oxford, 2020)

Suminoe Kinshi, 'Sakeshi ni kan suru ni san no chiken', *Nihon jōzō kyōkai zasshi*, LXV/9 (1970), pp. 770–74

Suzuki Yoshiyuki, *Nihonshu no kin-gendaishi: Shuzōchi no tanjō* (Tokyo, 2015)

Ueda Seinosuke, *Nihonshu no kigen: Kabi, kōji, sake no keifu* (Tokyo, 1999)

Uegaki Setsuya, ed., *Ōsumi no kuni fudoki*, in *Nihon koten bungaku zenshū*, vol. IV: *Fudoki* (Tokyo, 1997), pp. 564–5

Yamaguchi Shōzō, *Nihon no sakagura* (Fukuoka City, 2009)

Yokota Hiroyuki, *Horoyoibanashi: Sake no Nihon bunkashi* (Tokyo, 2019)

Yoshida Hajime, *Edo no sake: Tsukuru, uru, ajiwau* (Tokyo, 2016)

—, *Kindai Nihon no sakezukuri: Bishu tankyū no gijutsushi* (Tokyo, 2013)

—, *Kyō no sakegaku* (Kyoto, 2016)

—, *Sake* (Tokyo, 2015)

Yunoki Manabu, *Sakezukuri no rekishi, shinsōpan* (Tokyo, 2005)

ACKNOWLEDGEMENTS

Though I have been researching Japanese food culture for years now, one moment stands out as the symbolic beginning point of this study and that was when my wife, Kiyomi, created a *sakabayashi* and hung it from the eaves of the porch in our rural Kansas home. *Sakabayashi*, also called *sugidama*, are balls made from the branches of Japanese cedar and are traditionally hung under the eaves of breweries and sake shops. As the cedar ball ages, its colour fades from green to brown, a time-honoured sign that the sake is now ready to drink. Well, the *sakabayashi* that hung on my porch fell off and disappeared a long time ago, but it inspired my writing and also a few largely successful attempts at home brewing. Kiyomi has supported my work and life in other countless ways, which is why this book is dedicated to her, and I am grateful to her for creating several original watercolours as illustrations including the book's cover. I also appreciate the presence, talents and humour of my daughter Dana, which brighten my life in many ways.

I have learned a lot about the contemporary sake world and how the beverage is made from the writings of John Gauntner, Philip Harper, Gautier Roussille and others. In particular, John Gauntner's 'Sake Professional Course', which I took over a decade ago in Chicago, helped expand my horizons about sake and Japanese food culture. Notwithstanding the important work of these sake advocates, historical research on sake is a Japanese monopoly apart from a few articles in Western languages. There are no other histories of sake in English that I am aware of, and most textbook histories of Japan still make only passing reference to food and drink, if at all. My understanding of sake's past owes a great debt to the scholarship of Japanese experts, particularly Katō Hyakuichi, Suzuki Yoshiyuki, Yunoki Manabu and, above all, Yoshida Hajime. I was able to read this scholarship and more thanks to the efforts of University of Kansas Japanese Studies Librarian Michiko Ito, who has built up an impressive collection of resources on sake and Japanese food culture and who also maintains a useful resource webpage for sake studies, 'Guide to Japanese Sake', https://guides.lib.ku.edu. Michiko Ito also helped obtain some of the images for my book.

One of the most exciting parts of working on this book were my conversations with brewers in North America, mentioned in Chapter Eight, and I greatly appreciate their willingness to share their time and knowledge with me. I owe particular thanks to Weston Konishi, president of the Sake Brewers Association of North America (SBANA), for introducing me to these brewery pioneers and for his insights into the sake scene in North America. Elena Follador helped me to understand the sake scene in England and I appreciate her enthusiasm for my research.

I initially tried out some of the ideas that I developed further in this book in writings for the *Sake Times* and *Sake Today*, and I appreciate Saki Kimura and Ry Beville for their support of my work and for their enthusiasm for all things sake. Portions of my discussion of the history of kōji and my translation of the medieval *Sake Journal* (*Goshu no nikki*) first appeared in *Gastronomica: The Journal for Food Studies*. I am also grateful to Michael Leaman at Reaktion Books as well as Martha Jay and the very able editors and staff there.

Funding for a research trip to Japan came from the University of Kansas General Research Fund and travel awards from the Center for East Asian Studies, the College of Liberal Arts and Studies and the Department of International Affairs. The University of Kansas History Department helped pay for rights and reproduction of some of the photos. I appreciate the hospitality of the staff of the breweries and sake museums I visited, especially Ishimoto Tatsunori and everyone at Ishimoto Shuzō. The Department of Sakeology at Niigata University gave me a warm welcome and I am especially grateful to Professors Ono Yoshiko, Hata Yuki and Kishi Yasuyuki. Particular thanks are due to Professors Ono and Hata, who kindly took me to several remote breweries and shared their expertise with me.

Besides these folk, my fellow food scholars, sake lovers, friends, colleagues and a few anonymous strangers helped this project at various stages. I raise an overflowing choko to all of you and say, 'Kanpai!'

PHOTO ACKNOWLEDGEMENTS

The author and publishers wish to express their thanks to the sources listed below for illustrative material and/or permission to reproduce it. Some locations of artworks are also given below, in the interest of brevity:

AdobeStock: pp. 11 (Nishihama), 98 (funny face), 126 (Toru Kimura), 150 (JHVEPhoto); Art Institute of Chicago: p. 103; Bibliothèque nationale de France, Paris (MS Japonais 5343): pp. 96–7; The Cleveland Museum of Art, OH: p. 50; photos Alex Crawford, courtesy Proper Sake Co.: pp. 262, 297; courtesy Dassai Blue: p. 255; Flickr: p. 221 (photo bangdoll, CC BY-SA 2.0); photo Elena Follador: p. 300; courtesy Gekkeikan Sake (USA), Inc.: p. 293; International Research Center for Japanese Studies, Kyoto: p. 119; Los Angeles County Museum of Art (LACMA): p. 80; The Metropolitan Museum of Art, New York: p. 145; courtesy Ozeki Sake (USA), Inc.: pp. 247, 284; Philadelphia Museum of Art, PA: p. 194; photos Eric C. Rath: pp. 10, 14, 17, 20, 32, 127, 142, 147, 157, 161, 163, 164, 166, 172, 181, 184, 201, 204, 207, 231, 232, 235; courtesy Kiyomi Rath: pp. 73, 110, 193, 212; courtesy SakéOne: p. 280; courtesy Sawtelle Sake: p. 288; Smithsonian Libraries and Archives, Washington, DC: pp. 130, 131, 133, 134, 135; Tokyo National Museum, photos TNM Image Archives: pp. 24, 56, 58, 190; Waseda University Library: pp. 189, 191, 197; Wikimedia Commons: pp. 46 (photo Saigen Jiro, public domain), 123 (photo MoKu, CC BY-SA 3.0).

INDEX

Page numbers in *italics* indicate illustrations